Cultural Globalization and Language Education

Cultural Globalization
and
Language Education

B. KUMARAVADIVELU

San José State University

Yale University Press New Haven and London

Publisher: Mary Jane Peluso
Development Editor: Brie Kluytenaar
Manuscript Editor: Jeff Schier
Production Controller: Aldo R. Cupo
Designer: James J. Johnson
Marketing Manager: Timothy Shea

Set in New Aster type by Integrated Publishing Solutions.
Printed in the United States of America.

Library of Congress Cataloging-in-Publication Data

Kumaravadivelu, B., 1948–
Cultural globalization and language education / B. Kumaravadivelu.
p. cm.
Includes bibliographical references and index.
ISBN 978-0-300-11110-1 (pbk. : alk. paper)

1. Language and languages—Study and teaching.   2. Multicultural education.
3. Globalization.   I. Title.
P53.45.K86 2007
418.007—dc22
2007014831

A catalogue record for this book is available from the British Library.

The paper in this book meets the guidelines for permanence and durability of the
Committee on Production Guidelines for Book Longevity of the Council on Library
Resources.

10 9 8 7 6 5 4 3 2 1

To my children Chandrika and Anand
and to children everywhere.

As they learn to navigate their life
in this brave new global world,
may they be guided
by an ancient voice of wisdom:

யாதும் ஊரே யாவரும் கேளிர்

- கனியன் பூங்குன்றனார்

Every place, a home
Every person, a kin
—Kaniyan Poongunranaar
    (circa 500 B.C.)

Contents

Preface

Much water has flowed in the rivers of the world since I started working on this book nearly a decade ago. At the time I began thinking seriously about cultural concepts and cultural conflicts, the academic and social atmosphere was very conducive for critically reflecting on the subject. Words like multiculturalism, cultural diversity, cultural sensitivity were rapidly becoming prominent in the academic world. And, at least in the state of California, where I live and work, these words were already well on their way to becoming the buzzwords of public discourse.

Those were the days when corporations, government agencies, and educational institutions in California and other regions of the United States were seriously engaged in dealing with the challenges of cultural diversity. Discourses on diversity soon became a commercial venture with well-publicized seminars and workshops, at which highly paid diversity gurus were commissioned to help members of industries, city halls, colleges, and universities exorcise the little demons of discrimination supposedly residing in their body and soul. The diversity gurus were going around merrily making ex-cathedra pronouncements on sensitivity and tolerance. Mindful of the public interest, I wrote a newspaper column entitled "Our Prejudices, Our Selves" in the Sunday Perspective section of the *San Jose Mercury News*. In it I wondered aloud why for most of us, "sensitivity to diversity represented only an intellectualized concept, not an internalized conduct" (Kumaravadivelu, 1997, p. 4). In other words, why, when it came to cultural sensitivity, did most of us find it easier to talk the talk than to walk the walk?

At about the same time, I was getting ready to teach for the first time a core course on Intercultural Communication for my M.A.

students in the Teaching of English to Speakers of Other Languages
(TESOL) program. As part of my curricular and instructional
preparation, I surveyed the relevant literature in the field of applied
linguistics and TESOL. I selected from various sources what I considered to be useful materials and included them in a course reader.
During the first few semesters of teaching this course, I found myself
wildly experimenting with different methods and materials, learning from my frustrating failures as well as from my small successes.
My students supportively went along with the experiments.

I attended several conferences where issues related to culture
and intercultural communication were discussed. One in particular is worth mentioning—the national TESOL convention held in
St. Louis (February–March 2001). In a span of three days, I duti-
fully attended many of the sessions sponsored by the TESOL Interest Section on Intercultural Communication, looking for new ideas
and strategies to help me better teach my class on intercultural communication. While many of the presentations did enrich my understanding of the teaching of culture, I left the conference concerned
about what I considered to be an overly one-sided, Western representation of the cultural beliefs and practices of the Other. Upon my
return from the conference, I shared some of my concerns with the
readers of *TESOL Journal* in a short Perspectives piece titled, "Paying Attention to *Inter-* in Intercultural Communication" (Kumaravadivelu, 2002). I added an appendix of a list of books on culture
and intercultural communication written by non-Western professionals. Because of space constraints the editor decided to drop this
list; instead, he suggested that I include my e-mail address so that
interested readers could obtain a copy of the list by contacting me.
I agreed. I was soon overwhelmed by responses to my opinion piece
and requests for the list. Encouraged, I wrote a longer piece titled
"Problematizing Cultural Stereotypes in TESOL" for the Forum
section of *TESOL Quarterly* (Kumaravadivelu, 2003).

In the meantime, I had been working on possible curricular guidelines that might be of relevance for designing a culture-sensitive
language curriculum for the fast globalizing world. A first formal
opportunity to share some of my still-developing thoughts on the
subject came when I was invited to give the keynote address at the
13th Annual Educational Conference held in Fremantle, Australia,
in October 2000. In my talk, entitled "The Gift of One Another's
Presence: Culture and Language Teaching," I presented the rudi-

ments of my curricular guidelines, arguing that language educators cannot ignore their obligation to address the complex issue of the formation of cultural identity in the era of economic, cultural, and communicational globalization (Kumaravadivelu, October, 2000). Two more plenary addresses I had the honor of giving—one in Helsinki, Finland, in May 2003, and another in São Paulo, Brazil, in October 2004—provided additional chances for interacting with interested colleagues, which further solidified my thoughts. Interestingly, the Australian connection came full cycle when the Applied Linguistics Association of Australia invited me to give a plenary address at their International Conference on "Language and Languages: Global and Local Tension," held in Brisbane in July 2006. I used the opportunity to present a more fully formulated framework for the teaching of culture, drawing from the manuscript of this book, which I had just submitted to my publisher. For my talk I chose the title "(Ex)tensions: The Cultural Logic of the Global and the Local" (Kumaravadivelu, July, 2006).

It is the cultural logic of the global and the local, along with its unfailing impact on language education, that constitute the central theme of this book. The logic encompasses a variety of disciplines including anthropology, applied linguistics, cultural studies, history, politics, and sociology. Drawing from these and other areas, I have tried to critically and comprehensively examine, from the perspective of the emerging processes of cultural globalization, the major cultural concepts that have so far informed the learning and teaching of culture in the language classroom. I have also tried to go beyond the current practices in order to provide new and challenging ways to understand the complexity of the relationship between cultural globalization and language education.

The introductory chapter provides a gateway to the book. I then start with the concept of culture and its complexities (Chapter 2), followed by a review of the processes of cultural globalization (Chapter 3) and of the perils of cultural stereotypes (Chapter 4). In the following three chapters I discuss the prevailing cultural concepts of assimilation (Chapter 5), pluralism (Chapter 6), and hybridity (Chapter 7). Characterizing them as limited and limiting, I present a rationale for developing the concept of cultural realism (Chapter 8) followed by operating principles (Chapter 9) and instructional strategies (Chapter 10) necessary for developing global cultural consciousness in our learners. Then, I outline the problems and possibilities for intercultural communication in the era of cultural globalization (Chapter 11), before concluding with some final thoughts (Chapter 12).

I must admit that I found it to be a daunting task to pull together various strands of thought from varied disciplines that offer a plethora of definitions, descriptions, and interpretations. Given the range of academic disciplines and historical accounts, I had no choice but to be selective. I have focused on scholars whose work is representative of general trends in their fields in order to provide a comprehensive, and yet a comprehensible, narrative. Equally daunting was the challenge of writing in a style that is accessible beyond closed communities of specialized scholars. I have tried to achieve that by blending personal narratives with academic discourse without dumbing down the substance of my argument in the process.

Throughout the book, the reader will detect a critical undertone that is by no means accidental. For one who has migrated from one multicultural country to live in another, and for one who looks differently and speaks differently, living a "cultural" life that is rooted in one's tradition and yet open to new ways is an everyday imperative. For such a person, the personal is intertwined with the professional, and therefore it is nearly impossible to separate the two in a work of this kind. In that sense, this book represents a marriage of personal investment and professional commitment. The challenge has been to make sure that one does not erase the other.

This difficult yet rewarding project has been made possible because of the help I received from a host of people. First and foremost, I wish to express my particular gratitude to Mary Jane Peluso, an exemplary publisher. Mary Jane, thank you for your personal interest in this project and for your unfailing faith in my ability to finish it even though it dragged on for years. Many thanks go to Jeffrey Schier for his caring and careful editorial work. I'm lucky to have him as the manuscript editor for a second time (he edited my book *Beyond Methods* as well). His accomplished editorial skills made the manuscript clear and concise. Thanks also to the Yale University Press reviewers of the original manuscript for this book: Alistair Pennycook, University of Technology, Sydney; Robert Phillipson, Copenhagen Business School; and Thomas Scovel, San Francisco State University.

I am also thankful to San José State University, particularly the

Global Studies Institute, for offering me a fellowship that enabled me to work on this project. I also thank Jean Shiota, Faculty Lab Coordinator at the office of Academic Technology, who was always ready and willing to treat my computer illiteracy.

Finally, my family. To Revathi, who took a special interest in this book, for sharing her expertise in cultural studies and for offering constructive criticism. Thank you for helping me with the chapter on hybridity, especially in interpreting the poem included in Chapter 7. Chandrika and Anand, thank you for enduring my long spells at the computer ("Why are you working all the time?") and my brief spans of playing with you. Your experiences and explorations have provided me with valuable insights into the pain and pleasure of growing up in a culturally globalized world.

Cultural Globalization and Language Education

CHAPTER 1

The Lay of the Land

I invoke my authorial privilege to begin this book on cultural globalization and language education with a brief autobiographical note. I consider myself bilingual and bicultural. I was born in the state of Tamilnadu in South India, where I spent my childhood and a good part of my early adulthood. Tamil is my mother tongue. I began my never-ending process of learning English as a second language when I was about ten years old. Later, in 1984 (coincidentally the year made infamous by George Orwell), I uprooted myself from my native sociocultural soil looking for greener pastures in the United States.

In due course, the Immigration and Naturalization Services of the U.S. Department of Justice gave me what is popularly called a "green card," which is actually pink. The card characterized me as a "resident alien" with a nine-digit identification number prefixed by the letter A. Although I was initially amused by the label "alien"—a label normally associated with funny-looking fictional creatures from outer space—I had grown to feel comfortable with it particularly after watching heroic as well as hilarious deeds of aliens romanticized in popular movie series ranging from George Lucas's *Star Wars* to Mel Brooks's spoof of this genre. Once I sufficiently "naturalized" myself and became an American citizen, I was no longer officially considered alien.

Upon completing my formal educational voyages, which took me through the soaring halls of the University of Madras in India, the serpentine loops of the University of Lancaster in the United Kingdom, and the sprawling campuses of the University of Michigan in the United States, I eventually landed in the city of San Jose, located in the South Bay region of northern California, an area better known to the outside world as Silicon Valley. I teach at San José State University, proudly dubbed "the Metropolitan University of Silicon Valley." It is ranked as one of the region's most diverse campuses. At the dawn of the new millennium it boasted a student population of 30,104, with Asians (a politically convenient cover term for people who are as linguistically, culturally, and religiously as diverse as Chinese, Indian, Japanese, Filipino, Vietnamese, etc.) forming the single largest ethnic community (38 percent), followed by whites (30 percent), Latinos (14 percent), African-Americans (4 percent), and a sprinkling of others that include Native-Americans (less than 1 percent).

I live in the South Bay city of Cupertino, which prides itself as the global center for information technology by serving as the headquarters of several computer industries located there. It is truly a multiethnic city where many different hyphenated Americans—Chinese-Americans, Japanese-Americans, Indian-Americans, Mexican-Americans, and others—attempt to live together harmoniously with nonhyphenated Americans. My home, facing the foothills of Cupertino, is an "Indian" home in many respects. I speak Tamil in my home, I celebrate Indian festivals, I go to Indian temples, I frequent Indian cultural centers, I visit Indian families, and yes, I watch Indian movies. In these cultural discourse domains, what guides my behavior and my way of life is my Indian value system. But when I visit my American friends to socialize, I behave in a culturally appropriate way guided by a different value system. When I go to my workplace to practice my vocation and earn my living, I try to adhere to American cultural expectations. In other words, in spite of the geographical (dis)location, I draw from my *inherited* cultural tradition whenever I participate in Indian cultural discourse domains. I feel comfortable with that. I draw from my *learned* cultural experience whenever I participate in American cultural discourse domains. And, I feel comfortable with that, too.

I see a similar scenario being played out at a miniscule level with my two children—Chandrika and Anand, who are, at the time of this writing, seven and five years old, respectively. Weekdays they go to Faria, an alternative elementary school, where they interact with white American teachers and play with white American as well as Asian-American children. There they hear stories and sing songs that are deeply embedded in mainstream American sociocultural values. On weekends they go to Bala Vihar, a learning center run by the local branch of Chinmaya Mission, where they interact with Indian teachers and play with Indian children. There they hear stories and sing songs that are deeply embedded in Indian sociocultural values.

At home they practice what they learn from their teachers—when they are not watching Scooby-Doo or Winnie the Pooh, that is. At bedtime they read (or have read to them) both American and Indian storybooks and seem to enjoy them both. During Diwali, an Indian festival of lights, they enjoy lighting oil lamps, wearing new clothes, and eating special sweets. During Pongal, a Tamil Thanksgiving Day, they wonder why the ritualistic practices associated with it are "so funny" compared to those of American Thanksgiving Day, even though both are called the same. At Christmastime they have fun decorating our Christmas tree with colored lights and replicas of their favorite cartoon characters, and, like most other children, they get up early on Christmas day and anxiously run to see what Santa has brought for them.

As far as I can tell, they seem to feel comfortable with different cultural miniworlds they inhabit. In fact, they seem to enjoy the different cultural experiences that come with different cultural encounters. So far, that is.

I say *so far* because I recognize that things may change as my children grow up and assert their independence. Anecdotal evidence from my Indian friends who have older children suggests a U-shaped cultural phenomenon (see fig. 1.1). During their pre-teen years, children of recent immigrants joyously follow the cultural beliefs and practices introduced to them by their parents. But during their teenage years they experience severe peer pressure and often rebel against their inherited culture, hate everything associated with it, and even denounce their parents for making them look and behave culturally "deviant." And then, in young adulthood, they begin to realize the significance of being bilingual and bicultural, and they recognize the economic as well as the intellectual value of their cultural capital. Once that realization dawns on them, they begin to blame their parents for not bringing them up sufficiently bilingual and bicultural. This is by no means a universal phenomenon, but it seems to occur fairly frequently among the Indian immigrant population and, probably, among other ethnic communities as well. I will not be surprised if my children go through a similar cycle of cultural transformation.

Pre-teen   **Young Adult**
(Acceptance of   (Respect for
inherited culture)   inherited culture)

Teen
(Rejection of inherited culture)

Figure 1.1. U-shaped cultural phenomenon

To return to the adult world, the point I am trying to make is that it is not easy to understand or explain the complex formation of an individual's cultural identity, particularly when different cultures are in considerable contact. Several schools of sociological thought attempt to explain how an individual's cultural identity is constructed in a multilingual and multicultural environment. Most of these thoughts can be subsumed under three broad categories of cultural concepts: (a) cultural assimilation, (b) cultural pluralism, and (c) cultural hybridity. A detailed review of these concepts appears in subsequent chapters. Suffice it to say here that these concepts do not have adequate explanatory power to tease out the complex process of identity formation in an increasingly globalizing world.

In a nutshell, and to somewhat preempt the discussions that follow, proponents of cultural assimilation would expect me to adopt the behaviors, values, beliefs, and lifestyles of the dominant cultural community and become absorbed in it, losing my own in the process. In other words, they expect me to have metamorphosed into somebody with a totally different cultural persona. I do not see any noticeable evidence of such a metamorphosis in me.

Proponents of cultural pluralism would expect me to be a cultural snob, exhibiting superficial knowledge of, and shallow interest in, various cultural communities that I come into contact with as a citizen of a multicultural society. For instance, it would be considered politically correct for me, as an educated Bay area resident, to attend the Vietnamese Tet festival in January, recall African-

American heritage in February, revel in the Chinese lantern festival in March (depending on the lunar calendar), celebrate the Japanese cherry blossom festival in April, rejoice at the history of the Mexican *Cinco de mayo* in May, admire the Native-American powwow in June, etc. I would be expected to experience these rituals on an annual basis, although I am free to withdraw myself into my own cultural cocoon in the interregnums. I do not think I have become such a cultural snob.

Proponents of cultural hybridity would expect me to create a "third culture," or a "third space," without allowing either my inherited Indian culture or my learned American culture to fully determine my values and beliefs. They would expect me to live in a state of ambivalence, a state of in-betweenness that is supposed to result when individuals, voluntarily or involuntarily, displace themselves from one national/cultural context and get transplanted into another national/cultural context. I do not believe I am dangling in a cultural limbo.

Instead, I believe I live in several cultural domains at the same time—jumping in and out of them, sometimes with ease and sometimes with unease. I am certainly not unique, nor are my children. Thousands of people all over the world have crossed the borders of their native land for one reason or another; thousands of people all over the world are truly bilingual and bicultural. Like me, they live in different cultural domains at the same time, and at different levels of sophistication. In fact, one does not even have to cross one's national borders to experience cultural complexity. If we, as we must, go beyond the traditional approach to culture that narrowly associates cultural identity with national identity ("American culture," "Chinese culture," "Japanese culture," etc.) and take into consideration subcultural variations such as race, religion, class, and gender, then we easily realize that human communities are not monocultural cocoons but rather multicultural mosaics. Added to this equation is the astounding degree of cultural awareness that is being created because of the emerging process of cultural globalization, aided by information revolution.

What lies behind my lived experience, and that of a multitude of others, is a complex process of creating critical cultural consciousness through constant and continual self-reflection. What guides us in such a critical self-reflection is our inherited culture derived from the time-tested traditions of the cultural community into which each of us is born. Our learned knowledge and lived experience of other cultural discourse domains not only expand our cultural horizon but also clarify and solidify our individual inherited cultural heritage. This critical self-reflection helps us to identify and understand what is good and bad about our own culture, and what is good and bad about other cultures. In other words, in understanding other cultures, we understand our own culture better; in understanding our own, we understand other cultures better. This is the hallmark of an individual's complex cultural growth.

It is precisely the complexity of an individual's cultural growth that the language teaching profession has, in my view, almost completely ignored. Traditional approaches to culture teaching focus rather narrowly on helping second/foreign language (L2) learners develop the linguistic ability to use the target language in culturally appropriate ways for the specific purpose of performing certain speech acts (apologizing, requesting, thanking, etc.) in certain specified contexts. More recent approaches encompass an equally narrow focus on cultural arts and artifacts or cultural rites and rituals. Such approaches are clearly based on a simple and simplistic view of culture, culture learning, and culture teaching.

In order to be cognizant of the complexity of cultural identity, all we need to do is simply to look around and realize that we live in an increasingly globalizing world, a world that is in the firm grip of economic and cultural globalization. The relationship between cultural globalization and L2 learning and teaching is much closer and more complex than we in the language teaching profession have been hitherto willing to acknowledge. While we heartily talk about English as a global language, we hardly touch upon the complex process of globalization and its impact on learning and teaching culture in the language classroom of the twenty-first century.

The unfolding and the unfailing impact of cultural globalization on English as second/foreign language (ESL/EFL) learning, teaching, and teacher education constitutes the central focus of this book. Although I highlight ESL/EFL education, the book certainly has relevance to language education in general as well. Drawing on insights from anthropological, sociological, cultural, and applied linguistic studies, I first critique the notions of cultural assimilation, cultural pluralism, and cultural hybridity. The argument I make in this book is that these notions, conceived and constructed mostly by Western or Westernized scholars, offer only a limited and limiting relevance to L2 learning and teaching in a culturally glob-alized and globalizing world. Instead, I will explore the notion of cultural realism as one possible alternative guiding principle for the construction of individual identity that draws from global cultural consciousness.

I hope to show that any attempt to develop global cultural consciousness in the L2 learner must minimally take into account four realities that shape everyday life in the twenty-first century: (a) the global reality that marks dwindling space, shrinking time, and disappearing borders; (b) the national reality that nurtures robust (and, sometimes, militant) nationalism partly as a reaction to the onslaught of perceived global cultural homogenization, (c) the social reality that is created and sustained through social institutions such as families, cultural associations, youth clubs, and places of worship, and, finally, (d) the individual reality that depicts the individual as having multiple, contradictory, dynamic, and changing identities. I also hope to show that the global, national, social, and individual realities interweave and interact synergistically, resulting in a cultural whole that is greater than the sum of the parts. They constitute the fundamental elements needed for the construction of individual identity based on cultural realism.

In the following pages I provide a general road map pointing out certain highways that can possibly lead to global cultural consciousness among language learners, teachers, and teacher educators. In doing so, I take readers not only along the road well traveled (Western) but also along the road less traveled (non-Western). It is, of course, up to individual readers to use the road map in any way they deem fit in order to chart their particular path to their particular destination. This book, then, offers no more than a few baby steps toward that destination, and it does so in the true spirit of the Confucian wisdom that "a journey of a thousand miles has to start with a single step," and the Kantian maxim that "the only path that is still open is the critical."

CHAPTER 2

Culture and Its Complexities

"I think of my daughter and myself as having been born in different countries. We are actually born 30 years apart in the United States of America. That means we are born into massively different cultural environments."

"My Friends, this election is about much more than who gets what. It is about who we are. It is about what we believe. It is about what we stand for as Americans. There is a religious war going on in our country for the soul of America. It is a cultural war, as critical to the kind of nation we will one day be as was the Cold War itself."

"It is my hypothesis that the fundamental source of conflict in this new world will not be primarily ideological or primarily economic. The great divisions among humankind and the dominating source of conflict will be cultural. Nation states will remain the most powerful actors in world affairs, but the principal conflicts of global politics will occur between nations and groups of different civilizations. The clash of civilizations will dominate global politics. The fault lines between civilizations will be the battle lines of the future."

The parental voice belongs to anthropologist Mary Catherine Bateson (2000). She was responding to an interviewer's question on the issue of crossing cultures. She was highlighting the cultural gap between members of different generations within the same family and emphasizing the need to learn to deal with cultural strangeness in the home so that we know how to deal with cultural strangeness outside.

The political voice belongs to conservative columnist Patrick Buchanan (1992), who was twice a candidate for the Republican U.S. presidential nomination. The statement is part of the Republican National Convention speech he delivered in Houston, Texas, on August 17, 1992. He was referring to the ongoing culture wars between conservative and liberal activists in the United States and was entreating his conservative supporters "to take back our culture."

The professional voice belongs to Harvard political scientist Samuel Huntington (1993), who, in a controversial paper published in *Foreign Affairs,* argued that cultural fault lines are fast becoming global battle lines. He later elaborated his thesis in his best-selling book *The Clash of Civilizations and the Remaking of World Order* (Huntington, 1998). There are those who believe that 9/11 and the ensuing wars in Afghanistan and Iraq are but the latest examples of the clash of cultures and civilizations.

Three voices. One factor. Culture seems to possess an extraordinary power to sow the seeds of dissension between members of a family, between communities in a nation, and between nations in this world. What exactly is this entity called culture, which seems to have become an overbearing force that unites as well as divides individuals, communities, and nations?

2.1. The Idea of Culture

"Culture," said Raymond Williams, the author of *Keywords: A Vocabulary of Culture and Society,* "is one of the two or three most complicated words in the English language" (1976, p. 87). The reason is that the word has "come to be used for important concepts in several distinct intellectual disciplines and in several distinct and incompatible systems of thought" (p. 87). In highlighting the complex nature of culture, Williams was actually echoing the views of the eighteenth-century German philosopher Johann Herder, who wrote of the German word *Kultur:* "Nothing is more indeterminate than this word, and nothing more deceptive" (cited in Williams, 1976, p. 89). Although culture is one of the most studied and most used concepts in human history, it has stubbornly defied a clear-cut definition. There is also no consensus about what it really is. In fact, the concept is so elusive that the British cultural critic Stuart Hall came to the conclusion that there is not much point in trying to define culture (1997).

The elusive nature of the concept, however, has not prevented social scientists from attempting to define it. American anthropologist Clifford Geertz offered the widely used explanation that culture "denotes a historically transmitted pattern of meanings embodied in symbols, a system of inherited conceptions in symbolic forms by means of which people communicate, perpetuate and develop their knowledge about and attitudes towards life" (1979, p. 89). In its widest sense, then, culture stands for creative endeavors, such as art, architecture, theater, dance, music, and literature, that constitute the intellectual and aesthetic life of a community. It also stands for beliefs, morals, customs, norms, and values that govern the practice of everyday life. The former is generally referred to as Culture with a capital C and the latter as culture with a small c.

Such a distinction, however, is seldom maintained even among experts in the field, leading to the lamentation that "whenever a group of sociologists meets to discuss culture, it becomes quickly apparent that there is (still) no agreement on the meaning of this core term of sociological analysis. At one time or another, myths, values, eating and dressing habits, scientific theories, social norms, novels, and situated definitions have all been treated as elements of culture" (Mayntz, 1992, p. 219). Compounding this prevalent ambiguity is the fact that the word *culture* is used as a noun, giving the wrong impression that it is an object or a thing or a museum piece. Many scholars (e.g., Appadurai, 1996; Street, 1993) find the nominal usage of the word troubling. In a paper entitled "Culture Is a Verb," Brian Street (1993) argued that culture is a dynamic process of meaning-making, and therefore it carries the attributes of a verb rather than those of a noun. Agreeing with him, Hall emphasized that what is important is not what culture *is* but what culture *does*.

What culture does, according to Geertz (1973/2000), is to maintain as well as transform order in a society. In performing such a central function, culture provides individuals and groups of individuals with psychological structures that guide various aspects of their life. It steers them in their intellectual, spiritual, and aesthetic development. It offers them a rationale for their behavior, a prism through which to see it, and a measurement by which to evaluate it. It presents them with a basis for identity formation, thus helping them develop a sense of solidarity with other members of their community and the country. It shapes their aspirations and attitudes toward self and society. It equips them with a road map to explore the possibilities as well as the limits of their individual rights and responsibilities. In addition, it also nurtures in them prejudices and stereotypes that may prove to be detrimental to human understanding. Culture thus plays an overarching and overbearing role in the development of an individual.

Such an overarching notion of culture, as Williams noted (1977, p. 63), is "an interrelated configuration of archaic, residual and emergent cultures." The archaic dimension represents past historical patterns that are of symbolic value even if they are no longer considered relevant. They are manifested in proverbs and expressions used in everyday speech and also in rites and rituals followed during festivals, etc. The residual dimension represents patterns of behavior that are still considered relevant and effective. The emergent dimension, as the term suggests, represents nascent ways of behavior that are still in the process of being shared and established. This three-dimensional aspect of culture highlights the interaction between the old and the new in cultural patterns of individuals as well as communities.

Culture is also closely linked to *civilization,* yet another equally problematic concept. The two terms are used sometimes synonymously and sometimes hierarchically. Huntington, for instance, treated civilization as the broadest cultural entity. Thus, he pointed out, "the culture of a village in southern Italy may be different from that of a village in northern Italy, but both will share in a common Italian culture that distinguishes them from German villages. European communities, in turn, will share cultural features that distinguish them from Chinese and Hindu communities. Chinese, Hindus, and Westerners, however, are not part of any broader cultural entity. They constitute civilizations. A civilization is thus the highest cultural grouping of people and the broadest level of cultural identity people have short of that which distinguishes human from other species" (Huntington, 1996, p. 43). But he also added: "Civilizations have no clear cut boundaries and no precise beginnings and endings. People can and do redefine their identities and, as a result, the composition and shape of civilizations change over time" (p. 43).

Emphasizing the interconnectedness not only between civilizations and culture but also between cultures themselves, the Australian historian Robbie Robertson noted: "in reality, the grand cultures that civilizations are said to represent were never discrete. We cannot declare cultures independent and place them within an evolutionary hierarchy. In fact, what made cultures distinctive and gave them lasting meaning and significance was their interconnectedness" (2003, p. 49). Actually, cultures thrive in part because of the connections they forge with one another. It is meaningless to speak of a monocultural society, because, as the French anthropologist Claude Levi-Strauss has persuasively argued, "there never has been such a society. All cultures are the result of a mishmash, borrowings, mixtures that have occurred, though at different rates, ever since the beginning of time. Because of the way it is formed, each society is multicultural and over the centuries has arrived at its own original synthesis. Each will hold more or less rigidly to this mixture that forms its culture at a given moment" (Levi-Strauss cited in Borofsky, ed., 1994, p. 424). In other words, because no culture can exist in its purest form, every culture is, willy-nilly, a hybrid culture.

The interconnected nature of culture has been well analyzed by other European social scientists such as Mikhail Bakhtin, Pierre Bourdieu, and Michel de Certeau. They have all recognized that cross-fertilization of culture is as natural as it is endemic. Dismissing the illusion of cultural boundedness or cultural homogeneity, de Certeau (1997) talked about "culture in the plural." He invoked the artistic image of a bricolage to refer to cultural creativity that reuses and recombines disparate materials. Maintaining that "culture in the singular has become a political mystification" and therefore "deadly," he saw our challenge as "more than likely to be one of finding ourselves before the hypothesis of a plurality of cultures, that is, of systems of references and meanings that are heterogeneous in relation to each other" (1997, pp. 67–68). In a way, he anticipated the impact of economic and cultural globalization (see Chapter 3) when he asserted that "to the homogenization of economic structures there must be a corresponding diversification of cultural expressions and institutions. The more the economy unifies, the more culture must be variegated" (p. 68).

The plural character of culture is the result of the contact between cultural communities and of the consumption of cultural commodities, both of which create the conditions necessary for cultural change. Various forms of migration, some forced and some voluntary, have traditionally been the primary source of cultural contacts among people of different cultural beliefs and practices. In the past, industrial revolution triggered a mass movement of migrant workers. It was followed by information revolution that carried alien ideas into far-off places. Now, the emerging process of globalization has vastly increased the flow of capital and people across the world. All these developments accelerate culture change. But, culture change is not something that takes place instantly before our eyes; it matures over time. As Geertz put it so aptly, "culture moves rather like an octopus too—not all at once in a smoothly coordinated synergy of parts, a massive coaction of the whole, but by disjointed movements of this part, then that, and now the other which somehow cumulate to directional change" (1973/2000, p. 408).

2.2. Culture and Community

Clearly, any cumulative directional change is the result of complex interactions between the individual, the community he or she belongs to, and the larger society of which the community is a part. Operating at different levels of influence and interest, these three important players of cultural change function sometimes in tandem and sometimes at cross-purposes. The relationship between them, along with their relative importance, has long been the subject of sociological thought. With regard to the two larger entities, there seems to be a consensus on a distinction drawn by the nineteenth-century German sociologist Ferdinand Tönnies (1955) between what he called *Gemeinschaft* (community) and *Gesellschaft* (society). To put it simply, the former consists of a network of personal relationships based on extended kinship where individuals are bonded together in a close-knit web of mutual interdependence both for family life and for leisure activities. The latter, on the other hand, consists of laws, rules, and regulations that formalize social relationships and interactions in a more impersonal and formal fashion. Community thus presents a shared sense of individualized identity while society presents a general notion of institutionalized collectivity.

A society also gives its members a sense of belonging normally associated with the nation-state. But still, a society consists of several communities formed on the basis of factors such as ethnicity, religion, or language. Many of these communities do not have distinct boundaries; they overlap in beliefs and practices. In the United States, for instance, we speak of the white community, the black community, the Hispanic community, the Jewish community, the Catholic community, and so on. There are several markers of cultural identity that bind members of a community together. By and large, they speak the same language, worship the same God, tell the same stories, share the same memories, eat the same food, follow the same customs.

In spite of common cultural characteristics that unite its members, a community is an amorphous entity. It is made up of numerous individuals. Sometimes they operate within the confines of a community. Other times they are in blatant conflict with it. It is, however, the unrelenting efforts of individuals or groups of individuals that overcome resistance to culture change. The domination of individuals "results from the way they integrate, reflect upon, and modify their own cultural heritage and that of other people with whom they come into contact" (Gutmann, 1994, p. 7). The America of 1960s, for instance, presents a clear case. Mostly in response to what was perceived to be repressive sociocultural norms of the period leading up to the 1950s, a sustained countercultural movement gathered momentum particularly among the younger generation. This counterculture slowly and surely reshaped not only art and music, but also people's attitudes toward basic values regarding family, gender, morality, and sexuality. While the 1960s counterculture has left lasting legacies to the American society, it is not without its detractors, as evidenced in the ongoing culture wars that are ideologically and sometimes politically driven. Hot-button issues such as abortion and same sex marriage continue to pit the individual against the community as well as against the society at large.

An in-depth analysis of the dialectical relationship between the individual and the society comes from the work of the French social theorist Pierre Bourdieu (1977, 1991, 2000). According to him, individuals acquire a set of durable dispositions through intensive and extensive involvement in the practice of their everyday life. He calls these dispositions *habitus*. This acquired habitus in turn functions as a prism through which individuals see themselves and others. It conditions their words, their deeds, and their attitudes. It is at once a product of sociological forces and a creation of individual agency. It "restores to the agent a generating, unifying, constructing, classifying power, while recalling that this capacity to construct social reality, itself socially constructed, is not that of a transcendental subject but of a socialised body, investing in its practice socially constructed organising principles that are acquired in the course of a situated and dated social experience" (Bourdieu, 2000, pp. 136–37). It is through their agency, aided no doubt by their hierarchically situated conditions, that individuals accumulate what Bourdieu calls *cultural capital*. Very much like its economic counterpart, cultural capital is generated through various means, primarily socialization and education. The cultural capital so formed permits individuals to explore and establish alternative cultural practices and strategies that contribute not only to their own cultural growth but also to their community's cultural change.

To what degree individuals share the basic values of a given cultural community is a question that has perennially beset social scientists. One of the ways in which this question is often framed is in terms of individualism and collectivism, a familiar dichotomy that has been described as the single most important aspect of cultural behavior. According to Triandis (1988), collectivism represents a sociocultural pattern that consists of individuals who see themselves as parts of one or more collectives such as family, tribe, or nation. Their behavior is primarily motivated by the norms of and duties imposed by those collectives. They give priority to the goals of these collectives over their own personal goals. Individualism, on the other hand, represents a sociocultural pattern that consists of loosely linked individuals who view themselves as independent of the collective. They are primarily motivated by their own preferences, needs, rights, which are constantly negotiated with the collectives. They give priority to their personal goals over the goals of the collective.

Sociologists have neatly divided the world into two camps on the individualism-collectivism dimension, generally allotting the West to the individualism camp and the East to the collectivism camp. "European-American notions of personality," summarized Min-Sun Kim (2002, pp. 11–12), "are afforded and maintained by a great many cultural meanings, including the idea that difference among people is obvious and good; the belief that a person can be separated from society or the social situation; and the assumption that social behavior is rooted in, and largely determined by, one's underlying traits." In East Asian cultures, in contrast, she continued, "the self is defined predominantly in terms of relationships and group memberships. In this alternative view, the self is inherently social— an integral part of the collective. The key feature of interdependence is not distinctiveness or uniqueness, but a heightened awareness of the other and of the nature of one's relation to the other" (p. 13).

Such stark contrasts between the two sociocultural patterns are useful for the purpose of sociological analysis, but in reality they overlap both in the individual and across cultures indicating that they function more as a continuum than as a dichotomy (for more discussion on the problematic nature of this distinction, see Chapter 9). For instance, the Japanese sociologist Sugimoto (1997) argued that the culture of unbridled collectivism attributed to the Japanese society is more a matter of representation than of reality. Without denying that collectivism does play a role in Japanese cultural behavior, he questioned the notion that it is unique to the Japanese or to the Eastern societies. Pointing out that individuals and societies may possess this particular characteristic in varying degrees, he lamented that little attention is given to the possibility that some Japanese may have it in greater degree while other Japanese may have very little of it. Yet another misrepresentation, according to him, is the presupposition that the trait has prevailed in Japan for an unspecified period of time, independent of historical circumstances.

Simplistic characterizations of the Self and the society have also led to stereotypical representations of the Self and the Other (a reference to people who have been historically excluded and marginalized). "Otherization" is a crudely reductive process that ascribes an imagined superior identity to the Self and an imagined inferior identity to the Other. There is a general tendency among individuals and communities to portray themselves as having an identity that is desirable and developed while presenting the identity of people who are racially, ethnically, or linguistically different as undesirable and deficient. Most often a significant power differential is involved in the process of otherization, particularly cultural otherization.

Although the process of cultural otherization has been with us from the hoary past, it became much more pronounced during the colonial history of the twentieth century. Drawing from their personal experience with French colonialism in northern Africa, psychiatrist Frantz Fanon and philosopher Albert Memmi have theorized the relationship between the colonizer and the colonized, and in the process have elaborated on the process of cultural otherization. In two of his well-known works—*Black Skin, White Masks,* and *The Wretched of the Earth*—Fanon described how the colonizer deliberately creates "an inferiority complex" in the soul of the colonized by destroying and burying "local cultural originality" (Fanon,

1952/1967, p. 18), and how colonial domination oversimplifies and disrupts "in spectacular fashion the cultural life of a conquered people" (Fanon 1961/1963, p. 236). In a similar vein, Memmi in his oft-quoted book, *The Colonizer and the Colonized*, showed how colonizers systematically devalue the colonized and how this devaluation extends to every aspect of life. He pointed out that the devaluation of the Other is always presented as a contrast to Self. "Ethical, or sociological aesthetic or geographic comparisons, whether explicit and insulting or allusive and discreet, are always in favor of the mother country and the colonialist. This place, the people here, the customs of this country are always inferior— by virtue of an inevitable and pre-established order" (1957/1965, pp. 67–68).

Following Fanon and Memmi, cultural theorist Edward Said (1978) presented in his influential book *Orientalism* a critical interpretation of a number of literary, historical, sociological, and anthropological texts produced by colonial writers, and he argued that the colonized people are dehumanized, stereotyped, and treated not as communities of individuals but as an indistinguishable mass about whom one could amass knowledge. According to him, there are so many stereotypical observations which are made again and again about colonized countries and cultures that they cannot be attributed simply to the individual author's beliefs, but can only be products of widespread belief systems structured by discursive frameworks and legitimized by the power relations found in colonialism.

Said used the term *orientalism* to refer to the discursive field constituted by Western representations of the Other. Orientalism is a systematically constructed discourse by which the West "was able to manage—and even produce—the Orient politically, sociologically, militarily, ideologically, scientifically, and imaginatively" (Said, 1978, p. 3). It forms an interrelated web of ideas, images, and texts from the scholarly to the popular, produced by artists, writers, missionaries, travelers, politicians, militarists, administrators, that shape and structure Western understanding and management of colonized cultures/peoples. The discourse of orientalism, Said showed, is built on a binary opposition between the West and the East, Us and Them, that produces an essentialized and static Other. Maintaining that orientalism has produced a discourse or a structure of thinking about the Other, he explained that such a structure has created not only interested knowledge but also the very reality it seeks to describe. The works of Fanon, Memmi, Said, and other post-colonial thinkers clearly reveal that cultural images of other people that most of us have constructed in our minds may be no more than poor representations of reality.

To sum up this section, we learned that culture is an elusive concept. It plays a central function in the life of individuals, communities, and nations, all three of which are constantly locked in a dialectical relationship facilitating as well as constraining cultural change and cultural growth. While communities and societies as a whole do perform gatekeeping functions, it is individuals and groups of individuals that largely shape the contours of cultural transformation. We also learned that cultures are not an island unto themselves; they are all interconnected, making every culture, in effect, a hybrid culture. The concept of culture is so complicated and contentious that even scholarly representations of culture often reflect overgeneralized, stereotyped, and otherized representations. In all this, a tool that plays an instrumental role is language.

2.3. Culture and Language

The connection between language and culture has long been a subject of intellectual speculation. A theoretical articulation of its connection that is well-known and much debated is what has come to be known as the Sapir-Whorf hypothesis, named after American linguistic anthropologist Edward Sapir and his student Benjamin Lee Whorf. In a nutshell, the hypothesis states that *language determines thought*. That is, the way we think and behave is conditioned and constrained by the language we use. The hypothesis grew out of the conceptual foundation laid by Sapir and Whorf and their work on American Indian languages such as Apache and Hopi. Sapir maintained that "no two languages are ever sufficiently similar to be considered as representing the same social reality," and so "we see and hear and otherwise experience very largely as we do because the language habits of our community predispose certain choices of interpretation" (Sapir, 1949, p. 162). In other words, people speaking different native languages pay attention to different aspects of reality.

Along with Sapir, Whorf also believed that language is the shaper of ideas and a guide for all thought. In an oft-quoted statement, he categorically wrote:

> We dissect nature along lines laid down by our native languages. The categories and types that we isolate from the world of phenomena we do not find there because they stare every observer in the face; on the contrary, the world is presented in a kaleidoscopic flux of impressions which has to be organized by our minds—and this means largely by the linguistic systems in our minds. We cut nature up, organize it into concepts, and ascribe significances as we do, largely because we are parties to an agreement to organize it in this way—an agreement that holds throughout our speech community and is codified in the patterns of our language. The agreement is, of course, an implicit and unstated one, but its terms are absolutely obligatory; we cannot talk at all except by subscribing to the organization and classification of data which the agreement decrees. (Whorf, 1956, p. 213)

Formalizing his thoughts into a theoretical proposition, Whorf proposed what he called the principle of linguistic relativity, "which means, in informal terms, that users of markedly different grammars are pointed by their grammars toward different types of observations and different evaluations of externally similar acts of observations, and hence are not equivalent as observers, but must arrive at somewhat different views of the world" (1956, p. 221).

The invocation of grammar in the above statement is very instructive because Whorf, though an anthropologist, is not known to have undertaken any extensive ethnographic analysis of American Indians and their way of life. His conclusions about cultural thought patterns of Apaches, for instance, were derived from a linguistic analysis of Apache grammar and from translations of Apache sentences into English. Citing Apache grammatical structures, he provided several examples to show that, compared to speakers of English, the Apaches speak differently. He pointed out that the propositional statement *It is a dripping spring* is expressed in Apache as *As water, or springs, whiteness moves downward*. Similarly, the Apache equivalent of *He invites people to a feast* is *He, or somebody, goes for eaters of cooked food*. Based on similar linguistic analyses, he made an argument that is splendidly circular: Apaches speak differently because they think differently; they think differently because they speak differently.

Several critics have highlighted the problematic nature of the

Sapir-Whorf hypothesis. In a perceptive review, cognitive psychologist Steven Pinker (1995, pp. 58–59) concluded that there is no scientific evidence that languages determine their speakers' ways of thinking. He further noted: "the idea that language shapes thinking seemed plausible when scientists were in the dark about how thinking works or even how to study it. Now that cognitive scientists know how to think about thinking, there is less of a temptation to equate it with language just because words are more palpable than thoughts." Pointing to a major methodological flaw in Whorf's research, Pinker questioned the use of literal translation of sentences as a data source, and even charged that "Whorf rendered the sentences as clumsy, word-for-word translations, designed to make the literal meanings seem as odd as possible" (p. 61). He reckoned that the sentence *It is a dripping spring* could have been translated in Apache as *Clear stuff—water—is falling*. Turning the tables, he said, he could take the English sentence *He walks* and render it as *As solitary masculinity, leggedness proceeds*. Alluding to the fact that the Sapir-Whorf hypothesis, in spite of valid criticism, is still popular among certain sections of the academic community, Pinker asserted: "the discussions that assume that language determines thought carry on only by a collective suspension of disbelief" (1995, p. 58).

That the grammatical structure of one's language determines one's view of the world has been considered too strong a claim, and one with racial overtones as well. In an attempt to distance themselves from linguistic determinism, some scholars have developed a weak version of the hypothesis. Prominent among them was John Carroll, a cognitive psychologist who, in putting together a collection of works by Whorf, rephrased his linguistic relativity principle by stating that the hypothesis should be taken to mean that "the structure of a human being's language influences the manner in which he understands reality and behaves with respect to it" (Carroll, 1956, p. 23). In other words, the strong version of the Sapir-Whorf hypothesis claims that language *determines* thought, the weak version suggests that language *influences* thought.

Following the lead given by Carroll, other linguists have attempted to emphasize the fluidity of what are often seen as fixed cultural realities. Applied linguist Jim Gee, for instance, accepted the Whorfian dictum that different languages "cut up the world" in particular ways but offered a compromise: "The way a language cuts up the world will influence how we initially think about something, but it does not determine how we finish thinking about it. Under pressure we can think about things outside the categories of our language, because we find other people's ways of doing things senseful. We find them senseful because, at least where language is concerned, they are all chosen from the inventory of ways allowed by the human brain, which is, like the eye, everywhere the same across cultures" (1993, p. 11).

Yet another linguist who has vigorously pursued the Whorfian hypothesis is Anna Wierzbicka (1997). Although she acknowledged that "there is a good deal of exaggeration" (p. 6) in the Whorfian account of the language-culture connection, and that his examples and analytical comments are not convincing, she said that "language—and in particular, vocabulary—is the best evidence of the reality of culture" (p. 21). She believed that cultures can be studied, compared, and explained to outsiders through their key concepts expressed in key words such as *friendship, freedom,* etc. "Culture-specific words," she argued, "are conceptual tools that reflect a society's past experience of doing and thinking about things in certain ways; and they help to perpetuate these ways. As a society changes, these tools, too, may be gradually modified and discarded. In that sense, the outlook of a society is never wholly 'determined' by its stock of conceptual tools, but it is clearly influenced by them" (p. 5).

While it is true that certain key words can reflect the reality of culture, sometimes these words get tagged onto them additional semantic nuances with ethnocentric coloration. Consider how we use the pronoun *you.* It is rendered in different ways in different languages according to class, rank, number, degrees of politeness, etc. For instance, French pronouns *tu* and *vous* carry information about both grammatical concepts (singular, plural, or generic) and sociolinguistic functions (formal or informal, polite, or impolite). The same is true of Hindi pronouns *tum* and *aap.* Modern English, on the other hand, does not make such a distinction, although Old English did differentiate between an intimate/familiar *thou* and a more formal *you.* A polite linguistic fiction that seems to have gained quiet acceptance claims that the use of nondifferentiated *you* in English reflects the egalitarian, nonhierarchical nature of English-speaking societies. Nothing could be further from the truth. Whenever I talk to my university president, for instance, I use his first name, and the pronoun *you* to address him. Both of us are aware that this linguistic practice does not in any way diminish the hierarchical power differential between us. Similarly, when I was teaching in India, my students always called me *Sir,* consistent with the Indian sociocultural practice. In the United States, my students call me by my short name, Kumar, and use the pronoun *you* while talking to me. But that does not indicate—and they sure know it— that I have abdicated the hierarchical decision-making authority vested in me as a professor. As Helen Fox rightly pointed out, "to world majority students who have been raised to be comfortable with a certain degree of hierarchy, our efforts to act as though sta- tus differences do not exist can be both amusing and faintly em- barrassing" (1994, p. 54).

Given the problematic nature of language-culture connection, Pinker dismissed even the weak version, calling it banal and unsur- prising. "Language influencing a form of thought in some way," he said, "is hardly an example of incommensurable world views, or of concepts that are nameless and therefore unimaginable or of dissect- ing nature along lines laid down by our native languages" (Pinker, 1995, p. 66). The same sentiment has been expressed differently by sociolinguist Joshua Fishman, who noted that "we are far more valiant, nimble, experienced and successful strugglers and jugglers with language-and-communication problems than Whorf realized" (1980, p. 33).

It is safe to assume from the above discussion that language and culture are linked, but they are not linked inextricably. If the con- nection were inextricable, as the Whorfian hypothesis assumes, then we would not be able to translate successfully from one lan- guage to another, nor would we be able to engage in any fruitful cross-cultural communication. Moreover, the emergence of World Englishes, with their amazing functionality and spread along with the rich body of creative literature in varieties such as Indian En- glish and Nigerian English, proves, if any proof is needed, that cul- ture and language are not irrevocably linked. Novelists such as Chinua Achebe, V. S. Naipal, Salman Rushdie, and scores of others have so effectively and elegantly used the Western language, En- glish, for communicating sociocultural nuances that are alien to Western cultural traditions.

Some language educators have attempted to put the Whorfian theory to good use. Fishman used it to campaign for linguistic plu- ralism. Injecting a moral and ethical concern, he observed: "Pre- cisely because Whorf can be interpreted as believing that there are only limited number of language-based perspectives available to mankind he must also be interpreted as basically arguing for the benefits of language pluralism: the world will be a better place and humanity will be more successful in solving its ever more serious problems if we all master more (and more dissimilar) languages, because then we can share perspectives and shift perspectives more appropriately. The height of rationality, for Whorf, is the ability to select from among many language-dependent perspectives and to combine them productively" (1980, p. 27). Similarly, Fox (1994) urged language teachers, particularly teachers of writing, to learn something about the cultures that have informed their learners' views of themselves and the world. She is convinced that "when we have begun to understand not just that cultural differences exist, but how it feels to experience the world differently, it may be easier to see how culture underlies all the other interesting things that make writers human—gender, status, experience, interest, will, re- sistance, character" (p. 15). Clearly, the language-culture connec- tion has immense implications for language education.

2.4. Culture and Language Education

Culture has been an integral part of language education from time immemorial. In his classic book *Twenty-Five Centuries of Language Teaching*, Louis Kelly wrote that "the cultural orientation of lan- guage teaching has always been one of its unstated aims" (1969, p. 378). Unstated. That is to say, culture was not considered an overt part of language teaching curriculum. Cultural understanding was assumed to be a by-product of language learning. Such an assump- tion, of course, lacks empirical support. Only after World War II, when international commerce and communication became wide- spread, did language educators recognize the need for teaching culture explicitly. In the 1990s, its importance achieved greater awareness, partly because of extensive migration, exile, and dis- placement, and the renewed interest in multiculturalism.

A major thrust for the teaching of culture came from the field of foreign language education. A recent collection of papers aptly titled *Culture as the Core* (Lange and Paige, eds., 2003) presents a histori- cal narration of how the 1990s marked a turning point in the poli- cies and practices of teaching culture. After many years of painstak- ing work, the National Standards for Foreign Language Education

Project (1996) presented a comprehensive document on *Standards for Foreign Language Learning: Preparing for the 21st Century*. It lists five major goal areas referred to as the five C's of foreign language education: Communication, Cultures, Connections, Comparisons, Communities (see Lafayette, 2003, for more details), with eleven clearly delineated standards. Four of these standards pertain directly to culture:

> Standard 2.1: Students demonstrate an understanding of the relationship between the practices and perspectives of the culture studied.

> Standard 2.2: Students demonstrate an understanding of the relationship between the products and perspectives of the culture studied.

> Standard 3.2: Students acquire information and recognize the distinctive viewpoints that are only available through the foreign language and its cultures.

> Standard 4.2: Students demonstrate understanding of the concept of culture through comparisons of the cultures studied and their own.

An indirect reference to culture is also found in the fifth goal, Communities, which carries a call for participation in multilingual communities at home and around the world.

Standards defines culture in familiar terms, i.e., Culture with a capital C and culture with a small c. It defines the former as "the formal institutions (social, political, and economic), the great figures of history, and those products of literature, fine arts, and the sciences that were traditionally assigned to the category of elite culture" (1996, p. 40), and the latter as "those aspects of daily living studied by the sociologist and the anthropologist: housing, clothing, food, tools, transportation, and all the patterns of behavior that members of the culture regard as necessary and appropriate" (p. 40). Placing the concept of culture at the core of the language curriculum, *Standards* declares the rationale for teaching culture thus: "American students need to develop an awareness of other people's world views, of their unique way of life, and of the patterns of behavior which order their world, as well as to learn about their contributions to the world at large and the solutions they offer to the common problems of humankind. Such awareness will help combat the ethnocentrism that often dominates the thinking of our young people" (1996, p. 39). The driving force behind the rationale as well as the entire document is the concern that we live in a culturally complex world, and a true understanding of cultures other than our own is a basic ingredient in the development of twenty-first-century citizens.

Interestingly, about when American language educators were preoccupied with the task of redesigning the principles and practices of teaching culture, their European counterparts were engaged in a similar venture. Based on a decade of research by language educators from its various member states, the Council of Europe published in 2001 a document entitled *Common European Framework of Reference for Languages: Learning, Teaching, Assessment.* An important component of this comprehensive framework pertains to the development of what it calls *interculturality* in the language learner. It aims at promoting intercultural awareness that covers, in addition to objective knowledge of "the relation (similarities and distinctive differences) between the 'world of origin' and the 'world of the target community,'" an awareness of "how each community appears from the perspective of the other, often in the form of national stereotypes" (Council of Europe, 2001, p. 103). Toward that end, the *Framework* advises its users to consider the following (p. 105, italics as in original):

- *what cultural intermediary roles and functions the learner will need/be equipped/be required to fulfill;*
- *what features of the home and target culture the learner will need/be enabled/required to distinguish;*
- *what provision is expected to be made for the learner to experience the target culture;*
- *what opportunities the learner will have of acting as a cultural intermediary.*

Evidently, these recommendations are geared toward meeting the needs of a multilingual and multicultural Europe so that its citizens can communicate and work with each other across linguistic and cultural boundaries.

While the American *Standards* and the European *Framework* clearly represent a heightened awareness of as well as a sense of urgency for the effective teaching of culture, they have been critiqued for their conceptual imprecision. Focusing on the American proposal, Bennett, Bennett, and Allen (2003, pp. 241–42) noted that, although the definition of culture adopted by *Standards* is a significant advance over earlier definitions, it "still has the disadvantage of defining culture as something out there—a body of material to be explored and eventually mastered—as opposed to an interactive process between learners and cultural contexts." They also believed that while providing a sound conceptual overview of culture, "the five standards are far less explicit when it comes to suggesting how to structure culture learning" (p. 242). Similarly, with regard to the European proposal, Risager (1998) lamented that the intercultural approach that is dominant in Europe today "rests upon a concept of culture that presupposes an understanding of each of the cultures as a homogeneous entity—though perhaps geographically and socially varied—interacting with others. In my view, this approach is inadequate as an influential paradigm in language teaching, because it is blind to the actual multicultural (and multilingual) character of almost all existing countries or states" (p. 246).

Some of the questions and uncertainties raised about the teaching of culture in the field of foreign language education have been raised in the field of Applied Linguistics and TESOL (Teaching English to Speakers of Other Languages) as well. In a recent review, Holliday, Hyde, and Kullman (2004, p. 62) identified three "major difficulties" facing the field in both theoretical and practical areas: "firstly that the nature of these studies and programmes means that the focus is on problems and difficulties and so 'culture' or what we might call the 'cultural principle' is used in a 'celebration of communication.' Secondly, 'culture' is conceived of in a limited way to refer to resources, behaviour patterns and fixed values. And finally, 'culture' in the limited way described above becomes the necessary and sufficient explanation of intercultural encounters." Adding yet another dimension, Ryuko Kubota (1999, p. 11) noted that studies in Applied Linguistics and TESOL tend "to dichotomize Western culture and Eastern culture and to draw rigid cultural boundaries between them." These remarks echo Atkinson's (1999) conclusion that one of the prevalent views among TESOL educators sees culture as geographically and nationally distinct entities with systems of rules or norms that determine personal behavior. He believed that "if we can develop a notion of culture in the TESOL that takes into account the cultural in the individual, and individual in the cultural, then we will have a conceptualization that will stand us in good stead in the 21st century" (pp. 648–49).

2.5. In Closing

In this chapter I have attempted to bring out the complex and contentious nature of the concept of culture. Although it is famously vague, it undoubtedly shapes the life of individuals, communities, and nations. While cultures have certain distinctive features, they are interconnected so closely that each can be considered a hybrid culture. It is also closely but not irrevocably connected to language. Teaching it in a formal classroom context, therefore, presents both challenges and rewards for language educators, challenging because they do not seem to be fully equipped to cope with it, and rewarding because they have the opportunity to contribute to the development of their learner's cultural identity.

The task facing language educators is made even more formidable because of the forces of globalization that are currently shaping the global flows of interested knowledge and cultural capital. Cultural globalization is a huge elephant that has stealthily intruded into the arena of language education. Its dimensions have not yet adequately captured the attention of the language teacher. It is, however, having an enormous impact not only on real communities but also on "virtual" communities spawned by the Internet. The World Wide Web has given ordinary people an unprecedented capacity to collect and transmit information. It has fast become an astounding entity through which people in various parts of the world find cultural knowledge about communities and nations. And, they find not just the filtered and sanitized versions that government machineries propagate but almost everything—the good, the bad, and the ugly. The language teaching profession, therefore, cannot afford to ignore the emerging processes of globalization.

CHAPTER 3

Cultural Globalization and Its Processes

"Hi, this is Sandy. How may I help you?"

When hundreds of thousands of North Americans and western Europeans dial a toll-free number to book airline tickets, check their bank account, solve a computer glitch, or seek investment advice, they may not be aware that they frequently are talking to customer representatives who are some six to eight thousand miles away, in India, working in the dead of night in quiet offices with clocks showing time in places like New York, Los Angeles, Frankfurt, and London. Nor are they likely to know that the helpful person who answers and identifies herself as "Sandy" is in reality Lakshmi, a twenty-one-year-old who, after undergoing rigorous training to "neutralize" her Indian accent, has taken on a new workplace persona, including a pretend Western name and a pretend American or British accent.

Lakshmi (or Sandy), and thousands of others like her, are part of a new global business enterprise called call centers, which have grown in ever increasing numbers not only in India but also in countries such as China, Ireland, the Philippines, and Russia. These centers constitute just one aspect of BPO, or Business Process Outsourcing. It refers to the business practice followed by corporations and industries around the world that farm out a part of their operations to a third party inside the country or outside (called "offshoring"). These operations cover myriad business transactions such as maintaining accounts and audits, managing human resources databases, offering technical support, and handling customer complaints.

More than ever, offshore outsourcing has now become the hallmark of big business. As *BusinessWeek* (December 8, 2003, pp. 69–70) points out,

> few aspects of U.S. business remain untouched. The hidden hands of skilled Indians are present in the interactive Web sites of companies such as Lehman Brothers and Boeing, display ads in your Yellow Pages, and the electronic circuitry powering your Apple Computer iPod. While Wall Street sleeps, Indian analysts digest the latest financial disclosures of U.S. companies and file reports in time for the next trading day. Indian staff troll the private medical and financial records of U.S. consumers to help determine if they are good risks for insurance policies, mortgages, or credit cards from American Express Co. and J. P. Morgan Chase & Co.

It is not just the business and financial sectors that outsource essential operations, it is also done by governmental agencies (such as the U.S. postal service, and the food stamp programs) as well as medical establishments (such as Massachusetts General Hospital in Boston, which sends magnetic resonance images to be analyzed by radiologists in India). Even religious centers have not lagged behind. In an interesting article titled "Jesus! BPO has even come to Church," the popular English language daily *Indian Express* (dated January 3, 2004) reports that churches in the United States and Europe are outsourcing Holy Mass Intentions—requests for services such as thanksgiving, and memorial masses for the dead—to be performed at the parishes in India.

The primary motivation for outsourcing is, of course, cheap foreign labor. Without denying that outsourcing is a cost-cutting measure, American corporations stress its other advantages. They say it speeds up innovation and economic growth. For instance, as *BusinessWeek* (December 8, 2003, p. 66) points out, General Electric, which opened its John F. Welch Technology Center in Bangalore, India, in the year 2000 "employs 1,800 engineers—a quarter of them have Ph.D.s—who are engaged in fundamental research for most of GE's 13 divisions. In one lab, they tweak the aerodynamic designs of turbine-engine blades. In another they're scrutinizing the molecular structure of materials to be used in DVDs for short-term use in which the movie is automatically erased after a few days. In another, technicians have rigged up a working model of a GE plastics plant in Spain and devised a way to boost output there by 20%." Similarly, Oracle India, the Indian subsidiary of the Silicon Valley–

based high-tech company Oracle, has been the parent company's strategic core since 1996, when workers in India developed from scratch, and in record time, a new software product to access information stored on servers. Citing examples such as these, American corporations argue that offshoring will free up their resources to design and develop new products and ventures, which in turn will stimulate the American economy and ultimately benefit the American consumer.

A 2004 report titled "Choose to Compete," issued by the Computer Systems Policy Project, an arm of the top eight U.S. information technology companies, such as Intel and Hewlett-Packard, argued that U.S. companies must hire qualified workers around the world to meet customer demands and expand their capabilities. It also advised the U.S. government that it should, instead of banning outsourcing, improve the crumbling American school system in order to make American workers competitive. The report echoed an earlier editorial in *BusinessWeek* (December 8, 2003, p. 124): "Just as America reacted to the Soviet Union's sputnik in the 1960s and Japan's manufacturing prowess in the 1980s, so, too, the U.S. must today put into place new education, research, and innovation policies that move it to a higher competitive plane." During a hearing held in January 2004, the U.S. House of Representatives was sternly told by Carly Fiorina, then chief executive officer of Hewlett-Packard, that "there is no job that is America's God-given right anymore. We have to compete for jobs" (*San Jose Mercury News,* dated January 8, 2004, p. 2C).

While outsourcing has certainly boosted the national economy of receiving countries, it has come with mixed blessings for individual workers. It is apparent that outsourcing causes loss of jobs, thus hurting the ordinary worker, even if temporarily. Viewing offshore outsourcing as the root cause for unemployment, workers have started demonstrating against it, drawing comparisons between the loss of blue-collar manufacturing jobs to China, Japan, and South Korea during the second half of the twentieth century, and the loss of white-collar service sector jobs to China, India, and Ireland at the present. While acknowledging the individual sufferings, President Bush pointed out (*San Jose Mercury News,* dated February 23, 2006, pp. 1A & 5A) that "India's middle class is buying air-conditioners, kitchen appliances and washing machines, and a lot of them from American companies like GE and Whirlpool and

Westinghouse. And that means their job base is growing here in the United States."

The sufferings, it seems, are not confined to those who lose their jobs. According to a report in the monthly magazine *India Currents* (September 2003), a large number of call center workers in India, all of whom are between nineteen and twenty-one years old, suffer from severe psychological, social, and other health problems. Because most of them work at night (when it is daytime in the United States and Europe) and eat at odd hours, they exhibit health problems usually associated with people twice their age—indigestion, insomnia, fatigue, and stress. Some of them even exhibit signs of a split personality, as their jobs require them to pretend to be somebody else and speak in a false American or British accent for eight hours a day. They also lack a social life, since their work schedule necessitates that they sleep during the day and work at night. They do not get time off during important Indian festivals, so they hardly spend time with their families on days of cultural and religious importance. Instead, they are free on American holidays such as Fourth of July and Thanksgiving, when everybody else in India is working.

Clearly, the phenomenon described above has multiple dimensions creating multiple tensions: political, economic, social, and cultural. It, however, springs from one single source: globalization. In this chapter I provide a brief overview of globalization. I first explain the concept of globalization and sketch its historical development. Then I focus specifically on cultural globalization and its impact on contemporary life. Finally, I discuss the relevance of cultural globalization to the principles and practices of language education.

3.1. The Concept of Globalization

Globalization is a hotly debated multidimensional concept that cuts across several major academic disciplines such as economics, sociology, cultural studies, political science, and history. The subject is so vast and so varied that no single theoretical framework drawn from a single discipline can explicate it fully. As the preeminent cultural critic, Fredric Jameson (1998, p. xi), pointed out, globalization has become "the modern or postmodern version of the proverbial elephant, described by its blind observers in so many diverse ways." Simply stated, globalization refers to a dominant and driving force that is shaping a new form of interconnections and flows among nations, economies, and peoples. It results in the transformation of contemporary social life in all its economic, political, cultural, technological, ecological, and individual dimensions.

The term *globalization* is commonly used to refer to the process as well as the result of global interconnections, thereby creating unnecessary conceptual confusion. To address this ambiguity, sociologists such as Roland Robertson (1992) have suggested that we use the term *globalization* to refer to the process, and *globality* to refer to its result. In other words, the terms *globalization* and *globality* refer to the cause and effect of the same phenomenon. A consolidated definition that captures the essence of globalization states that it is "a multidimensional set of social processes that create, multiply, stretch, and intensify worldwide social interdependencies and exchanges while at the same time fostering in people a growing awareness of deepening connections between the local and the distant" (Steger, 2003, p. 13). In order to make sense of the concept of globalization, it is essential to understand its historical development.

3.1.1. A Historical Sketch of Globalization

The concept of globalization is so old and yet so new. The current phase of globalization, with its own distinctive features, is dramatically different from its earlier phases, as will become clear later. From a historical perspective, scholars talk about various periods of globalization with various points of departure. For our limited purpose, I shall highlight how a political scientist and a historian have treated the history of globalization in their fascinating books, both published in 2003. I am referring to *Globalization: A Very Short Introduction*, by American political scientist Manfred Steger, and *The Three Waves of Globalization: A History of a Developing Global Consciousness*, by Australian historian Robbie Robertson. I present in this section a bird's-eye view of the history of globalization mostly from their perspective.

Steger (2003, p. 19) believed that globalization "is as old as humanity itself." Accordingly, he identified five distinct historical periods starting with what he called "the prehistoric period" when small bands of hunters and gatherers reached the southern tip of South America. For him, this period lasted from 10,000 B.C.E. to 3500 B.C.E. The second, "the premodern period," covering 3500

B.C.E. to 1500 C.E., was characterized by the invention of writing in Mesopotamia, Egypt, and central China and roughly coincided with the invention of the wheel in southwest Asia. Steger felt that "these monumental inventions" moved globalization to a new level, and, "having contributed little to technology and other civilizational achievements before about 1000 C.E., Europeans northwest of the Alps greatly benefited from the diffusion of technological innovations originating in Islamic and Chinese cultural spheres" (p. 28).

The European contribution to globalization started during the "early modern period" (1500–1750), when Spain, Portugal, the Netherlands, France, and England "all put significant resources into the exploration of new worlds and the construction of new interregional markets that benefited them much more than their exotic 'trading partners'" (p. 29). It is during this period that the seeds of European colonialism were planted. The next period, "the modern period," covering 1750–1970, witnessed a spread of free market economy when Western capitalist enterprises gained power and prestige "fed by a steady stream of materials and resources that originated mostly in other regions of the world" (p. 31). Finally, "the contemporary period," from 1970 onward, marked "another quantum leap in the history of globalization" (p. 35) with "the dramatic creation, expansion, and acceleration of worldwide interdependencies and global exchanges" (p. 35).

Unlike Steger, who went back about 12,000 years and provided a more political history of globalization, Robbie Robertson traveled only about 500 years back and presented a more social history of globalization focusing, as the subtitle of his book promises, on the development of global consciousness. He identified three "waves" of globalization. The first wave centered on regional trade explorations led by Spain and Portugal; the second gained impetus from industrialization led by Britain; and the third is derived from the postwar world order led by the United States. Interestingly, taking a cultural studies perspective, postcolonial critic Walter Mignolo (1998, p. 36) also talked about "three previous stages of globalization under the banners of Christianization (Spanish Empire), Civilizing Mission (British Empire and French Colonization), and Development/Modernization (U.S. Imperialism)."

The first wave of globalization, according to Robbie Robertson, started after 1500 when two maritime powers, Spain and Portugal, sought trade routes to Asia to tap the resources of China and India, which were "already the world's largest and cheapest producers of a range of highly sought-after commodities" (Robertson, 2003, p. 106). In 1492, an explorer from Genoa, Christopher Columbus, with Spanish military and financial support, landed in the Americas, although he set out to find a way across the Atlantic to reach India. Six years later, driven by the fear of Spanish trade advantage, the Portuguese successfully explored their own route to the East when Vasco da Gama rounded Africa and opened up the sea route to India. According to Robertson, this first wave laid the foundation for European empires for modern global trade and finance and for the new global systems of production, all of which immensely benefited people across the European continent.

The second wave, beginning after 1800, is marked by the fruits of industrial revolution that Robertson dubbed the "child" of the first wave. He argued that competition from China and India "created the demand for mechanization" (p. 107), and Britain rose to the occasion with James Watt's steam engine, and his rotative engine that drove machinery. Mechanization promoted productivity, decreased cost, and increased profit. "There is no doubt," observed Robertson, "that industrialization broke China's and India's relative advantage" and "made Britain a powerful trading nation" (p. 116). Countries such as Germany, Japan, and the United States emulated Britain and benefited from the process of globalization that arose out of industrialization. But, "for the majority of the world's peoples, however, globalization meant only one thing: colonialism" (p. 131). Colonialism was extolled as a virtue by the imperial powers, which treated it as a civilizing mission they were destined to perform. "Schools, churches and mass circulation newspapers and magazines spread the word far and wide. So too music, theatre, literature, the visual arts, even postcards. Imperialism became part of the popular culture" (p. 141). Eventually, hegemonic rivalries and economic imperatives led the imperial powers into two world wars, the end of which also marked the end of the second wave of globalization.

The third wave of globalization, after 1945, marked a new era of international cooperation as well as international rivalry. The two major victors of the Second World War, the United States and the Union of Soviet Socialist Republics, sought to divide the world into two ideological camps—capitalist and communist—triggering an unprecedented arms race and untold misery to millions of people around the world. Both the superpowers were imbued with a sense of globalism deeply influenced by their own desire to seize the moment and secure political and economic advantages. They vied with each other to court several newly independent Asian and African countries that, through their intense freedom struggle, rendered the colonies more of a burden, economically and politically, than a blessing for the imperial powers. However, despite decolonization, "the 'civilizing' zeal of former imperialism was far from dead. In Britain and the United States a new mantra emerged. Western values, Western institutions, Western capital, and Western technology. Only by Westernizing could former colonies hope to achieve a modern future" (Robertson, 2003, p. 182). Of course, Westernization was presented largely as modernization.

In order to help modernize developing countries and rebuild war-torn European nations, the United States assumed leadership in establishing three new international economic organizations: the International Monetary Fund (IMF), in charge of administering the international monetary system; the International Bank for Reconstruction and Development (later known as the World Bank), in charge of providing loans for industrial projects; and the General Agreement on Tariffs and Trade (GATT, which in 1995 was transformed into the WTO, World Trade Organization), in charge of formulating and enforcing multilateral trade agreements. These financial institutions also helped create a stable money exchange system in which most nations' currency was pegged to the value of the U.S. dollar. All these measures were taken to ultimately promote American-style free-market economy around the world. This effort has only accelerated with the collapse of the Soviet Union in the 1980s, and with the economic liberalization in communist China and later in socialist India. Such a "triumph of markets over governments" (*BusinessWeek*, December 13, 1999) marks one of the distinctive features of the current phase of globalization.

3.1.2. The Current Phase of Globalization

Even though the concept of globalization is nothing new, the current phase of it is dramatically different from its earlier phases, in both intent and intensity. According to a 1999 United Nations Report on Human Development (p. 29), globalization is changing the world landscape in three distinct ways:

- Shrinking space. People's lives—their jobs, incomes and health— are affected by events on the other side of the globe, often by events that they do not even know about.

- Shrinking time. Markets and technologies now change with unprecedented speed, with action at a distance in real time, with
  impacts on people's lives far away. . . .
- Disappearing borders. National borders are breaking down, not
  only for trade, capital and information but also for ideas, norms,
  cultures and values.

What this means is that the economic as well as cultural lives of
people all over the world are more intensely and more instantly
linked than ever before. Whether we are aware of it or not, we all
are a microscopic mesh in a global web.

The most distinctive feature of the current phase of globalization is the global electronic communication force, the Internet. It
has become the major engine that is driving both economic and cultural globalization. In fact, without global communication, economic growth and cultural change would not have taken place with
"breakneck speed and with amazing reach" (U.N. Report, 1999, p. 30).
That is why Jameson (1998, p. 55) called globalization "a communicational concept, which alternately masks and transmits cultural
or economic meanings." The communicational revolution began in
1990 when Netscape opened up the Internet's World Wide Web and
email technology—hitherto available only to governmental agencies and scientific communities—into a user-friendly communication medium for people all over the world. In a development that is
unprecedented in human history, the Internet has become a unique
source that instantly connects millions of individuals with other individuals, private associations, educational institutions, and government agencies, making possible interaction at a distance and in
real time. In addition, the Internet-based technologies have also accelerated financial transactions. According to one estimate, in the
year 2000 dot-com and e-business firms traded about four hundred
billion dollars over the Web in the United States alone, and the
amount reached about six trillion dollars by the end of 2003 (Steger, 2003, pp. 44–45).

Yet another aspect of the current phase of globalization is the
rise of transnational corporations (TNCs) such as General Motors,
Hitachi, IBM, Mitsubishi, and Siemens, which control much of the
world's investment capital, technology, and access to international
markets. Some of the TNCs are so huge that they are economically
more viable and more powerful than several countries. An estimated fifty-one of the world's one hundred largest economies are
corporations, while forty-nine are countries; moreover, in 1999 one

hundred forty-two of the top two hundred TNCs were based in only three countries: the United States, Japan, and Germany (Steger, 2003, p. 48). The economic clout of these corporations is increasing even more because of the availability of cheap labor, foreign resources, and a deregulated global market. Although what they do affects people in faraway places—as the state of offshore outsourcing narrated in the beginning of this chapter reveals—their primary goal is to increase corporate profit. Considering their stranglehold on global economy, Robbie Robertson (2003, p. 11) declared that "by the close of the twentieth century, the corporate vision of globalism held center stage."

The steep rise in the power of transnational corporations signals a sharp decline in the power of nation-states, a decline that constitutes the third crucial feature of the current phase of globalization. Because of globalization, the world is fast becoming a "borderless world" in which political and economic power has been usurped by global institutions operating through global networks, rendering national sovereignty weak (see Chapter 8). Consequently, not only have nation-states lost their dominance, but, ironically, as the German sociologist Zygmunt Bauman (1998, p. 64) correctly pointed out, "there were now states which—far from being forced to give up their sovereign rights—actively and keenly sought to surrender them, and begged for their sovereignty to be taken away and dissolved in the supra-state formations." A case in point is the long and hard (and eventually successful) campaign mounted by Communist China to become a member of the World Trade Organization, subjecting itself to the enforcing authority of WTO on matters of trade.

As the brief historical narration demonstrates, the impact of globalization on national economies is astounding. Equally astounding is its impact on the sociocultural lives of people all over the world, as we will see. I shall briefly outline the imperatives of cultural globalization here. However, since the thematic focus of this book is cultural globalization and its relevance for language education, I shall take up some of the issues raised here for more detailed treatment in other chapters.

3.2. Cultural Globalization

Cultural globalization refers to the process of cultural flows across the world. It refers to how "contacts between people and their cultures—their ideas, their values, their way of life—have been growing and deepening in unprecedented ways" (U.N. Report, 1999, p. 33). Cultural images from far-off lands flashed across small screens in our living rooms and big screens in multiplex cinemas have made the world "a global neighborhood." Foreign cultures are no longer as foreign as they used to be. Local communities are no longer cultural islands unto themselves. Consequently, people all over the world are faced with unparalleled opportunities for their cultural growth, and with equally unparalleled threats to their cultural identity.

The impact of globalization on culture has become the topic of intense debate among scholars in different disciplines. A close and critical analysis of the relevant literature reveals the emergence of three schools of thought. One group, represented by political scientist Benjamin Barber, historian Francis Fukuyama, and sociologist George Ritzer, believes that some kind of cultural homogenization is taking place in which the American culture of consumerism constitutes the dominant center. Another group, represented by political scientist Samuel Huntington, sociologist Anthony Giddens, and cultural critic John Tomlinson, believes that some kind of cultural heterogenization is taking place in which local cultural and religious identities are being strengthened mainly as a response to the threat posed by globalization. A third group, represented by cultural critic Arjun Appadurai, historian Robbie Robertson, and sociologist Roland Robertson, believes that both homogenization and heterogenization are taking place at the same time, plunging the world in a creative as well as chaotic tension that results in "glocalization" where the global is localized and the local is globalized.

By encapsulating multifarious, and often cacophonous, views on cultural globalization into three schools of thought, I am not suggesting that they all neatly fall into these three categories; in fact, they are all linked together in an overlapping texture of dialectical discourse. Nor am I implying that the scholars I have associated with each school hold identical views without any differences of opinion among them. They all, however, tend to agree that "globalization lies at the heart of modern culture; cultural practices lie at the heart of globalization" and that globalization "cannot be properly understood until they are grasped through the conceptual vocabulary of culture" (Tomlinson, 1999a, p. 1). The classification is, therefore, made in order to facilitate a quick understanding of the ongoing process of cultural globalization. Let us briefly consider the main arguments of these three schools of thought.

3.2.1. Cultural Homogenization

The first group of scholars, whom Steger (2003) called "hyper-globalizers," presents a rosy picture of an emerging "global culture" that is rapidly changing the cultural profile of the world. Some of them are carnivalesque in their attitude and triumphalistic in their tone as they see in cultural globalization the supremacy of their own Western values and lifestyles. They tend to make a simple and direct equation: Globalization = Westernization = Americanization = McDonaldization. That is to say, they consider globalization predominantly as a process of Westernization, which, in their view, is not substantially different from Americanization, which can, in turn, be easily characterized as McDonaldization. The term *McDonaldization* was coined by American sociologist George Ritzer (1993) to describe the contemporary sociocultural processes by which the basic principles of the fast-food industry—creation of homogenized consumer goods and imposition of uniform standards—shape the cultural landscape in America and elsewhere.

In support of their worldview, the hyperglobalizers pointed out that ideas about American individualism and consumerism are circulated more freely and accepted more widely as evidenced in young people in various parts of the world wearing Levi jeans and Nike athletic shoes, sporting Texaco baseball caps and Chicago Bulls sweatshirts, watching music videos on MTV and blockbusters from Hollywood, and eating at McDonald's and Pizza Hut. They also stressed that such a cultural homogenization is facilitated by a global communications industry controlled mostly by American interests. It has been reported that, in the year 2000, "only ten media conglomerates—AT&T, Sony, AOL/Time Warner, Bertelsmann, Liberty Media, Vivendi Universal, Viacom, General Electric, Disney, and News Corporation—accounted for more than two-thirds of the $250–$275 billion in annual worldwide revenues generated by the communications industry" (Steger, 2003, p. 76).

The hyperglobalizers especially emphasized the role played by the American entertainment industry in spreading the gospel of American pop culture. As the 1999 U.N. Report stated, the single largest export industry for the United States is not aircraft, automobiles, or computers; it is entertainment. Although India's film industry, Bollywood, makes the largest number of movies each year, it is Hollywood that reaches every single market in the world, getting more than 50 percent of its total revenues from overseas. By the end of the 1990s, Hollywood claimed 83 percent of the film market in Latin America, 72 percent in Europe, and 50 percent in Japan. American cinema houses, on the other hand, are seldom open to foreign films, which take less than 3 percent of the U.S. market. The hyperglobalizers stressed that the spread of American popular culture is unstoppable and uncontestable because there is what Fredric Jameson (1998, p. 63) called "a fundamental dissymmetry" between the United States and others in terms of their ability to disseminate cultural values. He argued confidently that there can "never be parity" in this area because "other local entertainment industries are most unlikely to supplant Hollywood in any global or universally successful form" (p. 63).

Jameson would like us to remember that "Hollywood is not merely a name for a business that makes money but also for a fundamental late-capitalist cultural revolution, in which old ways of life are broken up and new ones set in place" (Jameson, 1998, p. 63). In other words, what Hollywood is exporting is more than entertainment; it is exporting cultural values as conceived and constructed by American cultural workers. It can potentially pose a threat to local cultural identities. That is why even Western countries like Canada and France have taken legislative measures to protect their artistic diversity and national identity by limiting the entry of American cultural goods into their societies. People hardly notice that there is an ongoing "struggle between immense US cultural interests, who want to open up foreign borders to American film, television, music and the like, and foreign nation-states who still place a premium on the preservation and development of their national languages and cultures and attempt to limit the damages— both material and social—caused by the leveling power of American mass culture" (Jameson, 1998, p. 59).

A clear reflection of this ongoing struggle is illustrated by a recent decision made by the General Conference of the United Nations Educational, Scientific and Cultural Organization (UNESCO). It adopted a new convention "to preserve and protect the diversity of cultural expressions" (see UNESCO Press Release No. 2005–128, dated 20 October 2005). The convention enables countries to take measures to protect their distinctive nature of cultural goods and services. It was approved by a vote of 148 to 2, with 4 abstentions. The United States was one of the two countries that voted against the convention, fearing that it could be used to block the export of

Hollywood films and other cultural exports. According to an on-line BBC report, Renaud Donnedieu de Vabres, the French culture minister, argued that "nations had a right to set artistic quotas because 85 percent of the world's spending on cinema tickets went to Hollywood" (BBC News, dated Oct. 20, 2005).

The benign form of cultural clashes between nations also finds expression in "cultural clauses" that are included in bilateral and regional trade agreements like the North American Free Trade Agreement (NAFTA). A not-so-benign form produces unpalatable, and sometimes unthinkable, results. The 9/11 terrorist attack that destroyed the World Trade Center in New York and shook the world is the most despicable manifestation of such a cultural clash. In fact, U.S. President George W. Bush declared that the attack was an attack on Western civilization. Even before 9/11, the hyperglobalizers had neatly divided the world into two camps: a silent majority that welcomes the homogenized "global culture," and a strident minority that is opposed to it. Their worldview was succinctly captured by sociologist Benjamin Barber (1996), who presented a dichotomized imagery of the world in his book *Jihad vs. McWorld.*

Although Barber (1996) claimed that he used "Jihad" only "as a generic term quite independently from its Islamic theological origins" (p. 299), he nevertheless explained it this way: "In its mildest form it betokens religious struggle on behalf of faith, a kind of Islamic zeal. In its strongest political manifestation, it means bloody holy war on behalf of partisan identity that is metaphysically defined and financially defended" (p. 9). Despite his invocation of the Arabic term and Islamic zeal, he hastened to add that he uses the term "in its militant construction to suggest dogmatic and violent particularism of a kind known to Christians no less than Muslims, to Germans and Hindis [*sic*] as well as to Arabs" (p. 9). Barber's McWorld, on the other hand, is very similar to Ritzer's McDonaldization in that it represents the "future in shimmering pastels, a busy portrait of onrushing economic, technological, and ecological forces that demand integration and uniformity and that mesmerizes peoples everywhere with fast music, fast computers, and fast food—MTV, MacIntosh, and McDonald's—pressing nations into one homogenous global theme park, one McWorld tied together by communications, information, entertainment, and commerce" (Barber, 1996, p. 4). Like other hyperglobalizers, Barber argued that the people of the world are presented with a stark choice between "the secular universalism of the cosmopolitan market and the everyday particularism of the fractious tribe" (p. 7). He, however, asserted that the forces of globalism and those of tribalism both undermine civil liberties and democratic values.

3.2.2. Cultural Heterogenization

If the first school of thought led by hyperglobalizers foregrounds the global aspect of cultural globalization, the second, led by what I call "localizers," foregrounds its local characteristics. For localizers, the most salient feature of cultural globalization is not homogenization but heterogenization, in which a multitude of local cultural identities are being revived and revitalized owing to real or perceived threats from the process of globalization. They reject the proposition about the cultural dominance of the West over the rest, and about the preeminence of the American cultural field. They see the emergence of several vibrant cultural hubs rather than a single vital cultural center. Their world is best described in the words of the celebrated Irish poet William Butler Yeats, who, writing at a different time and in a different context, stated that "the center will not hold, mere anarchy is loosed upon the world," or in the words of leading British sociologist Anthony Giddens (2000, p. 20), who says that our world "seems out of our control—a runaway world."

By "runaway world," Giddens denotes that globalization is becoming increasingly decentered. He even suggested, rather polemically, that "reverse colonization" is taking place. For him, "reverse colonisation means that non-Western countries influence developments in the West. Examples abound—such as the latinising of Los Angeles, the emergence of a globally oriented high-tech sector in India, or the selling of Brazilian television programmes to Portugal" (Giddens, 2000, pp. 34–35). If he were to rewrite this statement today, he might cite the recent rise of Al-Jazeera and Bollywood as cases in point.

Al-Jazeera is a Qatar-based Arabic language television network. During the 2002 Afghan military operation and the 2003 Iraqi war, it proved to be a noteworthy rival to the American-owned CNN news service in providing an alternative view of the wars. In fact, its mission was so effective that there were attempts to persuade the Qatari government to rein in Al-Jazeera. According to Steger (2003, p. 4), the Arabic network is now "offering its Middle Eastern audience a dizzying array of programmes, transmitted around the clock by powerful satellites put into orbit by European rockets and American space shuttles." It has grown so much in just three years that its broadcasts can be watched around the clock on all five continents. In addition, its Website attracts an international audience, with daily hits exceeding seven million. Al-Jazeera has definitely made a dent in the American dominance of global dissemination of current events. In a sign of expanding influence, it started an English-language international satellite television channel in November 2006.

Like Al-Jazeera's successful forays into the news media, the rise of Bollywood has caused a tiny crack in the armor of the American film industry. In a cover story on Bollywood, *Time* magazine (October 27, 2003) observed that "the sheer size of the Indian film industry— releasing an average 1,000 films a year, compared to Hollywood's 740; and attracting an annual world audience, from Kuala Lumpur to Cape Town, of 3.6 billion, compared with Hollywood's 2.6 billion—made it seem as though the West was the last to catch on." The magazine also pointed out that following 20th Century Fox's decision to distribute Bollywood films worldwide, other American companies such as Warner Bros. and Columbia TriStar Films, have also joined in the fray. In a critical analysis of such developments, Heather Tyrrell argued that "having largely failed to export Western product to India, Hollywood is now investing in Indian studios— putting money into Bollywood, not attempting to replace it with its own product" (Tyrrell, 1999, p. 264). Characterizing "Bollywood's resistance to colonisation by Hollywood" as "aesthetic and cultural as well as political" (p. 263), she viewed such resistance as proof that "the use of culture as a global force, and as a hegemonic force, is not confined to the West alone" (p. 273).

Turning to the impact of cultural globalization on common people, the localizers emphasize that the so-called global neighborhood does not really denote enhanced sociability but only what John Tomlinson (1999a, p. 105) called "enforced proximity." In other words, globalization has contributed only to the contraction of space, time, and borders and not to the expansion of communal harmony or shared values among the peoples of the world. In fact, it has only strengthened the forces of fundamentalism, which Giddens (2000, p. 68) described as "a child of globalization." Fundamentalism, whether it is of Buddhist, Christian, Hindu, Islamic, or any other persuasion, is premised upon a deep desire to protect and preserve local traditional beliefs and practices that are perceived to be threatened by global cultural flows.

No doubt global cultural flows have resulted in an extraordinary spread of Western consumption patterns, particularly among the growing middle class population in various regions of the world. Acceptance of Western consumer goods, however, does not necessarily mean acceptance of Western cultural beliefs. From a historical perspective Huntington (1996, p. 58) pointed out that "during the 1970s and 1980s Americans consumed millions of Japanese cars, TV sets, cameras, and electronic gadgets without being 'Japanized' and indeed while becoming considerably antagonistic towards Japan." He rhetorically and rightly asked: "What does it tell the world about the West when Westerners identify their civilization with fizzy liquids, faded pants, and fatty foods?" (p. 58).

Thus, the localizers vehemently dismiss the idea that a single, unified global culture is emerging. They insist that a diffusion of cultural fads from the West does not denote cultural domination on the part of the West. On the contrary, they see the grip of the West declining, and the grasp of the rest rising, although in a manner that is unequal and unbalanced. The reasoning of the localizers, as Tomlinson (1999b, p. 24) wisely cautioned, may "quickly take some of the wind out of the sails of the Westernisation argument, at least in its most dramatic, polemical formulations. However, they do not entirely resolve the issue of the contemporary cultural power of the West. For it could very reasonably be argued that, when all is said and done and all these criticisms met, Western cultural practices and institutions still remain firmly in the driving seat of global cultural development"—a point well taken by the proponents of cultural glocalization.

3.2.3. Cultural Glocalization

The third school of thought, represented by what I call "glocalizers," believes that cultural transmission is a two-way process in which cultures in contact shape and reshape each other directly or indirectly. They, therefore, assert that the forces of globalization and those of localization are so complex and overlapping that they cannot be understood from the narrow perspective of a center-periphery dichotomy. The two forces are, in fact, two sides of the same process in which the global is brought in conjunction with the local, and the local is modified to accommodate the global. In order to capture the essence of such an inextricably linked process, sociologist Roland Robertson (1992) coined a new term, "glocalization." The term is based on *dochakuka*, a Japanese word roughly meaning "global localization," which the Japanese business community often uses to refer to marketing issues, as in the popular slogan "think globally, act locally."

Cultural critic Arjun Appadurai's oft-quoted statement "the central problem of today's global interaction is the tension between cultural homogenization and cultural heterogenization" (1990, p. 5) broadly summarizes the stand taken by glocalists. How this tension is resolved may depend on whether a particular cultural transmission takes place in the appropriate context, and whether it is a "hard" or a "soft" cultural form. Hard cultural forms are defined as "those that come with a set of links between value, meaning, and embodied practice that are difficult to break and hard to transform. Soft cultural forms, by contrast, are those that permit relatively easy separation of embodied performance from meaning and value, and relatively successful transformation at each level" (Appadurai, 1996, p. 90).

Any tension concerning a soft cultural form can be easily resolved through a simple accommodation that meets the needs and wants of the receiving culture. Successful global marketing of consumer goods necessarily involves what is called micromarketing, in which products are tailored to suit religious, cultural, and ethnic demands. The American fast-food chain McDonald's, for instance, tries to be sensitive to local food habits conditioned by cultural and religious beliefs and practices. It serves Kosher food in Israel, conforming to the laws of the Jewish religion; or Halal food in Islamic countries, following Islamic religious traditions; or vegetarian food in India, where most people do not eat meat. At a deeper, harder level, "an acceptance of the technological culture of the West and of aspects of its consumerism may well co-exist with a vigorous rejection of its sexual permissiveness and its generally secular outlook— as is common in many Islamic societies" (Tomlinson, 1999b, p. 23).

In emphasizing the "the twofold process of the particularization of the universal and the universalization of the particular" (Roland Robertson, 1992, pp. 177–78), the glocalizers actually draw attention to the lofty ideal of human universality. They believe that the particularization of the universal "facilitates the rise of movements concerned with the 'real meaning' of the world, movements (and individuals) searching for the meaning of the world as a whole," just as the universalization of the particular facilitates "the search for the particular, for increasingly fine-grained modes of identity presentation" (Roland Robertson, 1992, p. 178). Such a search for global and local identities, historian Robbie Robertson (2003, p. 251) hoped, will ultimately display "dynamic signs of life in the great concert of this globalized planet." Calling for the creation of effective strategies to handle the challenge of cultural globalization, he urged educators to pursue all possible alternative pedagogies that will prepare our children in school to get ready to face the globalized world. In such a pursuit, language educators, it seems to me, have a special role to play.

3.3. Cultural Globalization and Language Education

More than any other educators, language teachers face distinct challenges and opportunities to help learners construct their own subjectivity and self-identity. This is mainly because, as Chris Weeden (1987, p. 21) pointed out, "language is the place where actual and possible forms of social organization and their likely social and political consequences are defined and contested. Yet it is also the place where our sense of ourselves, our subjectivity, is constructed." This is even more applicable to second language education, which brings languages and cultures in close contact.

Amid the centrifugal and centripetal pulls of globalization, the construction of self-identity becomes dauntingly difficult. As the relative security of tradition and custom slowly recedes, "the very basis of our self-identity—our sense of self—changes. In more traditional situations, a sense of self is sustained largely through the stability of the social positions of individuals in the community. Where tradition lapses, and lifestyle choice prevails, the self isn't exempt. Self-identity has to be created and recreated on a more active basis than before" (Giddens, 2000, p. 65).

It is my contention that in these days of cultural globalization, the edifice of an individual's identity can be constructed and reconstructed only on a strong foundation of global cultural consciousness. To my knowledge, there are very few second language education programs that seem to have fully grasped the imperative need to develop global cultural consciousness in the learner. Even the American *Standards* and the European *Framework* (see Chapter 2) that show an acute awareness of the connection between communicative competence and cultural competence present only a limiting and limited vision of teaching culture. How best to address the principles and practices of teaching culture in the globalized world will be the focus of chapters 9 and 10.

3.4. In Closing

In this chapter, I attempted a concise review of the emerging processes of globalization that have political, economic, social, cultural, and individual dimensions. I presented a brief historical sketch of the development of the concept of globalization with a particular emphasis on what is significant about its current phase. I then focused on cultural globalization and its twin processes of homogenization and heterogenization. In the last section, I briefly mentioned the relevance of cultural globalization to second language education, a strand that will be taken for a detailed treatment later.

If we are serious about preparing our language learners to face the challenges of the twenty-first century, we need to foster in them global cultural consciousness. We need to re-view our past and present practices of teaching culture in order to re-vision our future course of action. That is precisely what I set out to do in subsequent chapters.

CHAPTER 4

Cultural Stereotype and Its Perils

In March 1998 I was in Seattle, Washington, attending the 32nd annual conference of the Teachers of English to Speakers of Other Languages (TESOL), the flagship organization of the TESOL profession. One morning, as I walked by a newspaper display an article on the front page of the *Seattle Times* caught my attention: "Do Culture Factors Cause Air Crashes?" I have heard about culture causing so many hardships and heartaches, but never have I heard that it also could cause air crashes. Curious, I bought the newspaper and read the story with great interest.

The story was a follow-up to the crash of Boeing 747 Korean Air Flight 801, which slammed into the top of Nimitz Hill as it approached the Agana airport in Guam in August 1997. The crash killed 228 of 254 on board. The article reported on a meeting of crash investigators, who concluded that they were unable to determine the actual cause of the accident. The cockpit recorder, or "black box," did not reveal any mechanical malfunctioning. The investigators tried to reconstruct what might have happened in the cockpit moments before the tragedy: as the plane was approaching the airport, the pilot, a Korean, forgot that he had put the plane on autopilot. The co-pilot, another Korean, noticed this and also realized that the plane was flying at such a low altitude that it would not clear Nimitz Hill. Although he recognized the looming danger, the investigators surmised, he "failed to challenge the captain" because of his Korean cultural deference to command authority. They thought that, culturally, he is disposed to obey, not question, authority. His deference to the captain's authority, therefore, might have caused the accident.

Let us assume for a moment that the investigators got it right. That is, the Korean co-pilot knew the captain's fatal error but did not challenge him *because* of his cultural deference to authority.

Figure 4.1. Newspaper headline on the relationship
between cultural factors and airplane crashes

Armed with that assumption, let us try to imagine what might have gone through his mind during the last few fateful minutes of his life. Imagine I'm the Korean co-pilot. Since I have flown this sector many times before, I know the airport is fast approaching. I also know that the plane will be upon Nimitz Hill soon. I take a quick look at the control panels. I note the altitude. I note the speed. I also see that the aircraft is still on autopilot. The captain seems to be oblivious of the impending danger.

Alarmed, I quietly talk to myself. "Oh my God, what should I do? Should I alert the captain now? (pause) No, I can't do that. He is my commander. (pause) Wait a second. Is it not my duty, as a co-pilot, to alert the captain? Maybe, but (pause) I'm Korean. I can't challenge authority. I know my life and the lives of all the people on board are in danger. So what? I can't question my commander, can I? No way. I can't violate my Korean cultural beliefs. (pause) Oh, my darling wife, goodbye. Oh, my sweet little son, you are going to lose your dad. But when you grow up, you will learn that your dad sacrificed his life and the lives of 253 people to preserve and protect Korean cultural deference to authority and . . ." Crash! The plane hits the hill and disintegrates into a fiery ball, killing 228 people including the pilot and the co-pilot—all victims of Korean culture!

My fictional narrative of what might have gone through the mind of the co-pilot may sound ludicrous to some, but, to me, it is not as ludicrous as the investigators' suggestion that the co-pilot might have known what was happening but failed to alert the captain *because* of his cultural deference to authority. Such a suggestion defies common sense. But then, common sense and cultural stereotypes are not good companions. Cultural stereotyping is very common. People everywhere practice it, knowingly or unknowingly. It is an all-pervasive phenomenon that affects class, race, religion, gender, language, nationality, and ethnicity. We stereotype others, and others stereotype us. We are all victims as well as victimizers. Because cultural stereotypes are a fundamental trait of the human mind, we must try to understand their nature as well their cause, if we are serious about dispelling them.

4.1. The Nature of Stereotypes

The term *stereotype* originally referred to a particular method or process of printing in which a solid plate of type-metal cast from a plaster mold was used for making multiple copies. It signifies a standardized image that can be replicated with ease. Extending the term to human behavior, social scientists use it now to refer to how a society categorizes people by typecasting, or "stamping," them with a rigid set of characteristics that they may or may not share.

A stereotype, then, is a fixed, frozen, and often false image we retain about an individual or a group of individuals. It ranges from harmless caricatures ("The British are cold and reserved") to harmful characterizations ("Muslims are terrorists"). It can be found in popular children's ditties ("Sugar and spice and everything nice / That's what little girls are made of / Snips and snails and puppy dog tails / That's what little boys are made of") and in best-selling books about adults (*Men Are from Mars, Women Are from Venus*). It transcends such differences as nationality ("Japanese are hardworking"), religion ("Hindus are vegetarians"), profession ("Lawyers are greedy"), gender ("Women are weak"), age ("Young people are reckless"), etc.

A stereotype is socially constructed and is generally passed on from one generation to another. It is a simple and simplistic description of people about whom we have very little personal knowledge. Most of us implicitly accept it without clear understanding or critical reflection. As the celebrated American journalist Walter Lippmann (1922, pp. 54–55) rightly observed, "For most part we do not first see, and then define, we define first and then see. In the great blooming, buzzing confusion of the outer world we pick out what our culture has already defined for us, and we tend to perceive that which we have picked out in the form stereotyped for us by our culture." Because a stereotype is not a reflection of the true characteristics of individuals or groups, and is not a result of our own personal experience, it is considered "at once a substitute and a shadow" (Bhabha, 1994, p. 82).

What do stereotypes do? Stereotypes reduce an unmanageable reality to a manageable label. They exaggerate a grain of truth out of proportion until the reality is distorted into a simple image that makes us feel safe and superior. Once we accept stereotypes about people, we do not have to make a serious effort to understand them in all their complexity. Stereotypes represent the outward expressions of hidden beliefs and values of the members of a particular society, or a community within a society. In their extreme form, they can lead to prejudice and discrimination, even to hatred and violence. Stereotyping is a virus that replicates itself in one unquestioning mind and rapidly infects other unquestioning minds.

There are, however, those who believe that stereotypes can play a useful role. Nachbar and Lause (1992, p. 238), for instance, pointed out that "it is sometimes valuable to create classifications of individuals. The term 'freshman' on college campuses brings to mind a popular image of a rather naive newcomer who is not familiar with both the social and intellectual life of a campus. Of course, many freshmen don't fit this narrow picture. Nevertheless, the stereotype of the freshman serves the purpose of encouraging professors to construct introductory courses for those with no experience in the subject matter and it also encourages campus social organizations like fraternities and sororities to sponsor group activities planned especially for campus newcomers." The authors, however, hastened to add that even "useful" stereotypes are still oversimplified views of the group being stereotyped.

There are also those who believe that stereotypes can have a positive function. They cite the American stereotype about the so-called model minority as an example. Asian immigrants living in the United States are said to constitute the model minority because of their perceived work ethic, educational achievements, economic progress, and cooperative spirit. Students from Asian-American communities have been stereotyped as "overachievers," "nerdy," "great in math and science," "competitive," and "4.0 GPAs" (Lee, 1996). It has, however, been pointed out that this positive stereotype is a myth with mixed blessings. In exploring the stereotypes of Asian-American students, Kim and Yeh (2002), for instance, found that the model minority stereotypes attribute educational and economic success to all Asian Americans, with the danger that they ignore the between- and within-group differences of social, political, economic, and educational achievements. They cited a study, conducted by the Educational Testing Service in 1997, that found that twelfth-grade students from six major Asian groups (Chinese, Filipino, Japanese, Korean, South Asian, and Southeast Asian) had significant variations in their educational backgrounds and achievement. The study also demonstrated how such stereotypes "are reinforced in the school context and contribute to a biased and limited perspective of Asian Americans that does not reflect their within group heterogeneity" (Kim and Yeh, 2002, p. 2).

4.2. The Causes of Stereotypes

Why do we stereotype? There are several socio-psychological theories that address this question. One theory—called aversive racism theory—holds the view that stereotypes are ingrained by a racist system and are perpetuated by aspects of contemporary culture (Gaertner and Dovidio, 1986). According to this theory, even people with an egalitarian, nonprejudiced self-image can act prejudicially when interpretive norms guiding a situation are weak. In such a scenario, people easily justify their racially prejudicial acts and beliefs on the basis of some determinant other than race.

Another theory—called social identity theory—holds the view that we are more likely to use stereotypes if we perceive a threat to our self-esteem. According to Wolf and Spencer (1996, p. 177), this theory posits that we are all generally "motivated to maintain a positively valued social identity and we may do so by creating or taking advantage of favorable comparisons with other groups." They go on to observe that the need to maintain a positive distinction between ourselves and others can easily lead to stereotypes and attitudes that are biased in our favor and against others.

Contrary to sociologists and psychologists, postcolonial critics such as Albert Memmi and Edward Said saw in cultural stereotypes a binary opposition between Us and Them, one that produces an essentialized and static view of the Other. Recall from Chapter 2 that there are so many cultural representations that are made again and again about colonized countries and cultures that they can only be attributed to widespread belief systems structured by stereotypes (Said, 1978). Such structures of stereotypes resulted in what another postcolonial critic, Homi Bhabha (1994), has called *cultural fixity,* a paradoxical mode of representation that "connotes rigidity and an unchanging order" (p. 66), resulting in "an arrested, fixated form of representation" (p. 75).

Cultural fixity is not confined to public discourses or private conversations alone. It can be encountered in the academic arena as well. The profession of language education, where cultures come into contact, is not an exception. In the following section, I discuss the persistence of cultural stereotypes in the field of L2 education (Kumaravadivelu, 2003a).

4.3. Cultural Stereotypes in Language Education

A review of the literature on cultural stereotypes particularly in the field of TESOL reveals that, in spite of its widespread sensitivity to cultural diversity, it is full of stereotypes that are particularly associated with students from Asia. It is apparent that there exists in the field the practice of homogenization by which nearly three billion people belonging to cultures as contrasting and conflicting as the Chinese, the Indian, the Japanese, the Korean, the Vietnamese, and a host of others—are all thrown into a single cultural basket labeled *Asian.* Such a practice spawns stereotypes that, over time, develop a stubborn quality to persist. I outline below the cultural representation of students from Asia, and the conceptual limitation of research conducted in the field of TESOL.

4.3.1. Representations of Asian Students

Often repeated in the professional literature, in conference presentations, and in personal conversations are three common stereotypes about students from Asia: they show blind obedience to authority; they lack critical thinking skills; and they do not actively participate in classroom interaction. A critical analysis will easily show that a homogeneous body of Asian students who display these stereotypical characteristics seems to exist more in the imaginary homeland of the Western academia than in the actual classrooms of Asian societies.

It is not my contention that we never come across Asian students with the classroom behavior profile attributed to them. It is, however, my contention that the language teaching profession has shown a remarkable readiness to forge a causal connection between the classroom behavior of Asian students and their cultural beliefs even though research findings are ambiguous and even contradictory. I further contend that the classroom behavior profile attributed to Asian students is not confined to them alone; it can be seen among mainstream North American students as well. I briefly sketch below each of the three cultural stereotypes from the perspective of my personal experience and professional knowledge.

4.3.1.1. OBEDIENCE TO AUTHORITY

It is often asserted (e.g., Fox, 1994) that cultures in Asia have a long tradition of unconditional obedience to authority and, therefore, Asian students look at the teacher as an embodiment of knowledge, one who is to be obeyed and not to be questioned. Such an assertion is often made not based on robust research but on the popular sayings of some historical figures or the personal experience of some expatriate teachers. Citing familiar quotes from famous people, particularly taken out of context, cannot prove much because one can easily find opposite or contradictory quotes, sometimes from the same historical figures.

For instance, the Chinese philosopher Confucius is often cited to support the argument that the Chinese are nurtured to obey authority. He is often credited to advocate the need for maintaining status and authority, as is evidenced in his call for strictly maintaining the order of *jun jun chen chen, fu fu zi zi,* that is, the hierarchical order of emperor-citizen, and father-son. Another Confucius quote refers to the high authority and respect the Chinese have historically given to teachers: *yi re wei shi, zhong sheng wei fu,* meaning "if a person has been a teacher for me even for a day, then he is my father the rest of my life," implying that one should respect him as much as one respects one's father.

Contrary to common misconception, what the Chinese philosopher has advocated in statements such as the above is genuine respect for, not blind obedience to, teachers, elders, and other authority figures. As the Chinese applied linguist Xiaotang Cheng (2000, p. 440) wrote: "This is manifested in Confucius's well-known saying: *'shi bu bi xian yu di zi; di zi bu bi bu rushi'* which means the teacher does not always have to be more knowledgeable than the pupil; and the pupil is not necessarily always less learned than the teacher." Confucius had another saying that is known to virtually every household in China: *san ren xing, bi you wo shi,* meaning among any three persons, there must be one who can be my teacher. These historical accounts from China hardly support the stereotypical "Asian" image of unconditional obedience to the authority of the teacher.

The case of another ancient Asian nation, India, is not very different. In a comprehensive archival study on indigenous Indian education during the precolonial era, Dharampal (1983) showed that transfer of knowledge within the Indian educational system was distinctly marked by intellectual challenges and animated debates between the teacher and the taught. Similarly, in an analysis of the history of Indian philosophy of knowledge, Matilal and Chakrabarti (1994, p. 2) demonstrated that the traditional Indian attitude toward authority is precisely what is reflected in the oft-quoted declaration by Buddha (literally, "the Enlightened One"), who preached in his last sermon: "Do not trust my words, rely only upon your own light." Western scholars such as Immanuel Emeneau similarly argued that "intellectual thoroughness and an urge toward ratiocination, intellection, and learned classification for their own sakes should surely be recognized as characteristic of the Hindu higher culture" (Emeneau, 1955, p. 145).

Turning to my personal experience, I have taught in India for over ten years before coming to the United States. Indian schools and colleges have always faced, and still face, what is called "a perennial discipline problem." Many of my students were disobedient and disruptive. In fact, one of my constant complaints during my teaching days in India was that whenever Indian teachers met in the "staff room," they spent more time discussing strategies to handle unruly students than exchanging successful teaching strategies. Something similar seems to be happening in Chinese classrooms as well. Cheng (2000, p. 438) observed that many of his Chinese students "are extremely active and even aggressive."

4.3.1.2. PASSIVITY IN CLASS

Yet another stereotype about students from Asia is that they do not take active part in class discussion because of their cultural disposition (Sato, 1981; Flowerdew and Miller, 1995; Cortazzi and Jin, 1996). Several experimental studies cast doubts about such an assertion. For instance, Amy Tsui (1996) investigated the classroom action research carried out by thirty-eight English as a Second Language (ESL) teachers at the University of Hong Kong and reported that most teachers attributed student reticence to low English proficiency, lack of confidence, fear of making mistakes, and being laughed at. None of the teachers in her study cited culture as a contributing factor. Disputing the cultural connection that is made to explain the passive and reticent behavior of Chinese students, Pierson (1996, p. 55) argued that these characteristics are mainly the product of "the present colonial education system with its excessive workloads, centralized curricula, didactic and expository teaching styles, concentration on knowledge acquisition, examinations emphasizing reproductive knowledge over genuine thinking, overcrowded classrooms, and inadequately trained teachers."

In his study, British applied linguist William Littlewood, teaching in Hong Kong (2000, p. 33), came to the same conclusion: "if Asian students do indeed adopt the passive classroom attitudes that are often claimed, this is more likely to be a consequence of the educational contexts that have been or are now provided for them, than of any inherent dispositions of the students themselves." Likewise, Jun Liu (2001, p. 49) concluded that in order to understand Asian students' communication patterns in the classroom, we need to take into account, besides cultural beliefs, factors such as "the relevance of the topic under discussion, the instructor's presentation of the material, the students' familiarity with the subject, the students' motivation to participate, the students' anxiety and tolerance of risk-taking, and their speaking abilities and communicative competence."

4.3.1.3. LACK OF CRITICAL THINKING

The TESOL literature also presents the stereotype that Asian students do not think critically and that certain values underlying the notion of critical thinking are even incompatible with their cultural beliefs (e.g., Fox, 1994; Atkinson, 1997). Such a statement is often directly or indirectly contrasted with the perceived ability of American students to think critically and the contention that there is something inherent in the Western culture that promotes critical thinking. For instance, Fox (1994, p. 125) held the view that "this thing we call 'critical thinking' or 'analysis' has strong cultural components." She further argued that the importance given to critical thinking in the American educational curriculum "is based on assumptions and habits of mind that are derived from western—or more specifically U.S.—culture, and that this way of thinking and communicating is considered the most sophisticated, intelligent, and efficient by only a tiny fraction of the world's peoples" (1994, p. xxi). She asserted confidently that some of her ESL students "may be feeling a little ashamed about not being straight-line thinkers" (p. 114; see Chapter 5 discussion on "straight-line" thinkers).

Echoing a similar belief, Dwight Atkinson (1997, p. 72) added: "Not only is critical thinking a culturally based concept, but many cultures endorse modes of thought and education that almost diametrically oppose it." He proposed (p. 89) a catchy "aphorism" (his word): *"Critical thinking is cultural thinking"* (his italics). He further suggested that, even in the United States, critical thinking is a special characteristic of people belonging to particular strata of its society. Accordingly, he cautioned against teaching critical thinking to international and language minority students in the United States, and even doubted whether they will gain from such training. One is tempted to ask: is not the whole enterprise of education based on the basic premise that the human mind is trainable?

It appears that the view expressed by certain Western scholars about the non-Western mind is nothing new. Alastair Pennycook (2002, p. 100) cited an entry from *A Cyclopedia of Education*, compiled by a group of educators and published in New York in 1911: "There is nothing in the Chinese course of study in the way of mathematics or science, or indeed any line of thought, which will tend to develop the thinking faculties, such as reason or invention, and hence these faculties have lain dormant in the Chinese mind. They have never invented anything. They have stumbled upon most of the useful, practical appliances of life, and among these are the compass, gunpowder, and printing, and, though noted for their commercial astuteness, have lacked all power to develop into a commercial success." Is it not amazing that basic and useful scientific inventions like the compass, gunpowder, and printing are dismissed as being merely stumbled upon?

Such a contemptuous attitude is not inconsistent with the colo-

nial construction of the East. In his book *Decolonizing History* sociologist Claude Alvares (1979/1991) has provided a comprehensive
critique of Western interpretation of scientific and technological
knowledge in India and China. He has documented how Western
scholars have furthered their own vested interests by not only fail-
ing to acknowledge, but also by deliberately denigrating, the production and dissemination of local knowledge in these two ancient
nations. In a similar vein, historian Bernard Cohn (1996) in his
book *Colonialism and Its Forms of Knowledge* has documented how
British scholars and authorities "inferioritized" Indian indigenous
knowledge in order to package and rule India.

Pennycook (2002) also presented a detailed discussion on how
the cultural representation of the Chinese has affected their educational agenda, particularly language education. He showed how
language policy in colonial Hong Kong was linked to a discursive
construct of the Chinese as politically and culturally docile. Cheng
(2000, p. 441) questioned the widespread belief that the Confucian
philosophy discourages critical thinking on the part of the Chinese
and pointed out that, in Chinese, "the term for 'knowledge' is made
up of two characters. One is *xue* (to learn) and the other is *wen* (to
ask). This means that the action of enquiring and questioning is
central to the quest for knowledge." Similarly, Pierson (1996) drew
insights from ancient Chinese scholarship to support his contention that the idea of autonomy in learning has roots in Chinese
thought.

4.3.2. Common Characteristics of Student Behavior

An interesting and intriguing aspect of applied linguistic research is
that few systematic studies compare the classroom interactional
behavior of native speakers of English learning their L2 such as
Arabic, Chinese, or Japanese, and that of Asian students learning
English as their L2. The limited research that is available (Young,
1990; Loughrin-Sacco, 1992) clearly shows that English-speaking
North American students do not actively participate in the interactive activities of their foreign language classes. If and when they
talk, they do so by freely using their first language, English—a lux-
ury that they can afford mainly because of the English language
competency of their foreign language teachers, and the use of first
language (L1) in the teaching of an L2 in the United States. When

the American students are compelled to use their still developing foreign language, they report a debilitating level of anxiety. In the Young (1990) study, for instance, students reported that they hesitate to interact because "talking" in class is the most anxiety-provoking aspect of their foreign language learning. Similarly, in a detailed ethnographic study of a French language class, Loughrin-Sacco (1992) found that "speaking" was the highest anxiety-causing activity "for nearly every student" (p. 101).

Attempting to explain the differences between the real and the perceived images of the classroom behavior of Asian and American students as represented in the TESOL literature, Ryuko Kubota (2001) rightly pointed out that researchers in TESOL have falsely compared the ideal (not the real) images of American students with the perceived (not the ideal) images of Asian students. Comparing the negative images of U.S. classrooms presented in the literature on general education, and their positive images presented in the TESOL literature, Kubota concluded that "only this ideal image is exploited to accentuate cultural differences. Applied linguistics discourse of cultural differences indeed rarely mentions the other set of images, leaving the impression that positive images of U.S. classrooms are neutral, factual, and real" (p. 23).

A similar tendency can be found in terms of critical thinking skills. When I taught in India, I recognized that some of my students were critical thinkers but many were not. The same is true of my experience in the United States. For nearly twenty years I have taught undergraduate and graduate students in three U.S. universities. I have come across mainstream American students who are excellent critical thinkers. I have also come across mainstream American students who seem to believe that critical thinking is hazardous to their intellectual health. There are other educators (e.g., Boyer, 1987; Gimenez, 1989) who have made similar observations about American students who uncritically accept whatever their teachers say or whatever they read. Likewise, in a comprehensive study on critical thinking across the curriculum, Halpern (1997) cited a number of cross-national comparative studies that document how U.S. students lag behind their counterparts from other countries in using higher-order, analytical, and critical thinking skills.

Other studies conducted in the United States (e.g., Heath, 1983) show that students from economically and educationally deprived strata of the society have been found to be wanting in certain cognitive skills compared to students from more affluent sections of the society, and that a pedagogic practice that is sensitive to their needs and wants will enhance opportunities for the development of creative and heuristic devices in them. It has been pointed out that a lack of knowledge of instructional strategies on the part of the teachers themselves constitutes a major challenge in the teaching of critical thinking in the United States. According to researchers at the Center for Critical Thinking at Sonoma State University (see their Website, www.criticalthinking.org), an overwhelming majority (89 percent) of the faculty in thirty-eight public and twenty-eight private universities they surveyed stressed the need for helping American students develop critical thinking, and they claimed critical thinking to be a primary objective of their instruction. However, only a small minority (19 percent) could give a clear explanation of what critical thinking is. The researchers, therefore, recommended that if we are interested in having teachers with "a reasonable grounding in the rudiments of critical thinking based on a rich, substantive concept of it, or at least a minimalist, baseline concept, then we have a major task facing us, not the least of which is persuading the majority of the faculty that they do not already know what they confidently assume that they do know."

The above discussion suggests that critical thinking is a skill that learners develop through hard work, so long as optimal conditions for learning it and effective strategies for teaching it are present. Their success seems to depend more on a combination of their individual, socioeconomic, and educational opportunities than on their cultural disposition.

4.3.3. Limitations of Research Findings

It is fair to assume that classroom behavior of the L2 learner is the result of a complex interface between several social, cultural, economic, educational, institutional, and individual factors. It is almost impossible to control a multitude of intervening factors in order to isolate culture as the sole variable that can be empirically studied to determine its impact on classroom behavior. Most of the studies conducted to investigate the L2 learner's classroom behavior—whether they are experimental studies such as Liu (2001) or opinion surveys such as Cortazzi and Jin (1996)—are marked by a lack of robust research design that can separate culture as a variable in order to investigate its causal connection to classroom behavior. Therefore, looking at the classroom communicational behavior of the L2 learner predominantly through the cultural lens will result in nothing more than a one-dimensional caricature of the learner.

In a study that has implications for our discussion here, Ian Malcolm (1987) investigated the belief widely held among Australian teachers that "Aboriginal children in the classroom were shy, reluctant to initiate communication with the teacher, very hesitant in answering" (p. 39), etc. He recorded and analyzed lessons in over one hundred classes in Australian primary schools. Based on his extensive investigation, Malcolm declared: "the most powerful determinants of Aboriginal children's classroom interactional behaviours may not lie within their cultural background but rather within features of the structuring of the communicative situation" in the classroom (p. 56). For him, the prime factor governing classroom communication is the instructional strategy followed by the teacher. I came to a very similar conclusion in my study of ESL students in the United States. Based on my classroom-oriented study, I hypothesized that "the rules and norms governing L2 classroom interactional patterns will take on new dimensions depending as much on the teachers' pedagogic orientation and practical management of turn allocation as on the learners' disposition and motivation to participate in classroom communication" (Kumaravadivelu, 1990, p. 53).

A rewarding revelation about the inadequacy of the cultural explanation to classroom behavior emerges in the studies conducted in China by Cortazzi and Jin (1996) and by Cheng (2002). Using similar research methods, both Cortazzi and Jin, and Cheng investigated the attitudes, beliefs, and classroom behavior of Chinese university students. Cortazzi and Jin studied 135 non–English major students learning English while Cheng studied 167 English majors specializing in English language and literature. The Cortazzi and Jin study confirmed certain common cultural expectations: the Chinese students' preference for (a) the product of knowledge rather than the process of learning (p. 199), and (b) student passivity and teacher-centeredness rather than active participation and learner-centeredness (p. 199). Based on their findings, Cortazzi and Jin concluded: "Chinese expectations and behaviour in the language classroom seem to have their roots in a specific culture and social environment into which Chinese learners have been socialized from an early age" (p. 200).

Cheng's study yielded an entirely different set of findings. His subjects "are more concerned with the process of learning than with the product; they have realized that the ultimate goal of language learning is skills rather than knowledge; they prefer a student-centred approach to a teacher-centred approach; and they are willing to participate in interactive and cooperative language learning activities" (Cheng, 2002, p. 113). Finding the usual cultural explanation woefully inadequate to account for the differences in the findings of these two studies, Cheng argued that what shaped his subjects' expectations were factors such as learner motivation and the importance they attached to their major subject. In other words, studies investigating the classroom behavior of different groups of Chinese students majoring in different academic subjects yielded remarkably different results.

In addition, there may also be larger sociopolitical contexts that contribute to learner classroom behavior. South African applied linguist Keith Chick (1996) provided a classic example. He conducted a microethnographic analysis of his classroom data to find out why teachers as well as students in mathematics classes carried out through the medium of English as a second language in KwaZulu schools were reluctant to give up chorus responses, and were resistant to interaction associated with the communicative approach to language teaching. After microethnographically analyzing the data, he came to the interim conclusion that the behavior of Kwa-Zulu teachers and students was the result of their cultural disposition, that is, the interactional styles they exhibited are native to the Zulu-speaking community. This interim conclusion was the same as the one he arrived at in an earlier study conducted in 1985 in which he analyzed interethnic encounters between a White South African English-speaking professor and Zulu graduate students.

Later, however, he decided to reexamine the same set of classroom data because of his growing awareness of the limitations of microethnographic research that fails to show how the pervasive values, ideologies, and structures of the wider society condition and constrain microlevel behavior in the classroom. When he revisited the same data and analyzed them in terms of macrolevel issues of racist ideology and power structures of apartheid South Africa, he found that KwaZulu teachers and students actually colluded with each other to deliberately construct the kind of interactional pattern that he observed. He realized that the classroom discourse actually represented "styles consistent with norms of interaction which teachers and students constituted as a means of avoiding the oppressive and demeaning constraints of apartheid educational systems" (1996, p. 37). In other words, the interactional styles followed by KwaZulu teachers and students were not an example of their linguistic affiliation or cultural identity but an expression of their opposition to apartheid.

What is clear from the above literature review is that there is no empirical evidence to confirm any *causal* connection between the cultural beliefs and practices of students from Asia and their classroom behavior, precisely because, as I mentioned earlier, it is almost impossible to isolate culture to study its impact on classroom behavior. But still, cultural stereotypes persist.

4.3.4. Coping with the Unknown

The persistence of cultural stereotypes in the language teaching literature cannot be fully explained by invoking the social, psychological, and postcolonial theories (4.2 above) that address the causes of stereotyping. As language teachers, we recognize that when we deal with the psycholinguistic processes of L2 learning in a formal classroom context, we largely deal with the unknown and the unmanageable. And, in our attempt to deal with the complexity of our task, we embrace simple, sometimes even simplistic, solutions. We may be stereotyping our learners partly because it helps us cope with the unknown. Added to the complexity of language learning and teaching is the complexity of the concept of culture itself (cf. Chapter 2). So, if our students fail to perform or behave in class the way we expect them to, we readily explain their behavior in terms of culture and cultural stereotypes. In fact, what we do in the classroom is very similar to what we generally do in our public life as well. As Michael Guest (2002, p. 157) pointed out, "when we interact with people from our own culture, we tend not to 'culturize' them. That is, we do not search for cultural explanations in order to interpret their behaviour. Rather, we ascribe personalities to them." Why then, Guest wonders, do we interpret the behavior of a foreigner as though it "is entirely a product of his or her culture?" (p. 157).

Yet another factor that needs to be taken into consideration is that, with very few exceptions, published materials on culture used for L2 teaching purposes present only a narrow view of cultures, local and foreign (Kumaravadivelu, 2002). These materials are mostly based on traditional American anthropological approaches that put a premium on the anthropologist's own interpretation of what the cultural informants chosen for the study said about their cultures (see Chapter 11). The outsider's interpretation is ultimately framed as *the* cultural construct of a particular cultural community. The "mainstream" literature on culture and its impact on learning, teaching, and communication can be considered useful and usable only if it is augmented with literature written from nonmainstream perspectives as well.

Language educators need to be cognizant of the fact that there is "nothing so obdurate to education or to criticism as the stereotype. It stamps itself upon the evidence in the very act of securing the evidence. That is why the accounts of returning travelers are often an interesting tale of what the traveler carried abroad with him on his trip" (Lippman, 1992, p. 65). A critical awareness of the complex nature of cultural understanding and the problematic aspect of our investigative tools may help us open ourselves to alternative meanings and alternative possibilities, thereby restraining our rush to stereotype the Other.

4.4. In Closing

In this chapter I discussed the nature as well as the causes of cultural stereotypes. I pointed out how stereotyping has become a common practice in private lives, public discourses, and professional arenas. In spite of serious attempts at developing cultural understanding, stereotypes have a tendency to persist. Dispelling cultural stereotypes is an important and imperative task, particularly in the era of cultural globalization in which cultural identity formation is getting complicated. In the next chapter, we will see how cultural stereotypes, in part, shaped the development of the concept of cultural assimilation.

CHAPTER 5

Cultural Assimilation and Its Delusions

It was July 4, 1917—Independence Day in America. It was also graduation day for the students of English School, run by the Ford Motor Company of Detroit, Michigan. The school was entrusted with the task of not only teaching English as a second language to all the immigrant workers hired by Ford, but also helping them assimilate American cultural beliefs and practices, including "table manners" and "the care of their teeth."

As had been the annual custom, graduating students and nearly two thousand dignitaries including the legendary Henry Ford assembled in the well-lit and well-decorated open-air theater in the Highland Park Plant in Detroit. The graduation ceremony began promptly at 7 p.m.

The curtain on the stage opened. In the middle of the stage was a giant gray cauldron displaying the words "FORD ENGLISH SCHOOL MELTING POT." From one end of the gangway, the graduating students, wearing their colorful ethnic clothes, quietly entered the stage carrying a small piece of luggage similar to what they carried when they arrived in this country. Slowly and solemnly, they stepped into the huge pot. Next, some of the instructors of the Ford English School appeared on the stage, carrying long ladles. They inserted the ladles into the pot and started stirring. The lights on the stage turned red and the pot was gradually filled with what appeared to be steam. As the pot began to boil, the red lights brightened more and more.

Inside the pot, shrouded in the colorless, odorless, and presumably harmless steam, the men (yes, they were all men) shed their ethnic costumes and put on new blue suits gifted to them by the company. And, as the American patriotic song "Yankee Doodle" played in the background, the graduates climbed out of the caul-

Figure 5.1. Ford Museum Melting Pot (Picture No. 7227
Highland Park Plant, Ford Motor Company English School,
July 4, 1917 Copyright: Henry Ford Museum, Detroit)

dron and walked to the other side of the gangway, proudly waving
American flags. The audience cheered lustily. With that short and
symbolic ceremony, the immigrant workers of the Ford Motor Company were declared to have successfully completed their appren-
ticeship in American language and culture. They were now deemed
to have culturally assimilated themselves into their adopted land.

5.1. The Concept of Cultural Assimilation

The theatrical symbolism of the graduation ceremony presents a
simple and simplistic image of the process of cultural assimilation.
A critical analysis of the sociological literature on immigration in

the United States, however, reveals that the concept of cultural as-similation is anything but simple. Cultural assimilation, after all, is a long and laborious process. In an oft-quoted definition, two promi-nent American sociologists of the early twentieth century, Robert Park and Ernest Burgess, characterized cultural assimilation as "a process of interpenetration and fusion in which persons and groups acquire the memories, sentiments, and attitudes of other persons and groups and, by sharing their experience and history, are incor-porated with them in a common cultural life" (Park and Burgess, 1921/1969, p. 735). An interesting aspect of this definition is that it scrupulously avoids any explicit mention of which of the groups in contact was required to assimilate, for what purpose, and to what degree.

Over the years, the concept of cultural assimilation has been ar-ticulated variously by scholars, sometimes depending on their own political orientation and ideological stance. In a recent book Har-vard political scientist Samuel Huntington exhorted all immigrants to the United States to commit themselves to the Anglo-Protestant culture of the founding settlers, which, according to him, has al-ways been central to American identity. He lists the following as the key elements of that culture: "the English language; Christianity; re-ligious commitment; English concepts of the rule of law, the re-sponsibility of rulers, and the rights of individuals; and dissenting Protestant values of individualism, the work ethic, and the belief that humans have the ability and the duty to try to create a heaven on earth" (Huntington, 2004, p. xvi). He argued that "America was created as a Protestant society just as Pakistan and Israel were cre-ated as Muslim and Jewish societies" (p. 63), and went on to assert rather enigmatically that his is "an argument for the importance of Anglo-Protestant culture, not for the importance of Anglo-Protestant people" (p. xvii).

The Huntingtonian prescription is a clear echo of what sociolo-gist Peter Salins (1999, p. 6) previously described as "American style" assimilation. According to Salins, the "American style" assimilation is a three-part "contract between the existing settlers and all new comers." As per this contract, immigrants "would be welcome as full members of the American family" if and only if they (a) accept English as the primary language, (b) take pride in their American identity, and (c) live by the Protestant ethic. In spite of such strict stipulations that encompass linguistic, cultural, and religious as-pects of immigrant life, Salins stated without any sense of contra-

diction that the "American style" assimilation "has never demanded
that immigrants or their descendants "melt" into the general population or that they become indistinguishable from the mass of other
Americans" (p. 143). Such deliberate conceptual ambiguities have
plagued the concept of cultural assimilation for a long time, prompting sociologists Richard Alba and Victor Nee (1999, p. 137) to
lament that certain scholars in the field of sociology have committed what can be regarded as "intellectual sins."

One of the "intellectual sins" committed by sociologists is the
proliferation of terms that have been used to refer to the process of
cultural change newcomers undergo in their adopted land: accommodation, acculturation, adaptation, adoption, assimilation, enculturation, integration, etc. These terms clearly overlap in meaning
and in application. Focusing on two of the more commonly used
terms, acculturation and assimilation, sociologist Herbert Gans
(1999, pp. 162–63) noted that the distinction between the two was
formulated by the Chicago School of Sociology in the late 1940s.
According to this school of thought, "acculturation refers mainly to
the newcomers' adoption of the culture, that is, the behavior patterns or practices, values, rules, symbols and so forth, of the host
society (or rather an overly homogenized and reified conception of
it). Assimilation, on the other hand, refers to the newcomers' move
out of formal and informal ethnic associations and other social institutions and into the host society's non-ethnic ones" (Gans, 1999,
p. 162). In this sense, acculturation is faster and easier than assimilation because newcomers can acculturate on their own, if they
wish, but they cannot assimilate unless facilitated by the mainstream
community (more on this later).

While this distinction appears to be fairly simple, it is not common. Scholars in different disciplines use the terms sometimes synonymously, sometimes differently, and fairly inconsistently. Out of
frustration, Gans himself stated: "I did not know the origin of the
distinction, and some additional research for this essay has not reduced my ignorance" (Gans, 1999, p. 170). One source of so much
terminological and conceptual confusion is the complicated nature
of the assimilation process itself. Another source, it seems to me, is
the ideological as well as the political nature of that process. It is
clear for any perceptive reader of the relevant sociological literature
that there is so much semantic obfuscation aimed at concealing
real intentions and beliefs.

Recognizing such a problem, Alba and Nee (1999) observed that "if the terminology of assimilation is so freighted with bias and ambiguity, as many critics believe, then, perhaps it must be abandoned and a new vocabulary invented, even if this merely redeploys some of the assimilation's conceptual arsenal" (p. 159). Noting all the conceptual and linguistic deceptions that surround the concept of assimilation, sociologist Ruben Rumbaut (1999, p. 172) correctly pointed out that "few concepts have been so misused and misunderstood, or erected on such deep layers of ethnocentric pretensions. Few have so thoroughly conflated the real with the rhetorical, the idea with the ideal and the ideological, mixing descriptions of what is observable with prescriptions of what is desirable."

In spite of the terminological and conceptual ambiguities, early assimilationists elegantly and effectively captured the quintessence of the concept of cultural assimilation in a popular metaphor—the melting pot—that survives today. The melting pot theory, as the concept of cultural assimilation has come to be known, has at least two major strands—the ideal and the real. The difference between the two cannot be fully understood without understanding the history of immigration. Therefore, before discussing the melting pot theory, let us take a brief detour to understand the nature of immigration in the United States.

5.1.1. A Synoptic View of Immigration

There are several nations in the world that are indigenously multiethnic and multicultural. Some have become multiethnic and multicultural because of a steady inflow of immigrants from different parts of the globe. The United States, for instance, has come to be called "a nation of immigrants." It truly deserves the title because the growth of its population from a mere 4 million in 1790 to 300 million in 2005 has primarily resulted from the influx of immigrants and their resulting descendants. Compared to other developed countries such as Australia, Britain, and Canada, the United States continues to receive a record number of legal immigrants each year. As the editors of the 1999 *Handbook of International Migration* pointed out, the United States "is largely populated by persons whose ancestors lived elsewhere two centuries ago. This country's culture, as well as its politics and economy, has been continually expanded and remolded by successive waves of immigrants. It is hard to imagine any part of American history or popular culture that has not been touched by immigration" (*Handbook*, p. 1).

Sociologists generally identify four successive waves of immigration to the United States. The first wave began in the early seventeenth century when English-speaking pilgrims seeking religious freedom from the Church of England landed on Plymouth Rock and settled along the eastern shore. They were soon followed by more colonists from northern Europe, most of them from England, Ireland, Scotland, and Sweden, and also some from France and Germany. It has been estimated that by 1775, when the Revolutionary War started, nearly half a million immigrants had arrived. In addition, about 375,000 Africans were brought as slaves to work on large cotton and tobacco plantations in the South. This period lasted about one hundred and fifty years and coincided with the processes of colonization and economic growth under mercantile capitalism.

The second wave covered the period from about 1820 to 1875, during which more immigrants—an estimated eight million—arrived from northern as well as western Europe. At about the same time, nearly two hundred thousand Chinese came to California, initially to participate in the gold rush, and eventually to work on the railroads, in construction and manufacturing, and on the farms. This period lasted about half a century and coincided with the economic development of Europe and the spread of industrialism to former colonies in the New World.

The third wave witnessed a huge influx of immigrants. It covered the approximate period 1880–1960, during which nearly twenty-five million new immigrants arrived. A crucial aspect of this period is that a substantial number of these immigrants came from southern and eastern Europe, mostly Poles, Italians, Greeks, Slavs, Czechs, and Hungarians. They were largely of peasant- and of working-class origin. The new immigrants also included almost 150,000 Japanese who came to work in the rapidly expanding sugarcane plantations of Hawaii and the fruit and vegetable farms in California.

The fourth wave, which coincided with the postindustrial migration, began in the 1960s and continues to the present. By the end of the twentieth century, nearly twenty million new immigrants have arrived, this time mostly from Latin America (Mexico, Dominican Republic, Haiti, and Jamaica) and Asia (China, India, Korea, the Philippines, and Vietnam). This wave of immigration is dramati-

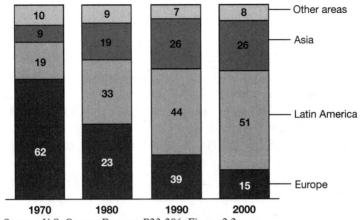

Source: U.S. Census Bureau, P23-206. Figure 2.2.

Figure 5.2. Foreign-born population by region of birth

cally different from the previous waves in at least two significant ways. First, the supply of immigrants, which was dominated by industrialized Europe in the past, shifted to the developing world, and in the process the country became more diverse—ethnically, culturally, linguistically, and religiously. A quick look at the profile of foreign-born population (i.e., those who are not American citizens by birth) during the last quarter of the twentieth century brings out this shift remarkably well. According to the U.S. Census Bureau, the estimated foreign-born population as of March 2000 was 28.4 million, half of whom (14.5 million) were from Latin America. The Europeans who constituted 62 percent of the foreign-born population in 1970 accounted for only 15 percent of the foreign-born population in the year 2000. Conversely, the percentage of foreign-born from non-European countries jumped from 38 percent in 1970 to 85 percent in 2000. That trend continues today.

Another significant aspect of the fourth wave of immigrants is that, with the exception of a segment of immigrants from Latin America, a large number of the new immigrants from Asia and Europe (although the Europeans constituted a small percentage) were high-status professionals in their country of origin. According to a report from Immigration and Naturalization Service (INS), more than two million engineers, scientists, university professors, doctors, nurses, and other professionals have arrived in the United

States in the last three decades alone. In fact, a special report on Asians in the United States issued recently by the Census Bureau states that about 45 percent of Asians were employed in management, professional, and related occupations, compared with 34 percent of the total U.S. population. The same report also shows that the median annual income of Asian immigrant families at the turn of the new century was much higher ($59,300) than the median for all families ($50,000), mainly because of their higher educational and professional status (*Census 2000 Special Reports*, Dec. 2004).

Throughout the history of immigration, except during the colonial era, the U.S. government has played a key role in regulating the flow of immigrants through legislative measures adopted due to economic exigencies such as the need to attract labor force, or due to political considerations such as the need to address popular backlash against immigrants. The first national immigration law was passed in 1875, for the sole purpose of restricting immigration. It was done primarily in response to a popular movement known as nativism (see below), which protested against the influx of Germans, Irish, and Chinese. Interestingly, the law also banned "convicts, prostitutes, lunatics and idiots." Within seven years, the U.S. Congress passed the Chinese Exclusion Act of 1882, fully blocking the entry of the Chinese, who were accused of taking away low-paying jobs from native citizens. For the same reason, a similar ban, called the Gentleman's Agreement, was put in effect in 1907 specifically to keep out Japanese laborers.

The state-sponsored regulation of immigration took a decisively racial turn in 1924 when Congress decided to use immigration policies to reinforce, rather than dilute, the racial stock of the early Americans. This law, known as the National Origins Act of 1924, stipulated stricter quotas on immigrants, mandating that new arrivals from any country could not exceed three percent of the people from that country who lived in the United States at that time. Its sole purpose was "to severely limit arrivals from eastern and southern Europe, with the explicit objective of preserving the character of the United States as a predominantly Anglo-Saxon, Protestant community" (Zolberg, 1999, p. 73). The 1924 Act was in force until 1965, when the Hart-Celler Act ended quotas based on nationality. Two subsequent amendments to the 1965 Act (the Immigration Reform and Control Act of 1986 and the Immigration Act of 1990) further loosened immigration restrictions. As a consequence, the number of legal immigrants has increased sharply, averaging over five hundred thousand per year, a large percentage of whom came from the Asia-Pacific region.

In addition to these measures, the U.S. government has, from time to time, permitted legal entry to refugees fleeing from their country due to political persecution or natural disasters. For instance, America accepted a huge number of Cuban refugees in the 1960s and Vietnamese refugees in the 1970s, both escaping communist regimes in their respective countries. Yet another aspect of immigration that has to be factored in is illegal immigration that has been taking place for a long time. According to a report from the Pew Hispanic Center, an immigration research organization based in Washington, D.C., as of March 2006 more than eleven million illegal aliens were living in the United States. To complete the picture of the current U.S. population profile, we must also add thirty-five million African Americans (12.3 percent of the total population), whose ancestors were brought from Africa, and two and a half million Native Americans (0.9 percent), whose ancestors were the original inhabitants of this land.

The synoptic view of the history and nature of U.S. immigration presented above shows the extent of ethnic, cultural, religious and linguistic diversity that makes America a nation of immigrants. Such a diversity can be expected to continue because, as Gans (1999, p. 169) rightly pointed out, "Unless political or economic conditions bring about a sudden halt to further immigration, many of today's immigration groups are going to be replenished by further sets of newcomers just as the second generation of the post-1965 arrivals enters adulthood in large numbers." Understandably, when immigrants from such diverse national, racial, and religious groups come to a common land seeking a common destiny, there are bound to be serious social, cultural, and political concerns about forging a common identity under a unified nation-state. These concerns are deeply reflected in the controversy surrounding the idea of America as a melting pot.

5.1.2. Melting Pot—The Ideal

The early waves of immigrants came to this country with an inimitable pioneering spirit and an indomitable will to build a new country that will be unrivaled in the annals of human history. For them, the melting pot represented a compelling image. Those "intrepid Europeans," as historian Arthur Schlesinger (1991, p. 13) called them, had a formidable task of forging an American identity out of a disparate group of people. They frequently raised, and constantly wrestled with, the question that resonates even today: who are we? (which, incidentally, is also the title of Huntington's 2004 book mentioned previously).

An initial answer to that question was provided in 1782 by a French immigrant, Hector St. John de Crevecoeur. In his *Letters from an American Farmer,* he portrayed America as a place free of cultural customs, social ills, and political conflicts that tormented European communities of his time. Attempting to define an American, Crevecoeur (1782/1912, p. 43) declared: "He is an American who, leaving behind him all ancient prejudices and manners, receives new ones from the new mode of life he has embraced, the government he obeys, the new rank he holds. . . . Here, individuals of all nations are melted into a new race of men, whose labours and posterity will one day cause great changes in the world."

The idealistic notion of "individuals of all nations" melting into "a new race" through a voluntary process of cultural assimilation captured the imagination of early immigrants, prompting leaders such as John Quincy Adams to declare in 1819 that immigrants "must cast off the European skin, never to resume it" (cited in Rishin, 1976, p. 47). It was, however, Israel Zangwill, an Anglo-Jewish author, who popularized the metaphor of the melting pot. In a play aptly titled *The Melting Pot,* Zangwill (1909/1923, p. 33) had his chief protagonist, David Quixano, proclaim loudly and proudly: "America is God's Crucible, the great Melting Pot where all the races of Europe are melting and reforming! Here you stand, good folks . . . here you stand in your fifty groups with your fifty languages and histories, and your fifty hatreds and rivalries, but you won't be long like that, brothers, for these are the fires of God. . . . Germans and Frenchmen, Irishmen and Englishmen, Jews and Russians—into the Crucible with you all! God is making the American. . . . The real American has not yet arrived. He is only in the Crucible, I tell you— he will be the fusion of all races, the coming superman." When the play was first performed on Broadway in New York in 1908, it became an instant success. It ran for months to packed audiences. Its appeal was attributed to the fact that it echoed the idealistic sentiments of some of the early Americans.

Idealism, in any place and at any time, is difficult to sustain. Particularly, idealism of the kind that demanded "the fusion of all races" is bound to confront opposition. In fact, Zangwill himself became skeptical about the possibility of racial and religious amalgamation. Within eight years after the staging of *The Melting Pot,* he observed, with a tinge of melancholy, that it was in vain to "declare that there should be neither Jew nor Greek. Nature will return even if driven out with a pitchfork, still more if driven out with a dogma" (cited in Glazer and Moynihan, 1963, p. 290). The opposition to the idealistic representation of the melting pot came from the so-called nativists. Like the idealists, the nativists too believed in cultural assimilation. Like the idealists, they too wanted people of different ethnic, cultural, and racial background to shed their past identity and construct a new one. Like the idealists, they too embraced the ever-popular metaphor of the melting pot—but all with a deceptive twist.

5.1.3. Melting Pot—The Real

As mentioned earlier, most who settled in this country in the seventeenth and early eighteenth centuries were escaping religious persecution. They came with the English language on their tongue, the Protestant faith in their heart, and a noble cause in their mind. They wanted to settle down to a life of "liberty, freedom and the pursuit of happiness." They considered themselves "original Americans." They came to be known as "old stock," "early Americans," or, more descriptively, "White Anglo-Saxon Protestants" (WASPs). They "had a frame in their minds, which became a frame in reality, that placed and ordered those who came after them. It was important to be white, of British origin, and Protestant. If one was all three, then even if one was an immigrant, one was really not an immigrant, or not for long" (Glazer and Moynihan, 1963, p. 15).

In other words, the "old stock" Americans readily and willingly accepted and absorbed immigrants of their own racial and religious stock. Others had to be Americanized. The process of "Americanization," another label given to the process of cultural assimilation in the early days, required the new immigrants to gradually and fully assimilate the cultural beliefs and practices, values and visions, that characterized the mainstream segment of their adopted society. From their classical assimilationist standpoint, the "old stock"

Americans saw any distinctive cultural traits, native languages, and ethnic enclaves as impediments to the construction and consolidation of a homogenized American national identity. They also viewed the cultural difference the immigrants brought with them as cultural deficiency.

The original nativists were confident of carrying out their classical assimilationist project rather smoothly and successfully, mainly because they thought that the immigrants from England and other northern European regions shared with them core cultural values and religious beliefs. They were, therefore, alarmed when, in the nineteenth and early twentieth centuries, a huge wave of immigrants from eastern and southern Europe crowded into major American cities. They were alarmed because they sincerely believed, according to a leading sociologist Oscar Handlin (1957, p. 96), that "the peoples of the Mediterranean region were biologically different from those of northern and western Europe and that the difference sprang from an inferiority of blood." They saw the changing racial and religious profile of immigrants as a change for the worse. In order to preserve and protect their original stock, they began a movement called nativism.

In *Strangers in the Land,* an authoritative book on the patterns of American nativism, sociologist John Higham defined nativism as "an intense opposition to an internal minority on the ground of its foreign origins and connections" (1955, p. 4). He identified three major characteristics that shaped American nativism of earlier times: opposition to Catholics, who were all considered incapable of the independent mind necessary to American citizenship; antipathy towards foreigners in general, who were all deemed to have a proclivity for political conflicts undermining American national stability; and a belief in the Anglo-Saxon origin and character of the American nation. In a later work, Higham (1999, p. 384) drew a distinction between nativism and racism, although he considered them closely related. Racism, according to him, "divided the whole of creation into hierarchized types. It was more consistently concerned with horizontal distinctions between civilization and barbarism than it was with boundaries between nation-states. In contrast, nativism always divided insiders, who belonged to the nation, from outsiders, who were in it but not of it. . . . Nativism signaled danger; racism spelled degradation. Nativism could espouse assimilation. Racism could not."

During the late nineteenth and early twentieth centuries, nativists became popular. Their political philosophy was propagated by several organizations such as the Know-Nothing Party and the American Protection Association. They successfully lobbied the U.S. government to pass a series of laws, including the National Origins Act of 1924 mentioned earlier, to restrict immigration and to preserve and promote their racial stock. Their mission was to mold the newly arrived European immigrants in their own image. Their battle cry was cultural assimilation. Their nativist sentiment continued to shape the contours of American history. It is this eighteenth century nativist sentiment that constitutes the central thesis of Huntington's twenty-first century book on American identity (Huntington, 2004), prompting a prominent reviewer of the book to call him a "native son" (Wolf, 2004). According to George Sanchez (1999, p. 377), right-wing political groups have, during the late twentieth century and in the new millennium, continued to articulate nativist sentiments by supporting the English-only movement, opposing bilingual education, and stoking economic fears about immigrants. In fact, referring to the national debate on immigration reform that was raging in the spring of 2006, and to the very stringent border controls proposed by some Republican Party (GOP) members of the Congress, William Kristol, himself a leading voice of the conservative movement, cautioned them against "the political and moral cost of turning the GOP into an anti-immigrant, Know-Nothing party" (2006, p. 7).

Historically, the nativists approached the concept of cultural assimilation fundamentally differently than the way the idealists did. The idealists visualized the emerging American identity as a true blend of sociocultural beliefs and practices drawn from many different ethnic groups. Everybody, including them, must consciously undergo cultural transformation. For them, assimilation was largely a two-way process. The nativists, on the other hand, dreamed of an American identity made up of a cultural core that is drawn from their own beliefs and practices. All others must undergo cultural transformation. For them, cultural assimilation was largely a one-way process.

Although both idealists and nativists used the metaphor of the melting pot, they treated it very differently. The idealists took the metaphor seriously. They considered themselves an active ingredient in the boiling pot. Along with all the other ethnic base metals, they were ready and willing to melt, forging a novel, sturdy alloy that was different from each of the ingredients. For the nativists, the pot was just a convenient metaphor. It boiled for others, not for them even though they were an integral part of it. They considered themselves no more than a catalyst that facilitated the required chemical reaction among the ingredients, without itself undergoing any change. All the other base metals were expected to melt and absorb the characteristics of the catalyst.

For nativists, cultural assimilation included linguistic assimilation as well. They expected the new European immigrants and their children to discard their home language and start learning and using English. Bilingual education was frowned upon. They were particularly worried about the spread of German-language programs in certain parts of the country. For instance, by 1880, fifty-two of the fifty-seven public schools in St. Louis had German-language programs that served not only German-speaking children but also English-speaking children who learned German as a second language (Lessow-Hurley, 1991). With concerted effort, the nativists successfully curtailed the advances made by German language programs in public schools. In fact, as suggested earlier, the current opposition to bilingual education in the United States can easily be traced, in part, to the nativist philosophy.

In the ideological conflict between the idealists and the nativists, the idealists lost out decisively. In one garb or another, it is the nativists' expectation of cultural assimilation that has largely shaped, and continues to shape, the American national psyche. In spite of the fact that ordinary Americans take pride in calling their country "a nation of immigrants," the American society at large has long been apprehensive about the immigrants' ability and willingness to adopt the cultural values of mainstream America. Attributing this apprehension to "the rhetoric of nativism," sociologists Hirshman, Kasinitz, and DeWind (1999, p. 130) find an unmistakable continuity in the antipathy expressed toward German and Irish immigrants in the eighteenth century, toward the southern and eastern European immigrants in the late nineteenth and early twentieth centuries, and toward Latin American and Asian immigrants in the late twentieth century and at present. There is a pattern here that is easy to see.

Classical assimilationists have all along assumed, rather simplistically, that assimilation involves a straight-line progression. That is, a progression from the disadvantages and discrimination endured by the first generation to considerable social and economic advancement by the second generation, and a disappearance of ethnic traits and early labor market disadvantages by the third generation (Portes, 1999, p. 30). They have also assumed that this progression is the result of "a natural process by which diverse ethnic groups come to share a common culture and to gain equal access to the opportunity structure of society; that this process consists of gradually deserting old cultural and behavioral patterns in favor of new ones; and that, once set in motion, this process moves inevitably and irreversibly toward assimilation" (Zhou, 1999, p. 196). After more than two hundred years of social experimentation, it is only proper to ask whether cultural assimilation of the nativist kind can take place at all. In other words, did the pot really melt? Or, did the nativists and their political descendants merely delude themselves about cultural assimilation?

5.2. Cultural Assimilation and Its Delusions

"The point about the melting pot is that it did not happen." That was the definitive conclusion reached by two prominent Harvard sociologists, Nathan Glazer and Daniel Patrick Moynihan (1963, p. 290). During the early 1960s, they conducted a detailed sociological study to trace the role of ethnicity in the lives of the Negroes (as African Americans were called then), the Puerto Ricans, the Jews, the Italians, and the Irish living in New York City. They found "the notion that the intense and unprecedented mixture of ethnic and religious groups in American life was soon to blend into a homogenous end product has outlived its usefulness, and also its credibility" (p. v). They presented the results of their study in an influential book titled *Beyond the Melting Pot*, published in 1963.

Within a decade another sociologist, Michael Novak, studied the lives of the descendants of the immigrants of southern and eastern Europe: Poles, Italians, Greeks, and Slavs. Discussing his findings in the book *The Rise of the Unmeltable Ethnics*, published in 1971, he declared that these ethnics were unmeltable because, in spite of the passage of time, they kept in touch with their ethnic roots and continued to harbor ethnic consciousness. According to him, their identification with their ethnic group turned out to be "a source of values, instincts, ideas, and perceptions that throw original light on the meaning of America" (p. 290).

Although much has been written about the fate of the melting pot, these two best-sellers by prominent scholars and published a decade apart stand out as outstanding contributions to our understanding of the concept of cultural assimilation. What also stands out is the apologetic tone of these scholars for having to come to the conclusions they did. Glazer and Moynihan thought it prudent to "ask a measure of forgiveness for talking up a subject which needs to be discussed, but which cannot be aired without giving pain to some" (p. vi) and to "ask the understanding of those who will be offended" (pp. 22–23). Similarly, Novak let it be known that the decision to go ahead and write his book caused him "several months of internal struggle" (Novak, 1971, p. xiii). Their apologetic tone indicates that sentiments about cultural assimilation continue to evoke strong emotional responses.

In order to fully understand why the kind of melting pot envisioned by classical assimilationists turned out to be more a myth than a reality, one has to address crucial questions such as "*who* is doing the assimilating, and *from what, to what,* and *for what*" (Rumbaut, 1999, p. 189, italics as in the original). Sociologists have provided intense and insightful responses to these questions, pointing out several interconnected factors, some of which are beyond the scope of this book. For the sake of simplicity and brevity, I shall touch upon three of them: (a) the selectivity of cultural assimilation, (b) the durability of ethnic affiliation, and (c) the responsibility of the mainstream community.

5.2.1. The Selectivity of Cultural Assimilation

It appears that most classical assimilationists treated the process of assimilation as a group-oriented zero-sum game. That is, they expected ethnic groups, as groups, to adopt the cultural beliefs and practices of the mainstream community fully or not at all. Cultural assimilation, however, is a selective process. This selectivity operates in two ways: individuals within an ethnic group may decide to assimilate although the group itself may not, and even those individuals who decide to assimilate may do so selectively, that is, they may assimilate certain aspects of the mainstream culture and not certain others.

One way of understanding the true nature of assimilation is to look at it as a powerful force that acts upon individuals and not necessarily upon ethnic groups. That is to say, its impact can be clearly seen and felt in individual cases rather than on a mass scale. As we discussed in Chapter 2, individuals, as against the group they belong to, may play a significant role in making cultural changes possible. Among immigrants, this occurs when, as Min Zhou (1999) pointed out, individuals choose to adopt the cultural beliefs and social values of the mainstream community depending on their educational level, exposure to mainstream society, aspiration in life, language ability, place of birth, length of residence, etc. In their individual effort, they may be helped or hindered by structural factors such as their racial status, family socioeconomic background, and place of residence. It is true that, over an extended period of time, more and more individuals belonging to a particular ethnic group may adopt the cultural beliefs and practices of the mainstream society, thereby giving the impression that the ethnic group as a whole has assimilated.

In order to explain the selectivity involved in cultural assimilation particularly among the second and third generation of immigrants, sociologists have coined the phrase "segmented assimilation." Alejandro Portes and Min Zhou, for instance, noted three distinct patterns of segmented assimilation among second generation immigrants. According to this pattern, some immigrants try and succeed in culturally and economically integrating into the mainstream community, deliberately losing their ethnic traits; some others move in the opposite direction of poverty and deprivation and end up in ethnic ghettoes in inner cities; and still others rapidly reach educational and economic advancement but deliberately preserve their ethnic values and ethnic solidarity (Portes and Zhou, 1993).

There are, of course, numerous factors that contribute to segmented assimilation. Zhou (1999, p. 210) summarized them in two categories: "factors external to a particular immigrant group, such as racial stratification, economic opportunities, and spatial segregation, and factors intrinsic to the group, such as financial and human capital on arrival, family structure, community organization, and cultural patterns of social relations." It is easy to understand how some of the factors identified as intrinsic to the group can ensure the durability of ethnic affiliation.

5.2.2. The Durability of Ethnic Affiliation

Ethnic affiliation, in one form or another, has proved to be durable as well as desirable. Even ethnic communities that have shown strong assimilationist tendencies in the past have found it useful to retain a measure of ethnic identity. For instance, immigrants from northern, southern and eastern regions of Europe eventually coalesced themselves into a broader European-American community, in spite of all the deep discords that characterized their interaction during the early waves of immigration. However, even with strong Judeo-Christian traits to bind them, European-Americans have taken pride in maintaining their ethnic affiliation. These "unmeltable ethnics," as Novak has called them, retained cultural practices that are particularly associated with family traditions and other ethnic institutions. They found their ethnic consciousness "exciting and valuable," and they were "in touch with their roots, secure in them even if long ago having transcended them" (Novak, 1971, p. 272).

The durability of ethnic affiliation can be seen even more pronouncedly among immigrants from non-European regions such as Asia and Latin America. As we saw earlier, the historical circumstances that characterized European and non-European migration were significantly different. The non-European immigrants, particularly those from Asia, came from a greater variety of racial and religious background and also with a greater sense of racial and religious cohesion within their ethnic community. There is, then, a greater tendency among them to preserve ethnic traditions and promote ethnic enclaves. They, along with other immigrants, have demonstrated that they can successfully participate in and contribute to the American society's educational, social, and political institutions while simultaneously retaining their ethnic affiliation. A detailed discussion on the close relationship between the durability of ethnic affiliation and the concept of cultural pluralism will be presented in the next chapter.

5.2.3. The Responsibility of the Mainstream Community

Yet another factor that severely minimized the chances of mass-scale assimilation is the role played by the mainstream cultural community that wanted assimilation to take place. The success of the assimilation project has depended as much on the willingness of the members of the ethnic groups to assimilate as on the willingness of the members of the mainstream community to accommodate. Ruben Rumbaut (1999, p. 185) put it succinctly: "It takes two to tango, after all—and to assimilate." Classical assimilationists failed to accomplish their desired goal, in part because they failed to tango.

Perhaps nobody has written more consistently and cogently about the American mainstream community's lack of accommodative spirit than the Harvard sociologist Nathan Glazer (Glazer and Moynihan, 1963; Glazer, 1993, 1997). He raised the question, "Is assimilation dead?" and answered it himself: "properly understood, assimilation is still the most powerful force affecting the ethnic and racial elements of the United States and our problem in recognizing this has to do with one great failure of assimilation in American life, the incorporation of the Negro, a failure that has led in its turn to a more general counterattack on the ideology of assimilation" (Glazer, 1993, p. 123). He pointed out that the assimilation project completely ignored a huge segment of the population—the African Americans and the Native Americans—and he found no references to them in the voluminous writings on the concept of assimilation in American history. He further noted that the African Americans were left out of the assimilationist project in spite of the fact that, until the mid-1960s, the dominant black ideal for their future in the United States was indeed assimilation. His argument, which is generally accepted by other sociologists, is that by making the assimilationist project Eurocentric, by ignoring other ethnic minorities in their midst, and by facilitating the growth of African-American and Native-American ethnic enclaves that led to other ethnic enclaves to emerge in due course, the classical assimilationists contributed directly to the failure of their own project.

The classical assimilationists not only kept certain ethnic groups out of the melting pot, they kept themselves out of it, too. Although they demanded fundamental cultural transformation on the part of the immigrants, they themselves wanted to remain unchanged and unaffected. As we discussed in Chapter 2, when cultures come into contact, they inevitably influence each other. That is true of cultural contacts between individuals, too. The classical assimilationists consciously attempted to insulate and isolate themselves from the cultural influences of ethnic minorities. The extent of their opening up to other cultural influences was limited mostly to superficial items such as the incorporation of Italian, Mexican, Chinese, or Indian cuisine into the American menu. But in reality, the powerful force of assimilation was having an impact on their lives, too. They seldom recognized that both they and the immigrants were contributing to a common American identity that has been evolving for a long time.

The narrative so far has focused on the larger historical, political, social, and cultural aspects of the concept of cultural assimilation. It has left its impact on second language education as well.

5.3. Cultural Assimilation and Language Education

Monolingualism and monoculturalism are two of the pillars of nativism. While the current opposition to bilingual education and support for the English Only movement in the United States can be seen as part of the living legacies of the concept of nativism, it has also had a perceptible impact on the development of theories of second language learning and teaching particularly in areas where language and culture intersect. In this part of the chapter, I focus on how the concept of nativism, in its various manifestations, has influenced contemporary theories and practices of English language education for immigrants and for foreigners. For illustrative purposes, I discuss two prominent theories in applied linguistics: (a) Kaplan's cultural thought patterns in intercultural education and (b) Schumann's acculturation model of second language acquisition. Although neither Kaplan nor Schumann has directly invoked nativism as a point of departure for their studies, any perceptive reader can easily find traces of nativistic philosophy deeply embedded in their theory construction, as we shall see below.

5.3.1. Kaplan's Thought Patterns

Robert Kaplan, a professor at the University of Southern California, is a prominent figure in the field of applied linguistics. He was president of the American Association of Applied Linguistics, which he co-founded with three other scholars. He also founded and edited the *Annual Review of Applied Linguistics,* a reputed journal that highlights scholarly developments in that field. He has authored or co-authored numerous publications. In 1966 he published an article titled "Cultural Thought Patterns in Intercultural Education" in *Language Learning,* a leading applied linguistics journal. There is perhaps no other single article in applied linguistics that has been so willingly canonized and so widely disseminated. In fact, it heralded the beginning of a subfield in applied linguistics called contrastive rhetoric, the study of how people's first language and culture shape their writing in a second language.

English   Semitic   Oriental   Romance   Russian

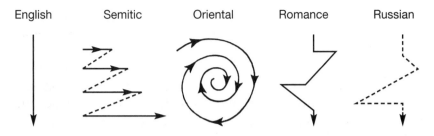

Figure 5.3. Cultural thought patterns (Kaplan, 1966)

Examining samples of expository essays written in English by foreign students enrolled at the University of Southern California, Kaplan found that even those students who have mastered the grammatical structure of English have been unable to compose academic prose in English following appropriate rhetorical styles. Based on his analysis, he identified five rhetorical patterns (that is, paragraph- and essay-level organizational patterns) linked to five broad lingua-cultural groups: "English," "Semitic," "Oriental," "Romance," and "Russian." According to him, the "Semitic" group follows a zigzag line with a series of parallel movements in paragraph development. The "Oriental" group follows an indirect spiral approach coming to the main point only at the end. The "Romance" group follows a digressive back-and-forth zigzag line, while the "Russian" group does the same but with a much higher level of digression. As for the "English" group, he reiterated the familiar rhetorical pattern which, according to popular writing style manuals, follows a straight line linear development. He graphically presented these observations in a diagram (Kaplan 1966, p. 15).

Kaplan then posited a simple and symmetric relationship between linguistic rhetorical patterns and cultural thought patterns. That is, he said, the straight arrow that stands for the linear development of the English paragraph also signifies logical thinking on the part of native speakers of English. Such thought patterns, he argued, "have evolved out of the Anglo-European cultural pattern" (Kaplan, 1966, p. 3). Likewise, he said, the "Oriental" rhetorical pattern is spiral because the Orientals (i.e., Asians) think in circles, while the speakers of Semitic, Russian, and Romance languages take various forms of a zigzag route in paragraph organization because they think in a zigzag manner (for a detailed discussion of cultural stereotypes in the field of applied linguistics, see Chapter 4).

Researchers such as Connor (1996), Connor and McCagg (1983), Kowal (1998), Kubota (2004), Martin (1992), Mohan and Lo (1985), Zamel (1983), and others have pointed out that Kaplan's study is fundamentally flawed from methodological as well as conceptual points of view. I compile below four of the major problems cited by them (for a more comprehensive critique, see Kowal, 1998). First, Kaplan collected essays written as a class exercise by foreign students writing in their second language, English, which they were still in the process of learning, and compared them with the writings of highly educated native speakers of English including that of Thomas Macaulay, who was a reputed historian and a British administrator in colonial India. In other words, Kaplan was comparing apples and oranges. A robust research study aimed at investigating the language-thought connection via writing samples would have minimally required the comparison of same type of texts across cultures, composed by people of comparable linguistic competence, and written under comparable circumstances. Kaplan did none of these.

Second, Kaplan did not take into consideration the fact that the rhetorical deviation he found in the essays written in English by foreign students was very similar to the rhetorical errors made by native speakers of English when they are in the process of learning to write in their first language. Rhetorical errors are indicative of the developmental phase one goes through in learning to write, whether in the first language or in the second. In justifying this omission, Kaplan invoked the notion of a "native reader" whose expectations of writing, he said, the foreign students did not fulfill. He assumed, quite wrongly, that all native speakers, by virtue of being native speakers, also know how to read critically and write appropriately in their language. In making such an assumption, he conflated the distinction between naturally acquired language skills (i.e., listening and speaking) and formally learned literacy skills (i.e., reading and writing). As is well known, the Chomskyan notion of linguistic competence in one's native language refers to the child's innate capacity to naturally acquire the ability to speak in the first language. Unlike speech, reading and writing skills are not biologically endowed. In other words, there are only native *speakers;* there are no native *readers* and there are no native *writers.* That is why almost every college in the United States has a writing program or a writing center to help native speakers of English develop and improve their reading and writing skills.

Third, Kaplan's classification of five lingua-cultural groups, for which he provided no working definition, was an arbitrary exercise that did not take into account linguistic and cultural variations within each group. Equally arbitrary was his underlying assumption that the complex language-culture relationship (see Chapter 2) can be gleaned from a single essay or a single paragraph. He went ahead with that assumption even though he acknowledged that paragraphs like the ones written by foreign students "do exist in English," and he cited "circular" paragraphs written by the American poet Ezra Pound, and "wildly digressive" paragraphs written by the American novelist William Faulkner, as examples of "literary" and not "expository" paragraphs (Kaplan, 1966, p. 14). But, as Braddock (1974) showed, even nonliterary professionals who are native speakers of English do not often follow a linear, straight line paragraph development, and as Leki (1991) stressed, members of different discourse communities (such as lawyers, scientists, journalists, etc.) using the same language follow different writing conventions.

Finally, in deriving the cultural thought patterns of the five lingua-cultural groups, Kaplan appeared to have relied less on the analysis of his database and more on his faith in a particular interpretation of the Sapir-Whorf hypothesis. Recall from Chapter 2 that the strong version of the hypothesis asserted that language controls human thought while the weak version maintained that language merely influences it. According to this hypothesis, the worldview of a person or a group of people using the same language is determined by that single language. Considered highly ethnocentric, the hypothesis was often criticized by linguists as well as by psychologists. Critics such as Martin (1992, p. 54) have argued that Kaplan's attempt to postulate cultural specificity of rhetorical patterns is the result of a direct application of the strong version of the Sapir-Whorf hypothesis. Kaplan himself has used the term "neo-Whorfian" to refer to the underlying assumptions of his work (Kaplan, 1988, p. 279). The ideological basis of Kaplan's assertions have continued to trouble several scholars in the field of applied linguistics.

In a paper published in 1987, two decades after the publication of his 1966 article, Kaplan modified some of his earlier positions. Saying that his 1966 article (he called it his "doodles" article) came home to haunt him, he said: "I admit having made the case too strong. I regret having done so, though I in no way regret having made the case (Kaplan, 1987, p. 10). He further admitted that "all of the various rhetorical modes identified in the 'doodles article' are possible in any language" (p. 10), that "any native speaker of any particular language has at his disposal literally hundreds of different mechanisms to signify the same meaning" (p. 10), that "written language is different from spoken language" (p. 12), and that writing, unlike speech, is a "post-biological evolutionary step" (p. 12). These acknowledgments notwithstanding, he declared without any sense of contradiction that he became even "more convinced that there is some validity" (p. 9) to the notion that he expressed in his 1966 article.

In spite of all the valid criticisms and of his own modified positions, Kaplan's hypothesis continues to hold sway among a large segment of English language teaching professionals. It is still cited as an authoritative source of how international students think and write (see, for instance, Panetta, ed., 2001). There are practicing teachers who connect the rhetorical deviation in the essays written by their L2 students to their native cultural traits, and who see contrastive rhetoric as an answer to ESL dilemmas. In this context Alastair Pennycook (1998) narrated an interesting episode that testifies to the abiding influence of Kaplan's cultural thought patterns. While teaching in China, he came across an Anglo-Australian woman married to a Chinese man taking a distance-learning class from Australia while living in China. Her Australian instructor, who never met her and who knew her only by her Chinese last name, commented on her writing assignment that she was writing in the circular Chinese style as described by Kaplan.

The conceptual foundation of Kaplan's contrastive rhetoric is clearly consistent with the nativist ideology, especially with two of its fundamental tenets: (a) language and culture are inextricably interconnected, and (b) cultural difference is cultural deficiency. Besides, as Pennycook (1998) and Kubota (2004) rightly argued, Kaplan's emphasis on cultural difference and an implicit assumption of the superiority of English rhetoric tend to reinforce a colonialist construct of culture that depicts a static cultural binary between the Self and the Other (cf. Chapter 2). For more than a quarter century, applied linguists have continued to practice contrastive rhetoric "within a ruling paradigm suggested by Kaplan's first research"

(Connor, 1996, p. 6). In fact, it was only in 1996 that a book-length work arguing for and presenting "a different contrastive model" appeared in the market for the first time. It was written, not without significance, by a non-native speaker of English, Ulla Connor.

Unlike Kaplan, who equated linguistic structure with cognitive ability, and connected linguistic rhetorical styles to cultural thought patterns, Schumann focused on the power of social psychological integration in fostering successful second language acquisition. His ideas, too, dovetailed nicely with some aspects of the nativist philosophy although he himself has not explicitly stated it.

5.3.2. Schumann's Social Distance

John Schumann, a professor of applied linguistics at the University of California, Los Angeles, is an internationally reputed scholar who specializes in the neurological aspects of second language acquisition (SLA). He has done extensive research on the socio-psychological features of SLA as well. In 1978 he published a research paper titled "The Acculturation Model of Second Language Acquisition," which was, in effect, an attempt to formulate a *causal* connection between classical cultural assimilation (he used terms such as assimilation, acculturation, enculturation, and adaptation with varying shades of meaning) and successful learning of a second language in the specific context of immigrant life. Unlike Kaplan's study, Schumann's was based on a more rigorous experimental design. Like Kaplan's work, however, it too has traces of nativism and has its own methodological problems, but, on both counts, its flaws are much less severe, as will become clear below.

During the 1970s, as part of a team of researchers at Harvard University, Schumann conducted a ten-month longitudinal study to investigate untutored acquisition of English by a small group of native speakers of Spanish consisting of two children, two adolescents, and two adults. He took a particular interest in one of the adults, Alberto, a thirty-three-year-old lower-class Costa Rican immigrant worker, because, compared to the other five, Alberto made very little progress in English language learning. Schumann connected Alberto's poor performance to the social and psychological distance between him and the members of the mainstream community. He explained the social factor as the individual learner's willingness to integrate culturally and socially with the members of the target language (TL) community, and the psychological factor as the individual learner's personal comfort level in learning the second language. For Schumann, social and psychological contact with the TL group "is the essential component in acculturation" (1978, p. 29).

According to the *Routledge Encyclopedia of Language Teaching and Learning,* edited by Michael Byram (ed. 2000), acculturation theory originated with sociologist Linton's ethnographic work published in 1960. Linton investigated the social and psychological changes Native Americans needed to make in order to integrate themselves culturally with mainstream American society. In that context he identified the notion of social and psychological distance. According to him, social distance related to the opportunities for actual contact available between the members of the two cultures, while the psychological distance related to the extent to which minorities wanted to adapt to the dominant culture. Successful learning of the target language was seen as an important part of the assimilation process.

Following a similar line of reasoning, Schumann argued that Alberto failed in his English language learning because he failed to integrate with the TL community. In other words, he failed to acculturate. Defining acculturation as "the social and psychological integration of the individual with the target language group" (1978, p. 29), Schumann argued that "any learner can be placed on a continuum that ranges from social and psychological distance to social and psychological proximity with speakers of the TL, and that the learner will acquire the language only to the extent that he acculturates" (p. 29). He went even further in his claim, stating that "the degree to which the learner acculturates to the TL group will *control* the degree to which he acquires the second language" (p. 34, emphasis added). In making such a strong causal connection between social psychological proximity and successful second language learning, Schumann dismissed several other known factors that govern successful second language learning as "less important variables or simply minor variables" (p. 44). Even formal teaching, he concluded, will be of extremely limited benefit to the second language learner who lacks social and psychological proximity to the members of the TL community.

Although Schumann's acculturation model successfully drew researchers' attention to the relevance of social and psychological factors to informal language learning, it has been criticized for its lack of methodological as well as theoretical rigor. The idea of constructing a theoretical model based on the data collected from one individual learner itself is a risky proposition. Besides, there is no reliable method by which the key causal factor—social psychological distance—can be objectively measured or interpreted (Larsen-Freeman and Long, 1991). For instance, as Bonny Norton (2000) pointed out, in order to measure Alberto's psychological distance from the members of the mainstream community, Schumann asked him to complete a questionnaire on his attitude and motivation. Alberto's responses indicated that he "seemed to have a positive attitude and good motivation, and hence little psychological distance" (Schumann, 1976, p. 403), but Schumann still dismissed this evidence because he thought Alberto might not have been candid in his response.

Questioning Schumann's interpretation, Norton suggested the possibility that Alberto was indeed telling the truth and that he probably did not learn English to the expected level partly because the members of the mainstream community had an ambivalent attitude toward him, thus offering him limited opportunities to practice English with them. She went on to argue: "if Schumann found that Alberto's lack of progress in language learning was due to the social and psychological distance between Alberto and Anglophones, it may be because the dominant power structures within society had relegated Alberto to a marginalized status and then blamed him for his inability to acculturate" (Norton, 2000, p. 116). Norton's interpretation is consistent with the position adopted by sociologists about the responsibility of the mainstream community in maximizing opportunities for cultural assimilation, as discussed in section 5.2.3 above.

Schumann's acculturation model echoes, in part, the nativist belief that language and culture are inseparable entities, and that second language acquisition and cultural assimilation are interconnected processes. The greater one's cultural integration with the mainstream group, the more successful would be one's attempt to learn the target language. The model lends implicit support to the nativistic tendency to minimize the importance of the immigrants' own language and culture. Such an assertion is contrary to recent research findings that show that maintenance of the mother tongue among immigrant children can in fact facilitate their successful learning of the target language (see, for instance, Cummins, 2000).

The model also suggests, as was maintained by nativists, that cultural assimilation is a one-way process in which immigrants adopt the cultural values and beliefs of the mainstream community. Like the nativistic orientation, Schumann's model puts the entire onus for linguistic and cultural assimilation on the immigrants, and pays scant attention to the role played by the inequitable relations of power that exist between second language learners and target language speakers (Norton, 2000).

In both immigrant and foreign language learning contexts, the acculturation model received only limited support in empirical studies (see Larsen-Freeman and Long, 1991). In spite of its problematic nature, the model is considered to be very influential in addressing social psychological factors in SLA. Although it was specifically constructed to address the context of immigrant life, researchers have attempted to apply it to other language learning contexts as well.

5.3.3. The Teaching of Culture

The nativist approach to cultural assimilation dovetailed neatly with the early approach to cultural anthropology. They both put a premium on the culture of the Self and looked down upon the culture of the Other. They both treated cultural difference as cultural deficiency. These thoughts shaped the teaching of culture in the second-language classroom during the 1960s and the early part of the 1970s.

Before the 1960s, L2 teachers focused primarily on the big C, that is, history, arts, and literature of a particular culture. During the 1960s, the emphasis slowly moved to the anthropological aspects of culture with a small c, that is, the personal aspects of culture (see Chapter 2). Consequently, several scholars argued for a strong component of culture in the language curriculum. Most prominent among them is Nelson Brooks, who introduced a chapter on "Language and Culture" in his influential book *Language and Language Learning* (Brooks, 1964). "Language," he argued, "is the most typical, the most representative, and the most central element in any culture. Language and culture are not separable; it is better to see the special characteristics of a language as cultural entities and to recognize that language enters into the learning and use of nearly all other cultural elements" (p. 85). The language teacher, who is invariably the native speaker, "is presumed to be a cultured person and the learner is presumed to enhance his own culture as he learns a second language" (p. 83).

Arguing that "knowledge of culture is best imparted as a corollary or an obbligato to the business of language learning," Brooks (p. 89) characterized knowledge of culture as knowledge of topics that bring out "identity, similarity, or sharp differences in comparable patterns of culture" (p. 89). Accordingly, Brooks provided a list of sixty-four topics and questions that "may be considered as items for such "hors d'oeuvres" in the language classroom" (p. 90). They include (pp. 90–95)

- Greetings, friendly exchange, farewells: How do friends meet, converse briefly, take their leave?

- Patterns of politeness: What are the commonest formulas of politeness and when should they be used?

- Verbal taboos: What common words or expressions in English have direct equivalents that are not tolerated in the new culture, and vice versa?

- Festivals: What days of the calendar year are officially designated as national festivals? What are the central themes of these occasions and what is the manner of their celebration?

- Races, circus, rodeo: What outdoor events are in vogue that correspond to our auto or horse races, circuses, and similar spectacles?

The teacher is supposed to collect and present such cultural knowledge in the form of incidental talks, thereby establishing in the classroom "a cultural island made up of both materials and nonmaterial elements" (p. 96). Clearly, the emphasis here is on fragmented cultural tidbits that may not be sufficient to understand the unity and the character of a cultural community. Nor does this teaching strategy recognize the cultural capital second language learners bring with them (cf. Chapter 9).

5.4. In Closing

This chapter pertained to the concept of cultural assimilation with particular reference to the United States, a nation of immigrants. However, the concept and the challenges it has posed are not unique to American society. They are shared, in different degrees, by other multiethnic, multicultural, and multilingual societies such as Australia, Britain, and Canada. They are also shared by nonimmigrant societies such as India, Singapore, and South Africa, which have a racially and religiously diverse population. In fact, as we saw in the previous chapter on cultural globalization, even a society that is not multilingual and multicultural cannot hope to remain a cultural island unto itself.

The fear of cultural homogenization and the anxiety about maintaining one's cultural identity have rendered classical cultural assimilation a questionable concept. It is particularly questionable in the context of the emerging cultural globalization we discussed in Chapter 3. The classical assimilationist path has left many people disillusioned, making them wonder whether it is desirable to lose one's cultural identity, and to get cut off from one's own roots, even if it is possible to do so. They find it difficult to accept the argument that they cannot fully realize their human potential unless they uncritically assimilate the core values of the dominant cultural community. These sentiments resulted in the emergence of cultural pluralism, which has its own challenges, opportunities, and deceptions.

CHAPTER 6

Cultural Pluralism and Its Deceptions

Headscarf.

Female attire? A religious symbol? A cultural icon? A mark of identity?

Whatever it is, a piece of cloth called *hijab*, worn by Muslim women, has recently become the focal point of an agonizing national debate across some Western nations. Consider the following news story I have paraphrased from BBC News that appeared on 2 February 2005 (http://news.bbc.co.uk/2/hi/europe/4223307.stm):

> "You are a bad Belgian and you have signed your own death warrant."
>
> That was the chilling message Rik Remmery got when he opened his mail one morning just before Christmas. For this quiet and unassuming factory owner in the small, sleepy town of Ledegem in West Flanders, Belgium, the nightmare was just beginning. Further letters put a 250,000 euro ($326,000) price on his head. Soon, a package containing a bullet arrived.
>
> Rik's crime? He employed Naima Amzil, a Muslim woman who wore a headscarf to work. Her job included packing prawns and other delicacies produced by the factory.
>
> Rik was repeatedly warned that he would face death unless he sacked Naima. But he stood firm. "She's worked here for eight years. I accepted her with a headscarf and I will not change my mind because of one sick person," he said.
>
> Naima was horrified to learn that someone would react to her simple white headscarf in such a hateful manner. Originally from Morocco, and now a Belgian citizen, she had done everything to integrate into Belgian society—including learning to speak French and Dutch.
>
> But as the letters kept coming, the pressure and fear grew. In the end, Naima decided to act. She removed her headscarf to work on

the factory floor. "It was very, very difficult," she said with a tinge of sadness in her voice. "It was like a piece of me was taken away."

Belgium's King Albert, who was on a holiday in France, saw a report about events in Ledegem on television. Upon his return, he invited Rik and Naima—in headscarf—to the royal palace for a televised audience. He wanted to send a message out that religious intolerance was unacceptable.

Unlike Naima, who quietly opted for the path of least resistance, a pair of French teenagers, Lila and Alma Lévy-Omari, decided to challenge the secular credentials of the country of their birth— France. In October 2003, the two sisters from Aubervilliers, an industrial suburb of Paris, were kicked out of school for wearing a headscarf. According to a 1989 court ruling based on the secular principle of the French state, it is not illegal to wear religious symbols to school. But the law forbids ostentatious religious signs that constitute pressure, provocation, proselytizing, or propaganda. The teenagers chose to wear a full headscarf, covering their ears, hairline, and neck. The school considered it provocative and expelled them. For these two teenagers, wearing the headscarf to school is a mark of religious liberty and individual identity. In fact, it's their decision. Nobody imposed it on them. Their Algerian-born mother does not wear a headscarf, and their father is Jewish.

The controversy created by Lila and Alma touched a nerve in France, which has a Muslim population of about five million. Declaring that secularism is nonnegotiable, President Jacques Chirac set up a twenty-member high-level commission on secularism. One of the contentious subjects it considered was whether to ban veils completely, not only in schools but also in all public places. In its report released in December 2003, the commission recommended that all "conspicuous" signs of religious belief—specifically including Jewish skullcaps, oversized Christian crosses, Islamic headscarves, and Sikh turbans—be outlawed in state-approved schools.

The commission's recommendations were fully endorsed by Chirac, French legislators, as well as the general public (70 percent of the public including 40 percent of Muslim women supported them). In October 2004 the recommendations were passed into law by a massive parliamentary majority, 494–36. A few religious leaders of Catholic, Jewish, and Islamic persuasions expressed opposition to the legislation. For the proponents of the ban, the principles are simple. The French Republic is rooted in secularism, in a reaction against Catholicism's domination of the state before the French

Revolution, and the Church's opposition to liberal values into the early part of the twentieth century. Faith is a private matter that belongs only in places of worship and in private domains. In this predominantly Christian society, even nativity scenes or Christmas carols are not allowed in public schools. For the opponents of the ban, the *hijab*, the cross, the skullcap, and the turban are foundations of individual liberty and religious freedom. Once the law was passed, however, there was a consensus that the rule of law must prevail. Even the Union of French Islamic Organizations, which had previously urged schoolgirls to defy the ban, recommended that pupils now refrain from openly flouting the law.

Other Western countries tackled the same issue in a different way. In Germany, with a Muslim population of 3.2 million, women seem to have won their headscarf battle. In September 2003, the German Supreme Court ruled that Stuttgart school authorities had no legal right to deny a teacher her job because she insisted on wearing a headscarf to school. The school argued that the teacher had violated the country's religious neutrality. The teacher countered it by saying that it was her constitutional right to practice her religion. The Supreme Court agreed with her.

In Britain, an Appeals Court judge ruled in March 2005 that it was illegal for Denbigh High School, Luton, England, to exclude Shabina Begum from school for wearing a traditional Muslim gown. The judge declared that the school violated Britain's Human Rights Act and called for more guidance for schools on complying with the law. According to a BBC News report, dated 2 March 2005 (http://news.bbc.co.uk/2/hi/uk/news/england/4310545.stm), Shabina was pleased with the court verdict and said, "it is amazing that in the so-called free world I have to fight to wear this attire." However, a year later, in March 2006, Britain's highest court overturned the lower court's ruling declaring that the school was within its rights to impose a school uniform and to bar Shabina from wearing her Muslim gown to school (http://www.nytimes.com/2006/03/23).

In the United States, Benjamin Franklin Science Academy in Muskogee, Oklahoma, banned a sixth-grader, Nashala Hearn, from wearing a headscarf to school. The school district argued that her headscarf clearly violated a systemwide ban on the wearing of hats, caps, bandanas, or jackboots. The Justice Department intervened to revoke the ban, pointing out that the school was infringing on Nashala's constitutional right to practice her religion freely.

As the above-mentioned cases reveal, some countries expect

their citizens to show allegiance to secular values above religious loyalties. Others emphasize a constitutional right to freedom of expression and religion. The *hijab* issue is symptomatic of the challenges faced by certain Western democracies. To what extent can a liberal democratic society accommodate cultural and religious diversity? What are the limits of democratic ideals of liberty and equality? What is the nature of multicultural citizenship that does not pose a threat to national cohesion? What are the ways in which minority cultural practices get represented within a nation-state? These and other related questions are only part of an infinitely more complex narrative affecting everyday life in pluralistic societies. In order to gain a proper perspective on these issues, we need to understand the concept of cultural pluralism.

6.1. The Concept of Cultural Pluralism

There are several nations that are linguistically and culturally pluralistic, each with its own version of pluralism that suits its genius. Consequently, there are many forms of cultural pluralism. Even within the Western liberal democratic societies, pluralism is understood and practiced in many different ways. In this chapter I focus primarily on the American version of cultural pluralism—its origin, its growth, its manifestations, and its deceptions.

6.1.1. The Origin of Cultural Pluralism

The American version of cultural pluralism originated as a reaction to the stridency of nativism, which, in its strong version, demanded from immigrants allegiance to the cultural characteristics of the mainstream community accompanied by erasure of one's own cultural heritage (see Chapter 5). Alarmed by the mounting popularity of nativism, particularly during the late nineteenth and early twentieth centuries, several prominent American intellectuals dedicated themselves to work toward a nation where linguistic and cultural diversity would be recognized and respected. Foremost among them were John Dewey and Horace Kallen.

Dewey, America's preeminent educational philosopher, deplored the nativistic project of Americanization. In a strongly worded speech delivered before the National Education Association in 1916 he said, "No matter how loudly anyone proclaims his Americanism, if he assumes that any one racial strain, any one component culture . . . is to furnish a pattern to which all strains and cultures are to conform, he is a traitor to an American nationalism. . . . I find that many who talk the loudest about the need of a supreme and unified Americanism of spirit really mean some special code or tradition to which they happen to be attached. They have some pet tradition which they would impose on all" (Dewey, 1916, cited in Kallen, 1924, pp. 131–32).

Dewey was also critical of those who attacked "hyphenated Americans." He argued that Americans are indeed hyphenated persons in the sense that they are international and interethnic in their makeup. He further observed: "The point is to see to it that the hyphen connects instead of separates. And this means at least our public schools shall teach each factor to respect every other, and shall take pains to enlighten us all as to the great past contributions of every strain in our composite make-up" (Dewey, 1916, cited in Kallen, 1924, pp. 13–132).

Kallen, a Jewish-American philosopher, pursued the same theme even more vigorously. In 1915 he wrote a two-part essay, entitled "Democracy Versus the Melting-Pot," that was published in the popular magazine *The Nation* and later reprinted in his 1924 book *Culture and Democracy in the United States*. In his essay, Kallen argued that it is the very nature of democracy to encourage the development of cultural consciousness and a sense of cultural autonomy especially among ethnic minorities within a society. He further questioned the validity of the melting pot theory and denounced nativism as fundamentally misguided. He emphasized the strong bond associated with one's ethnic heritage and declared unequivocally: "Men may change their clothes, their politics, their wives, their religions, their philosophies, to a greater or lesser extent; they cannot change their grandfathers. Jews or Poles or Anglo-Saxons, in order to cease being Jews or Poles or Anglo-Saxons, would have to cease to be" (Kallen, 1924, p. 116). In his 1924 book he proposed and popularized the term "cultural pluralism" and argued persuasively that ethnic diversity can only enrich the American nation. He saw America "as a federation or commonwealth of national cultures . . . cooperating voluntarily and autonomously through common institutions . . . a multiplicity in a unity, an orchestration of mankind" (Kallen, 1924, p. 122). Like a symphony orchestra, each ethnic group can preserve and protect its own integrity and identity yet produce harmonious music with other groups.

Kallen and his ideas became influential in solidifying the concept of cultural pluralism at the initial stages of its history. However, as historian David Hollinger reminded us, his cultural pluralism "was defined less sharply as a positive program than as a negative reaction to conformist versions of the melting pot" (1995, p. 92). Furthermore, as another historian, Arthur Schlesinger, pointed out, "Kallen was unclear on the question of how to encourage ethnic separatism without weakening the original idea of a single society" (1998, p. 42). Rather than his ideas on cultural pluralism, it was his clarion call for the recognition of diversity and its potential to enrich a democratic society that had an immense appeal. As a Jewish immigrant from Germany, Kallen certainly sympathized with immigrants' resistance to cultural assimilation and their desire to maintain their religious, linguistic, and cultural heritage, but in practice the cultural pluralism he espoused "came to little more than the 'celebration' of cultural difference of the kind which characterized the activities of the settlement workers in the early years of the twentieth century" (Grillo, 1998, p. 192).

Although both Dewey and Kallen emphasized the importance of spreading the value of cultural pluralism through public schools, their ideas seem to have had little impact on public education. As sociologist Glazer (1997, p. 87) pointed out, in the public schools of the 1920s, 1930s, and 1940s, "Americanization was the order of the day." He recalled that when he attended New York City schools from 1929 to 1944, "not a whiff of cultural pluralism was to be found" (p. 87). While this may be true, there is no gainsaying the fact that both Kallen and Dewey challenged the cultural standardization and social engineering represented by the Americanization project, and laid the foundation for the concept of cultural pluralism to grow.

6.1.2. The Growth of Cultural Pluralism

The concept of cultural pluralism evolved into its more active phase during the latter part of the twentieth century. The Second World War provided an immediate impetus for its steady growth. As Schlesinger (1998, pp. 45–46) put it: "Hitler's racism forced Americans to look hard at their own racial assumptions. How, in fighting against Hitler's doctrine of the Master Race abroad, could Americans maintain a doctrine of white supremacy at home? How, with China a faithful American ally, could Americans continue to forbid

Chinese to become American citizens? If the war did not end American racism, at least it drove much racial bigotry underground. The rethinking of racial issues challenged the conscience of the majority and raised the consciousness of minorities." As a result, well-meaning members of the mainstream community reflected on possible ways of spreading cultural sensitivity among the public. There was even a short-lived movement for what was called "intercultural education," aimed at teaching people something about ethnic and racial groups that constituted the American society.

More than any other ethnic minority, it was the African-American community, or the Negro community as it was called then, whose consciousness was raised to a significantly higher level. Recall from Chapter 5 (see section 5.2.3) that the assimilation project of the nativists failed in part because of their refusal to incorporate African-Americans and Native-Americans within the American mainstream society. Ironically, it was not just the nativists who kept the huge African-American community out of their favorite melting pot; cultural pluralists too considered them unworthy of inclusion in their pluralistic agenda. As historians (e.g., Schlesinger, 1988), sociologists (e.g., Glazer, 1997), and others rightly pointed out, even liberal-minded intellectuals such as Dewey and Kallen made no reference whatsoever to African-Americans or Native Americans in their plea for cultural pluralism. Their pluralistic vision was limited to immigrants of European origin. For them, the proposed transition from an Anglocentric to a Eurocentric approach to cultural diversity was pluralistic enough. Fully excluded from the pluralistic vision were black, brown, red, and yellow people. The exclusion of African-Americans, in particular, took place in spite of the fact that they themselves wanted to assimilate.

Their personal and historical experience of racial segregation along with their successful civil rights movement in the 1960s prompted African-American activists to look for effective ways of affirming and asserting their ethnic identity. As a protest against the Anglocentric bias in the construction of American culture, they revived what could only be called Afrocentrism. Their slogan was simple: back to the roots! That is, they turned to their African origin in order to raise racial consciousness and ethnic pride among ordinary African-Americans and to help them regain a sense of identity and self-respect. They made renewed efforts to increase their contact with Africa, including organized trips to the land of their origin. But their attempt to trace their way of life to Africa resulted in utter disappointment when they learned that they have more in common with America than with Africa.

In fact, several leading African-American thinkers such as Frederick Douglass, W. E. B. Du Bois, and Ralph Ellison had, from time to time, rejected the notion that Africa is the home of African-Americans. Du Bois, for instance, was categorical when he wrote as early as in 1940: "Once for all, let us realize that we are Americans, that we were brought here with the earliest settlers and that the very sort of civilization from which we came made the complete absorption of Western modes and customs imperative if we were to survive at all; in brief, there is nothing so indigenous, so completely 'made in America' as we" (Du Bois, 1940, p. 116). The same sentiments were expressed nearly a quarter century later by Ralph Ellison: "The American Negro people is North American in origin and has evolved under specifically American conditions: climatic, nutritional, historical, political and social. It takes its character from the experience of American slavery and the struggle for, and achievement of, emancipation; from the dynamics of American race and caste discrimination, and from living in a highly industrialized and highly mobile society possessing a relatively high standard of living and explicitly stated egalitarian concept of freedom" (1964, p. 262). Following the same tradition, contemporary scholars such as Henry Louis Gates Jr., and Cornel West, who were instrumental in establishing and popularizing the department of Afro-American Studies at Harvard University, have also rejected Afrocentrism. They all realized, quite correctly, that Afrocentrism is as ethnocentric as Anglocentrism, or Eurocentrism.

When the Afrocentric campaign failed to take off, the African-American community opted for an expanded version of the concept of pluralism, one that would include non-European ethnic minorities well, one that would recognize and respect ethnic heritage and ethnic identity of all. An important development in this context was the formation of the National Coalition for Cultural Pluralism, which defined cultural pluralism as: "a state of equal co-existence in a mutually supportive relationship within the boundaries or framework of one nation of people of diverse cultures with significantly different patterns of belief, behavior, color, and in many cases with different languages. To achieve cultural pluralism, there must be unity with diversity. Each person must be aware of and secure in his own identity, and be willing to extend to others the same respect and rights that he expects to enjoy himself" (cited in Grillo, 1998, p. 192).

In 1972, largely influenced by the African-American attempt at cultural pluralism, the American Association of Colleges of Teacher Education established a Commission on Multicultural Education. In its report, entitled *No One Model American,* the commission rejected the prevailing view that schools should seek to melt away cultural differences or merely tolerate cultural pluralism. Instead, it stated that multicultural education "recognizes cultural diversity as a fact of life in American society, and it affirms that this cultural diversity is a valuable resource that should be preserved and extended. . . . To endorse cultural pluralism is to endorse the principle that there is no one model American. . . . Cultural pluralism is more than a temporary accommodation to placate racial and ethnic minorities. It is a concept that aims toward a heightened sense of being and wholeness of the entire society based on the unique strengths of each of its parts" (cited in Bullivant, 1983, pp. 124–25).

The commission used the terms *cultural pluralism* and *multiculturalism* interchangeably, thereby signaling an important conceptual connection between the two. In this book I also treat multiculturalism as an extension of cultural pluralism and treat the terms interchangeably. Clearly, in order to distinguish from the original concept of cultural pluralism that included only people of European origin, the concept of multiculturalism, while adhering to the basic philosophy of pluralism, has been formulated, as the African-American community intended, to include people of non-European origins as well. From the perspective of the African-American community, the newly created multicultural awareness yielded concrete results, including the designation of February as Black History Month, and the establishment of African-American studies programs in leading universities and colleges. As a result of these developments, African-Americans have begun to play a significant role in the presentation of their life histories from their own perspective, and also in the teaching of their contribution to American art, music, and literature.

The role played by African-Americans in the development of multiculturalism is so vital that they have been called "the storm troops in the battles over multiculturalism" (Glazer, 1997, p. 94). However, when the expanded version of cultural pluralism metamorphosed into multiculturalism, and was seen as an all-inclusive concept, other immigrant communities, particularly Asian and Hispanic, jumped on the multicultural bandwagon. Soon, the mainstream American community too followed suit. The tension created by a multitude of players and a multiplicity of agendas is reflected in the many manifestations of multiculturalism.

6.1.3. Manifestations of Multiculturalism

Multiculturalism emphasizes, at least in its theoretical core, certain lofty humanistic principles. Going beyond a mere assertion of tolerance and coexistence of different cultures, multiculturalism contends that preservation and protection of ethnic heritage is a fundamental right and responsibility of all members of a pluralistic society. Without treating ethnic identity and national identity as conflicting entities, multiculturalism seeks to promote among the general public a genuine understanding of the value of cultural diversity in shaping national identity. It believes that discrete ethnic identities can be preserved within a larger national identity that unites disparate ethnic groups. It also stresses, more than anything else, the importance of equality in the public domain: equality of cultures, equality of status, equality of treatment, and equality of opportunities. Accordingly, it calls for active participation by governmental, political, social, cultural, and educational institutions to create the conditions necessary to facilitate meaningful interactions between individuals and communities of different ethnic origins so that they can all march toward a common destiny.

Given such broad principles, multiculturalism appealed to various segments of the population and soon grew into a large movement. During the 1980s and early 1990s, multiculturalism became a fashionable field of academic, political, and social activity. Its lasting impact can be seen in the academic arena. Following the model of African-American studies, other ethnic programs such as Asian-American studies and Latin-American studies sprouted in several institutions of higher education. The impact was even greater at the school level. Several states, beginning with two of the biggest ones—California and New York—introduced new curricula for grades one through twelve, significantly increasing the class time allotted for the learning and teaching of ethnic histories and cultures. The importance of multiculturalism to school education is such that it has been described as "one of the shaping forces in American education today" (Glazer, 1997, p. 33).

The perceived success and spread of multiculturalism alarmed a section of the mainstream community. Influential voices from the right wing of the political spectrum represented by columnists such as Pat Buchanan, commentators such as Lynne Cheney, politicians such as Newt Gingrich, and educators such as Diane Ravitch vigorously derided multiculturalism and equally vigorously defended Eurocentrism. They saw in multiculturalism a force that is bent on diluting America's European inheritance by injecting into it undesirable elements from non-Western cultures. Some of them even argued, appropriating the positive sentiments associated with the popular principles of multiculturalism, that they are also multiculturalists because, according to them, the mainstream American culture became multicultural in character when it moved away from an Anglocentric emphasis to a Eurocentric emphasis. Their fear is that the carefully constructed edifice of American culture will collapse if its Eurocentric foundation is weakened.

Their conservative voice found a surprise ally in Schlesinger (1998), who is considered to be a liberal intellectual. He saw in the spread of multiculturalism an "ethnic upsurge" (p. 49) that he characterized as "a cult" (p. 49). This "cult of ethnicity," he argued, "exaggerates differences, intensifies resentments and antagonisms, drives even deeper the awful wedges between races and nationalities" (p. 106). Cautioning that such "ethnic cheerleading" will eventually lead to the disuniting of America, he suggested that public schools should not be saddled "with the mission of convincing children of the beauties of their particular ethnic origins. Ethnic subcultures, if they had genuine vitality, would be sufficiently instilled in children by family, church, and community" (p. 96). Ironically, however, he did not see anything wrong in saddling public schools with the task of teaching children the cultural values of the American mainstream community. Stephen May (1999, p. 20) pointed out the obvious inconsistency in such an argument: "on the one hand, Schlesinger derisively describes group-based affiliations as mere 'ethnic cheerleading' and argues that these are essentially preservationist rather than transformative. And yet, on the other hand, he ends up, as we have seen, invoking a majoritarian version of the same process."

Thus, both conservatives and liberals commend as well as condemn different aspects of multiculturalism depending on their own overt and covert agendas. It is worthwhile to recognize that the developmental path taken by American multiculturalism—its avowed opposition to cultural assimilation, its ritualized and racialized representations, and its liberal and conservative confrontations—all have striking similarities to the one experienced by other immigrant nations such as Australia, Britain, and Canada. Partly due to the conservative onslaught on multiculturalism, and partly due to their own dissatisfaction with the way multiculturalism has been evolving, a group of educationists from pluralistic democracies such as Australia (e.g., Bill Cope and Mary Kalantzis), Britain (e.g., Stephen May), Canada (e.g., Will Kymlicka), and the United States (e.g., Peter McLaren) began propagating a new brand of multiculturalism called *critical multiculturalism.*

Rejecting both conservative and liberal versions of multiculturalism, critical multiculturalism "interrogates the construction of difference and identity in relation to a radical politics. It is positioned against the neo-imperial romance with monoglot ethnicity grounded in a shared or 'common' experience of 'America' that is associated with conservative and liberal strands of multiculturalism" (McLaren, 1994, p. 53). Referring specifically to the North American context, McLaren asserted: "conservative attacks on multiculturalism as separatist and ethnocentric carry with them the erroneous assumption by White Anglo constituencies that North American society fundamentally constitutes social relations of interrupted accord. The liberal view is seen to underscore the idea that North American society is largely a forum of consensus with different minority viewpoints accretively added on. We are faced here with the politics of pluralism which largely ignores the workings of power and privilege" (McLaren, 1995, pp. 126–27). In other words, multiculturalism, as widely practiced, has not changed the unequal social status or the unequal power structure between mainstream and minority communities.

Determined that the best way to effect desired change is through education, critical multiculturalists ask for educational reforms that are oriented toward sociopolitical access. Drawing mostly from the critical pedagogy of the Brazilian educator Paulo Freire, critical multiculturalists maintain that classroom reality is socially constructed, politically motivated, and historically determined. Therefore, any serious multicultural education must attempt to transform the relationship between the classroom and the sociopolitical forces operating in the wider community. Although there are subtle variations in their emphasis, they generally agree that education should be made less informative and more performative. Toward that end, they call for an education in which

- multicultural ethics are performed through the practice of everyday life rather than through the practice of merely reading texts (McLaren and Torres, 1999);
- students are encouraged and enabled to engage critically with various ethnic and cultural backgrounds so that they can recognize and explore the complex interconnections, gaps, and dissonances that occur between their own and other ethnic and cultural identities, and how these identities are situated in the wider framework of power relations (May, 1999); and
- curriculum and teachers stand in an authoritative rather than an authoritarian position in relation to students, that is, authoritative in representing expert knowledge about their disciplinary areas, yet not authoritarian in negating the critical dialogue that marshals differences as a resource for access without prejudice to the integrity of those differences (Kalantzis and Cope, 1999).

These ideas remain a point of lively discussion within the academic discourse community, and it is not clear to what extent they have captured the imagination of educational authorities and classroom practitioners.

As the discussion so far attests, there are many forms and phases of cultural pluralism. Even in its current form of multiculturalism, it manifests in many ways. Proponents of different strands of multiculturalism grapple with the complex issue of cultural diversity unable or unwilling to determine what kind of diversity is desirable, how much, on what matters, and on what basis. It is not at all surprising that, with a multiplicity of approaches and a multitude of constituencies, multiculturalism lacks a governing, unifying principle. As Christopher Clausen (2000, p. 158) aptly put it, it is irresistible to think of the ship of multiculturalism "as a modern replica of Noah's Ark—proved to have more sail than rudder and scudded unsteerably before a succession of powerful winds." Consequently, multiculturalism has been rendered a deceptive concept with deceptive practices.

6.2. Cultural Pluralism and Its Deceptions

The deceptive nature of various forms of cultural pluralism (a.k.a. multiculturalism) can best be understood in terms of exclusivity, superficiality, and inequality. Recall that pluralism's early proponents such as John Dewey and Horace Kallen had openly excluded non-European minorities from their pluralistic tent. Later forms of pluralism, however, appear to have embraced exclusivity in a different way: by particularizing the beliefs and practices of specific cultural or ethnic communities and by bestowing rigid and exclusive identity markers to each of them. What is being sidelined here is the fact that cultural communities overlap in their belief and practices, shaping and reshaping each other's cultural life in myriad ways. The very usage of the hyphen, as in African-American, Asian-American, and Hispanic-American, indicates that people have overlapping cultural identities.

Part of the rationale for such exclusivity comes from cultural essentialism. It treats culture as an immutable given that stays stable across historical and social contexts. It fails to recognize that cultural boundaries are fluid rather than fixed (see Chapter 2 for details). Multiculturalism, in spite of its desire for diversity, engages in a totalizing discourse that unhelpfully essentializes and reifies ethnic and cultural differences. Even the most positive aspect of multiculturalism—helping marginalized minorities to preserve and protect their cultural heritage—assumes cultural fixity. As Kivisto (2002) argued, a truly multicultural society needs broadly shared sociocultural norms to sustain it, and such a society can grow only if cultural communities unite around a common view of life. The treatment of each cultural community as a more or less homogeneous and coherent whole forbids, rather than facilitates, the emergence of a multiculturally constituted society.

As a consequence of their essentialistic approach, multiculturalists put a premium on group identity rather than on individual identity. They treat individuals as members of discrete communities with clearly identified and identifiable characteristics, ignoring the distinct possibility that individuals may develop multiple identities, belongings, and loyalties, some of which may even appear contradictory to each other. Besides, by positing a binary opposition through which the self and the community are conceptualized, multiculturalism "breeds an enthusiasm for specific, traditional cultures that can sometimes mask a provinciality from which individuals are eager to escape through new, out-group affiliations" (Hollinger, 1995, p. 107). In the name of cultural diversity, then, multiculturalism solidifies cultural exclusivity to the detriment of individual cultural growth.

Even the much-fancied celebration of cultural diversity is marked more by superficiality than by sensitivity. A detailed analysis of the practice of multiculturalism will show that what started as a grand project has been reduced to no more than ethnic rites and rituals. Incorporating a few ethnic stories written by ethnic writers in the school curriculum came to be considered a mark of multiculturalism. Ritualized celebration of difference has become an end in itself. Several public schools in California, for instance, routinely celebrate diversity in the form of the Vietnamese Tet festival in January, Black History Month in February, the Chinese lantern festival in March (depending on the lunar calendar), the Japanese cherry blossom festival in April, Mexican Cinco de Mayo in May, the Native-American powwow in June, etc. Students quickly get used to the routine. They know what to expect in these months, and they enthusiastically participate in these events. After the festivities are over, they slip back into their own cultural cocoon—only to return to the same old tiring rituals the following year. Thus, multiculturalism has been "aestheticized and packaged as an exciting consumable collage: brown hands holding yellow hands holding white hands holding male hands holding female hands holding black hands in a spirit of post-historical contemporaneity" (Radhakrishnan, 2003, p. 40).

Such superficial and cosmetic form of multiculturalism has been called "boutique multiculturalism" by literary critic Stanley Fish (1999). Boutique multiculturalists "admire or appreciate or enjoy or sympathize with or (at the very least) 'recognize the legitimacy of' the traditions of cultures other than their own; but boutique multiculturalists will always stop short of approving other cultures at a point where some value at their center generates an act that offends against the canons of civilized decency as they have been either declared or assumed" (p. 56). They will oppose the force of a minority culture "at precisely the point at which it matters most to its strongly committed members—the point at which the African American tries to make the content of his culture the content of his children's education, the point at which a Native American wants to practice his religion as its ancient rituals direct him to" (p. 57). Unwilling to compromise their own cultural values that they believe are unique and superior, and unable to resist the experience and practice of multiculturalism in the social arena, boutique multiculturalists engage in what has been called political correctness—parrotlike repetition of meaningless labels that conceal, rather than reveal, one's real intentions. Many advocates as well as adversaries of multiculturalism encode their public discourse in terms of a politically correct vocabulary that is full of platitude.

Furthermore, multiculturalism has become, as Kwame Anthony Appiah (1991) rightly pointed out, an object of commodification where ethnic diversity is treated as a commodity to be bought and sold. Even marginalized groups go along with such commodification by manipulating and marketing ethnic arts and artifacts in novel and expressive ways in order to sell them to eager patrons. Academic and corporate sectors too use multiculturalism as a commercial tool, with well-publicized diversity workshops and sensitivity training sessions where "diversity gurus" were regularly commissioned to help the members of industries, schools, and colleges exorcise, on a periodical basis, the little demons of discrimination that are supposed to reside in their body and soul. Goldberg (1994) called this brand of multiculturalism "managed or corporate multiculturalism." The task is seen here as one of designing opportunistic strategies aimed at "maintaining a constriction of diversity that otherwise might be unmanageable and overwhelming from the standpoint of bureaucratic and administrative technologies" (p. 29).

More than exclusivity and superficiality, what has rendered multiculturalism a disappointing concept is its failure to address in any meaningful way the sociopolitical inequality that exists between the mainstream and minority communities. One of the cardinal principles of multiculturalism that distinguishes it from the earlier forms of pluralism is precisely its emphasis on equality. In spite of all its good intentions, multiculturalism has ended up "doing nothing either to change the mainstream or to improve the access of those historically denied its power and privileges" (Kalantzis and Cope, 1999, p. 251). Critics fault both conservatives and liberals for losing sight of the equality dimension of multiculturalism. "It is a significant irony," noted May (1999, pp. 20–21), "that conservative and liberal commentators fail to recognize that ethnic conflict and fragmentation arise most often not when compromises are made between ethnic groups or when formal ethnic, linguistic and/or religious rights are accorded some degree of recognition, but when these have been historically avoided, suppressed, or ignored."

It has also been pointed out that multiculturalism seeks to promote equality only up to a point. In the context of American multiculturalism, cultural critic Trinh Minh-ha (1989, cited in Yuval-Davis, 1997, p. 55) has commented that there are two kinds of social and cultural diversity: one that threatens the mainstream power structure and one that does not. American multiculturalism is aimed at nourishing and perpetuating the kind of differences that do not loosen the firm grip on power and privilege that the mainstream community has historically enjoyed. In the same vein, McLaren and Torres (1999) have suggested that American multiculturalism has not been informed by a principled ethics of compassion and social justice. From Britain, Paul Gilroy (1987) and others have observed that British multiculturalism has not effectively addressed the structural inequalities faced by minority communities, and that it has left the life chances of minority community unchanged and the hegemony of majority community unchallenged. Similarly, Andrew Jakubowicz (1984, p. 42) pointed out that the policy of multiculturalism pursued by the Australian government "gives the ethnic communities the task to retain and cultivate with government help their different cultures, but does not concern itself with struggles against discriminatory policies as they affect individuals or classes of people."

Overall, then, the deceptive nature of multiculturalism is very much reflected in how its adherents of all hues interpret the concept in their own way and appropriate it to suit their own agenda. Thus, there is a "weak" version of multiculturalism whose adherents are preoccupied with ethnic rites rather than ethnic rights; a "muscular" version whose adherents are engaged in using it as a colorful costume to cover their covert ethnocentrism; and a "critical" version whose adherents are engrossed in the academic, thus far ineffectual, discourse of sociopolitical equality. The concept of multiculturalism has thus been rendered so diffuse that a leading sociologist declared rather gleefully: "We are all multiculturalists now" (Glazer, 1997). But, he hastened to add: "Of course we are not *all* multiculturalists, but one would be hard put . . . to find someone who is not. The expression 'We are all multiculturalists now' harks back to others that have been pronounced wryly by persons who recognized that something unpleasant was nevertheless unavoidable; it is not employed to indicate a wholehearted embrace" (Glazer, 1997, p. 160, emphasis as in original). It is to such a deceptive, diffused, and divisive concept that educators in general, and language educators in particular, turned for curricular inspiration.

6.3. Cultural Pluralism and Language Education

Although the language-culture connection has engaged the minds of language educators for a long time, the multicultural movement provided an extra impetus for them to make the connection even more explicit. During the 1980s and 90s, the field of foreign language education preoccupied itself with the task of locating culture at the core of the language curriculum. The publication of ACTFL Proficiency Guidelines in 1986, and the National Standards in 1996, made clear the central role of culture as a curricular content. Similarly, in the field of TESOL, cultural understanding and cross-cultural comparisons were declared to be a necessary component of language teaching (Stern, 1983). Consequently, multicultural issues were deemed to be a part of the knowledge-base of TESOL teachers who were advised to include "certain activities or materials that illustrate the connection between language and culture" (Brown, 1994, p. 25).

In a typical and popular approach to culture teaching, Stern (1992) proposed a "cultural syllabus" that included cognitive, affective, and behavioral components. Cognitive component relates to various forms of knowledge—geographical knowledge, knowledge about the contributions of the target culture to world civilization, knowledge about differences in the way of life, as well as an understanding of values and attitudes in the L2 community. Affective component relates to L2 learners' curiosity about and empathy for the target culture. Behavioral component relates to learners' ability to interpret culturally relevant behavior, and to conduct themselves in culturally appropriate ways. The cultural syllabus focuses on six topics covering major aspects of cultural knowledge the average learner is most likely to require: (1) *Places*—describing "how the geography is perceived by native speakers" (Stern, 1992, p. 219); (2) *Individual persons and way of life*—making personal contact with a native speaker's everyday life because only "by observing it, and asking questions about it, the learner can get attuned to the customs of the community" (p. 220); (3) *People and society in general*— identifying "significant groups indicative of social, professional, economic, and age differences, as well as those which reflect regional characteristics" (p. 220); (4) *History*—knowing "the historically significant symbols, notable events and trends, and the main historical personalities as well as critical issues" (p. 221); (5) *Institutions*— understanding "the system of government—central, regional, and local—the educational system, social welfare, economic institutions, the military and the police, religious institutions, political parties, and the media including television, radio, and the press" (p. 221); and finally, (6) *Art, music, literature, and other major achievements*— acquiring "knowledge about and an appreciation of artists, musicians, and writers and their works" (p. 221). To help learners become aware of these six content areas, Stern advocates a problem-solving teaching method in which "the learner is not simply presented with information, but is confronted with a culturally significant situation which may present a problem to a foreigner visiting the country. These are usually questions of manners or customs, for example, what to say or what not to say in a given social situation" (p. 226).

The phrase "what to say or what not to say in a given social situation" fairly captures the basic orientation taken by second language educators toward culture teaching—an orientation inspired largely by studies in sociolinguistics. These studies (see Kasper and Blum-Kulka, eds., 1993; and Rose and Kasper, eds., 2001) focus on cultural aspects of speech act performance in order to identify the basic linguistic structure of, say, politeness formulas in the target language as contrasted with politeness formulas in the learners' first language and/or in their still developing second language (i.e., interlanguage). The goal is to predict areas of cultural adjustments for the L2 learner and to suggest strategies of pedagogic intervention for the L2 teacher. These studies have no doubt helped us understand how pragmatic aspects of learners' interlanguage performance can be related to the way certain speech acts are realized across languages and cultures. They, however, do not explore the complexities of cultural beliefs and practices (see Chapter 9).

Furthermore, a focal point of the cognitive, affective, and behavioral components of teaching culture has always been the native speaker of the target language. As Stern (1992) reiterated, "one of the most important aims of culture teaching is to help the learner gain an understanding of the native speaker's perspective" (p. 216). It is a matter of the L2 learner "becoming sensitive to the state of mind of individuals and groups within the target language community" (p. 217). The teacher's task, then, is to help the learner "create a network of mental associations similar to those which the items evoke in the native speaker" (p. 224). The overall objective of culture teaching, then, is to help L2 learners develop the ability to use the target language in culturally appropriate ways for the specific purpose of empathizing and interacting with native speakers of the target language.

Such an approach is based on a limited view of multiculturalism in at least two important ways. First, it narrowly associates cultural identity with national identity or linguistic identity. That is, it considers all the people belonging to a particular nation (e.g., America) and speaking a particular language (e.g., English) as belonging to a particular culture. It ignores multicultural and subcultural variations within national or linguistic boundaries. Second, it also ignores the rich diversity of worldviews learners bring with them to the language classroom. As Scarcella and Oxford (1992, p. 186) pointed out, "the ESL classroom is typically a cultural microcosm of the world. Not only are ESL students exposed to US culture, but they are also often exposed to the cultures of many lands throughout the world." Besides, even if a group of learners, as in most other educational contexts, appears to belong to a seemingly homogeneous national or linguistic entity, the life values, life choices, and lifestyles of these learners and, therefore, their worldview, may vary significantly. In that sense, most classes are not monocultural cocoons but rather are multicultural mosaics. With its exclusive emphasis on a homogenized target language community and its cultural way of life, the approach has failed to capitalize on the rich linguistic and cultural resources that characterize most L2 classes.

Yet another area of multicultural teaching that has not received adequate attention is the designing of culturally appropriate teaching materials. As I have argued elsewhere (Kumaravadivelu, 2003b), textbooks are not a neutral medium; they represent cultural values, beliefs, and attitudes. They reflect "a social construction that may be imposed on teachers and students and that indirectly constructs their view of a culture. This aspect often passes unrecognized" (Cortazzi and Jin, 1999, p. 200). The hidden cultural values embedded in textbooks are rarely recognized and redressed. Referring to English language textbooks used in Canada, which has officially endorsed the principles of multicultural education, Nicholls (1995, p. 113) pointed out that "a uniformity of middle-class, anglocentric values still informs the themes and characters in these texts. So, for example, while Canadians featured in these texts are now more likely to be members of a minority than ever before, these characters almost always embrace the values, manners and mores, religion and socioeconomic status of members of Canada's Anglo majority." What is true of the Canadian context is also true of other ESL contexts as well.

In fact, the cultural orientation weighted in favor of the target language speakers is not unique to textbooks used in the ESL context. Giving a view of the Asian English-language classroom, Tickoo (1995) lamented the absence of culturally appropriate materials for use in teaching English in cross-cultural contexts of multilingual/multicultural countries of Asia. As McKay (2000) pointed out, teachers and students coming from the same linguistic and cultural background use textbooks that draw heavily on a foreign culture, as in the case of classrooms in Thailand or in Korea, where local teachers use culturally loaded materials written in the United States or the United Kingdom. A survey of learners of English as a foreign language (Prodromou, 1992) revealed that learners themselves are dissatisfied with the culturally inappropriate materials used in their classroom. They look for richer multinational, multicultural input than they find in their textbooks.

Faced with such limitations in terms of concepts, methods, and materials, L2 teachers find themselves inadequately prepared to carry out the goals of multicultural education. Recognizing the problem, and asserting that "preparation for teaching in the 21st century should require that all teachers gain an appreciation for and acceptance of cultural pluralism, along with confidence in teaching all students," Watkins and Butler (1999, p. 27) have attempted to develop what they call a Cultural Implications Role Play for both in-service and pre-service teachers. The goal of the role play, usually conducted by a knowledgeable colleague playing the role of a facilitator, was "to introduce teachers to the array of cultural patterns represented in classrooms" (p. 28). The specific objectives are to

- Sensitize teachers to the subtle cultural meanings that children with a different view of social reality bring to the classroom setting.
- Provide teachers the opportunity to explore the implications of their responses to ethnic and socioeconomic differences within the classroom setting.
- Provide teachers an opportunity to investigate and analyze a variety of responses to cultural implications and learning styles.
- Focus on cultural issues that interfere with or enhance students' education.

The role play uses preselected cultural typologies (some might call them cultural stereotypes) on students from various linguistic and cultural backgrounds, and includes information related to nonverbal communication such as eye contact, silence, head nods, and physical proximity. According to the authors, the role play helps teachers recognize "the need to develop teaching techniques that are responsive to a range of cultural realities, to look beyond their taken-for-granted assumptions when interpreting student behavior, and to be more adaptive and sensitive to their students. Such awareness can provide the basis for respecting differences and synthesizing similarities that would help the classroom become a true community of learners" (1999, p. 30).

To sum up this section, language education informed by multiculturalism, in spite of some of its laudable intentions, exhibits several drawbacks. It essentializes culture. It offers fragmented cultural tidbits. It valorizes mainstream cultural beliefs and practices. It museumizes minority cultures. It disregards the cultural capital L2 learners bring with them. It channels its energy toward educating the members of the minority communities as if members of the mainstream community have little to learn and gain from it. It ignores the processes of cultural globalization that make the teaching of culture a critical as well as a challenging task facing our profession today.

6.4. In Closing

In this chapter I have dealt primarily with the American version of cultural pluralism. I have briefly traced the origin of the concept of cultural pluralism and its gradual evolution into multiculturalism.

I have also discussed how multiculturalism manifests in many ways. Attracted by the appeal of multiculturalism, its proponents—whether they have practiced a weak or a strong version—have interpreted the concept in their own way and have appropriated it to suit their own sometimes overt and sometimes covert agenda. Consequently, multiculturalism has become a deceptive, diffused, and divisive concept challenging educators everywhere to come to terms with certain realities that have been best summarized by Kalantzis and Cope (1999, p. 269): "Just as geopolitics have shifted, so schools have to service linguistic and cultural diversity. Their fundamental role has changed. The meaning of literacy pedagogy has changed. Local diversity and global connectedness not only mean that there can be no standard; they mean that the most important skill students need to learn is to negotiate dialect, register and semiotic differences, code switching, interlanguages and hybrid cross-cultural discourses."

The dissatisfaction with the concept of multiculturalism as professed and practiced today; the dispersion of people, ideas, and goods across the borders of nations and cultures; and the dissemination of postcolonial and poststructural thoughts to the field of language education have directed the attention of the profession toward yet another cultural concept: cultural hybridity.

CHAPTER 7

Cultural Hybridity
and Its Discontents

Point of convergence
Union of way back then, back home and home
Where I depend neither on memory or desire
Where I am neither mendhi, baigan, or steelpan
Nor
Mindless of these

Seemless juncture
As in mulligatawny that cooks long and slow
Neither Jeera, cardamom, hurdi, nor clove
stand alone

Hybridity
As in: "Offspring of tame sow and wild boar
Child of freeman and slave"
Some concoction, some new stew of callallaoo
Spotted variegated deformed crude new

Calcottawarima
Persimangorangegrapear
Pomeracappleplummecythere
Gorakpurcarapachaimavancouverlaromainottawa

Where neither Nepalese great-grandmother
Mother, lover, nor government can define I
Nor
am I
Mindless of these

Aptly titled "Hybridity," this poem was written by Shani Mootoo
(1999, p. 106), who was born in Ireland to parents of Nepalese/Indian
origin and raised in the Caribbean island of Trinidad. She later mi-

grated to Canada, which she now calls home. In all her work as a visual artist, filmmaker, poet, and novelist, Mootoo starkly confronts the issue of authenticity and ambivalence associated with hybrid identity.

The poet represented identity as irretrievably hybrid, a comingling of diverse and divergent cultures. Meditating on the process of her own becoming, Mootoo excavates the various fusions through which her own consciousness has been forged. She unearths the sediments of a family history that brings a Nepalese great-grandmother's offspring, an indentured laborer forcibly uprooted by British colonialism, from the Indian subcontinent to the Caribbean. In the new (dis)location, Nepalese meets African meets Native American meets European, giving birth to new possibilities of being and becoming. The poet therefore located her consciousness in an in-between space composed of ingredients from each of these cultures, but belonging to none exclusively.

Mootoo used several culinary metaphors in the poem. She compares herself to mulligatawny soup, a dish made by boiling various ingredients together until they can no longer be separated even though it is possible to detect or taste each of them in the soup. She cooked up some novel linguistic concoctions by inventing compound words that mirror the process of cultural amalgamation. She elegantly combined names of places and fruits associated with the different locations that have contributed to her identity:

Calcottawarima
Persimangorangegrapear
Pomeracappleplummecythere
Gorakpurcarapachaimavancouverlaromainottawa

In doing so, she represented the process of fusion as natural, spontaneous, "seamless." There is not much tension here. No loud celebration of hybridity either. Only a quiet affirmation of identity—an identity that belongs to no one but herself. Hybridity is seen as a net gain, something that not only makes the poet unique but also enables her to slip past all restrictive definitions. Thus, "neither great grand-mother, mother, lover nor government" can define the "I" who is free, free to be me. Rather than producing a sense of loss, the poet's sense of not belonging exclusively to any one culture actually makes her free to belong anywhere.

The formation of hybrid identity that the poet so elegantly articulates is not as unproblematic as she portrays. It fact, it has long been the subject of academic argumentation. The struggles and strategies followed by individuals and communities to meet the challenges of cross-cultural experiences have been described variously as hybridity, strategic essentialism, cosmopolitanism, and critical cosmopolitanism. To discuss its complexities I consolidate these insights under the rubric of cultural hybridity.

7.1. The Concept of Cultural Hybridity

The word *hybrid* has a biological and botanical origin. The *Oxford English Dictionary* defines it as "the offspring of two animals or plants of different species, or (less strictly) varieties; a half-breed, cross-breed or mongrel" (1971, p. 1354), and by nature, such a half-breed is incapable of reproduction. The word was scarcely in use until the nineteenth century, when it was extended to include human beings and quickly took on a racial or, more precisely, a racist, tone aimed at maintaining intraracial purity and at discouraging union between interracial partners. The debate about "human hybrids" centered around the issue of whether people of different races were actually members of different species—a debate that was fully exploited, for instance, by Adolf Hitler, who argued that Nature's rule consists of "the inner segregation of the species of all living beings on this earth," and if this rule is infringed upon, then, Nature will resist "and her most visible protest consists either in refusing further capacity for propagation to bastards or in limiting the fertility of later offspring" (Hitler, 1925/1969, p. 258, cited in Young, 1995, p. 8).

  In the twentieth century, the physiological phenomenon of hybridity was increasingly applied to the cultural arena. Although, as we discussed in Chapter 2, every culture is inherently a hybrid culture, certain historical forces accelerate the formation of cultural hybrids in expressed and explicit ways. Colonialism with its "civilizing mission" is one of them. Not surprisingly, then, the concept of cultural hybridity is closely connected to colonial and postcolonial projects. In fact, the concept has been studied so much that it "has now acquired the status of a common-sense term, not only in academia but also in the culture more generally. It has become a key concept in cultural criticism, in post-colonial studies, in debates about cultural contestation and appropriation and in relation to the concept of the border and the ideal of the cosmopolitan" (Coombes and Brah, 2000, p. 1). It is, therefore, fitting to discuss how the concept of hybridity is treated in the discourses of colonialism, postcolonialism, and cosmopolitanism.

7.1.1. Colonialism and Cultural Hybridity

In the context of colonial studies, hybridity is defined as "the creation of new transcultural forms within the contact zone produced by colonization" (Ashcroft, Griffiths, and Tiffin, 2001, p. 118). The conflicts and consequences arising out of the cultural mixing of different races of people during colonial encounters presented a fertile site for sociologists and anthropologists to construct theories about cultural hybridity. Latin America is one of those sites where the focal point of sociological and literary discourse centered around the notion of *mestizaje,* or *mestizo*—a popular term that refers to a racial category of people with noticeable European and Amerindian ancestry. In order to make sense of the culturally hybridized beliefs and practices resulting from these interminglings, several Latin-American cultural anthropologists explored the *mestizaje* phenomenon with remarkable intellectual rigor. Foremost among them was the renowned Cuban historian and anthropologist Fernando Ortiz.

Precisely during the period (i.e., early to mid twentieth century) when notions of cultural purity and biological determination of race were reigning supreme in Europe, the Americas, and elsewhere, Ortiz conceptualized and coined the term *transculturation* and vigorously defended *mestizaje* and hybridity. In *Cuban Counterpoint: Tobacco and Sugar,* an anthropological classic first published in Spanish in 1940, made available to the English-speaking world in 1947, and republished by Duke University Press in 1995, Ortiz critiqued the prevailing notion of acculturation for its inability to capture the uneven tensions that characterize the transformations of people in intense cultural contact. In the colonial history of Latin America, Ortiz saw a long intermeshing process of transculturation among people of different race and color—brown (Indians from the mainland), white (the conquering Spaniards who themselves were torn lose from the Iberian Peninsula), and black (Negroes from the coastal regions of Africa across the Atlantic)—"all of them snatched from their original social groups, their own cultures destroyed and crushed under the weight of the cultures in existence here, like sugar cane ground in the rollers of the mill" (Ortiz, 1995, p. 98). All of them "had to readjust themselves to a new syncretism of cultures" (p. 98) while at the same time "exerting an influence and being influenced in turn" (p. 98).

Unlike traditional anthropologists, Ortiz moved away from racial consideration of cultural hybridity and toward what he called "the social life of things." For him, *mestizaje* was more than just a mixing of color; it was, indeed, a synthesis of different ways of life. He viewed transculturation as a phenomenon that has impacts on the lives of people in cultural contact regardless of whether they are members of the colonizing or colonized communities (or of the mainstream or minority communities in immigrant contexts). He declared unequivocally: "I am of the opinion that the word trans-culturation better expresses the different phases of the process of transition from one culture to another because this does not consist merely in acquiring another culture, which is what the English word acculturation really implies, but the process also necessarily involves the loss and uprooting of a previous culture, which could be defined as deculturation. In addition it carries the idea of the consequent creation of new cultural phenomena, which could be called neoculturation" (1995, pp. 102–3). Notice that Ortiz's trans-culturation involves the uprooting of oneself from one's own cultural milieu, the erasure of one's traditional cultural traits, and the acquisition of new cultural beliefs and practices. The resulting cultural persona is, in significant ways, the product of an amalgamation of past history and present reality.

Following the lead given by Ortiz, Nestor Garcia Canclini, a Mexican sociologist, saw in the concept of transculturation a creative and energetic tension between the traditional and the modern. In his book *Culturas Hibridas,* published in Spanish in 1990 and translated into English in 1995, Garcia Canclini provided a comprehensive and critical analysis of sociocultural formations in Latin America. Based on his understanding that "tradition has not yet disappeared and modernity has not yet completely arrived" in Latin America, he hypothesized that "the *uncertainty* about the meaning and value of modernity derives not only from what separates nations, ethnic groups, and classes, but also from the sociocultural hybrids in which the traditional and the modern are mixed" (1995, p. 2, italics as in original). Maintaining that contemporary Latin-

American societies are the product of the intercrossing of Indian traditions, of colonial Catholic hispanism and of modern political and educational practices, Garcia Canclini argued that the modern has not only not replaced the traditional, but has actually rearticulated and reaffirmed it.

The Latin-American view of transcultural hybridity has been duly recognized in certain intellectual circles as something that "subsumes the emphasis placed on borders, migrations, plurilanguaging, and multiculturing and the increasing need to conceptualize transnational and transimperial languages, literacies, and literatures" (Mignolo, 2000, p. 220). However, postcolonial critics presented yet another perspective on intercultural interrogations that lead to what has been dubbed as the Anglophone version of cultural hybridity.

7.1.2. Postcolonialism and Cultural Hybridity

Along with American anthropologist James Clifford and British cultural critic Stuart Hall, India-born postcolonialist Homi Bhabha is among the most influential theorists of cultural hybridity. In a series of articles published during the 1980s and put together as a collected volume entitled *The Location of Culture* in 1994, Bhabha exorcised the concept of hybridity from its racialized and racist formulation of the past, relocated it within a nonracial site, and used it to psychoanalytically examine the inner mechanisms of colonialism. Without looking at colonial power as "the noisy command of colonialist authority or the silent repression of native traditions" (1994, p. 112), Bhabha saw in colonial encounters no less than "the production of hybridization" (p. 112) that impacts both the colonizer and the colonized. In this respect, Bhabha clearly echoed Ortiz.

To put it simply, Bhabha hypothesized that, in a colonial context where cultures collide, the dominant as well as the dominated undergo subtle and sustained cultural transformations. A similar phenomenon may occur, in a less forceful and forthright manner, in an immigrant context where individuals uproot themselves from one cultural soil and get transplanted into another. According to Bhabha, what eventually results from these encounters is a "third culture," or a "third space." The third space suggests that "the meaning and symbols of culture have no primordial unity or fixity; that even the same signs can be appropriated, translated, and rehistoricized anew"

(Bhabha, 1994, p. 37). It offers freedom for people to continually negotiate and translate all available resources in order to construct their own hybrid cultures and, consequently, reconstruct their own individual identities. By displacing the histories that constitute it, hybridity enables new and recognizable positions to emerge.

For Bhabha, hybridity is not an object to own, nor is it a goal to achieve. It is not a culminating product; rather, it is a continual process. It is a way of understanding and perceiving the ambiguous cultural transition that carries no promise of perceptible closure. He believed that "the theoretical recognition of the split-space of enunciation may open the way to conceptualizing an *inter*national culture, based not on the exoticism of multiculturalism or the *diversity* of cultures, but on the inscription and articulation of culture's *hybridity*. To that end we should remember that it is the 'inter'—the cutting edge of translation and negotiation, the *in-between* space—that carries the burden of the meaning of culture" (p. 38, italics as in original).

In carrying that burden, hybridity does not resolve any tension between two cultures in contact, nor does it recognize cultural pluralism or cultural superiority. On the contrary, it represents a state of ambivalence, of in-betweenness, of border-crossing—all of which are considered to be liberating. Instead of getting imprisoned in one cultural space, one can now belong everywhere. Thus, Bhabha's postcolonial interpretation of hybridity clearly treats it as a positive force both for the postmodern individual and for the postcolonial society. Mootoo's poem presented above clearly reflects such a view.

In enunciating cultural hybridity, Bhabha focused on the dialectical relationship between the dominating and the dominated. Hybridity is considered to reverse "the effects of the colonialist disavowal, so that other 'denied' knowledges enter upon the dominant discourse and estrange the basis of its authority—its rules of recognition" (p. 114). He claimed that because hybridity "entertains difference without an assumed or imposed hierarchy" (p. 4), and because it disrupts power asymmetries rooted in hierarchical relationships, it is just another "name for the strategic reversal of the process of domination" (p. 112). Whether such a sanguine representation of colonial (or immigrant) encounters will stand historical scrutiny or not is an issue we will take up later.

Unlike Bhabha, who takes a psychoanalytic approach to hybridity, Hall, without distancing himself from Bhabha's interrogations, added a sociological dimension to his analysis. He focused on contemporary postcolonial communities that are characterized by multicultural diasporas, that is, mixed and minority communities caused by displacement (e.g., Jewish diaspora), exile (e.g., Kurdish diaspora), and migration (e.g., Indian diaspora). Bemoaning that the term *hybridity* has been widely misunderstood, Hall asserted, not unlike Bhabha, that it "does not refer to hybrid individuals, who can be contrasted as fully-formed subjects with 'traditionals' and 'moderns.' It is a process of cultural translation, which is agonistic because it is never completed, but rests with its undecidability" (2000, p. 226). The nature of hybridity is such that it "neither remains within one boundary, nor transcends boundaries" (p. 226). Hall illustrated his view by referring to contemporary British society: "the besuited Asian charted accountant . . . who lives in suburbia, sends his children to private schools and reads *Readers Digest* and the *Bhagavad Gita,* or the black teenager who is a dance-hall DJ, plays jungle music but supports Manchester United or the Muslim student who wears baggy, hip-hop, street-style jeans but is never absent from Friday prayers, are *all,* in their different ways, 'hybridized'" (2000, p. 226, italics as in original).

According to him, these hybridized individuals are not simply engaged "in slow transition to full assimilation" (p. 221), but, in fact, "represent a novel cultural configuration—'cosmopolitan communities'—marked by extensive trans-culturation" (p. 221). Clifford (1993) had earlier expressed similar views in the context of local ethnographic informants who, contrary to their representations as "natives," have always been multilingually and interculturally savvy, indicating their complex "inside/outside" position vis-à-vis the community they are called upon to represent. Pointing out that cultural arenas are "sites of displacement, interference, and interaction" (p. 101), Clifford developed the notion of cultures as traveling—unrooted and unstable. Such an analysis by Clifford and Hall recalls the cultural reconfiguration of the particular and the universal that has been the hallmark of cosmopolitanism.

7.1.3. Cosmopolitanism and Cultural Hybridity

Cosmopolitanism is nothing new. In the Western tradition, it is closely associated with the Enlightenment of the eighteenth century, and is best represented by Immanuel Kant's notion of perpetual peace. It seeks to promote "citizens of the world" who transcend ethnic, racial, or national boundaries and embrace universal values. Unlike multiculturalism or cultural pluralism (see Chapter 6), cosmopolitanism rejects the essentialist notion of culture that assigns fixed and frozen cultural traits to majority as well as minority groups in a society. As Hollinger (1995, pp. 3–4) succinctly put it: "Pluralism respects inherited boundaries and locates individuals within one or another of a series of ethno-racial groups to be protected and preserved. Cosmopolitanism is more wary of traditional enclosures and favors voluntary affiliations. Cosmopolitanism promotes multiple identities, emphasizes the dynamic and changing character of many groups, and is responsive to the potential for creating new cultural combinations. Pluralism sees in cosmopolitanism a threat to identity, while cosmopolitanism sees in pluralism a provincial unwillingness to engage the complex dilemmas and opportunities actually presented by contemporary life." Bhabha, Hall, and others saw hybridity as one form of radical cosmopolitanism that is responsive to the lived experiences of diasporic communities.

The radical form of cosmopolitanism may be looked upon as the cause as well as the consequence of hybridization. That is, exigencies and experiences connected to exile, migration, or displacement may trigger in individuals or groups of individuals a cosmopolitan consciousness that in turn may accelerate the process of hybridization, which may further consolidate their cosmopolitan outlook. In addition, hybridity theorists claimed that a continual process of hybridization has the capacity to undermine the center's cultural imposition perpetrated on the periphery and to unsettle the concept of nation-states formulated on the basis of identifiable and isolatable national cultures. As Pheng Cheah (1998, p. 297) explained, "the hybrid revival of cosmopolitanism therefore has two steps: an antilocalist/antinationalist argument and an argument that new radical cosmopolitans already exist." The first recognizes the demand or the desire to detach oneself from the obligations and affiliations linked to local or national ethos so that one can enjoy the freedom offered by as well as shoulder the responsibilities required by such a detachment. The second acknowledges the presence of transnational, transcultural migrant individuals who may be called cultural hybrids, like the British chartered accountants, black teenagers, and Muslim students mentioned in the quote from Hall.

To this debate on cosmopolitanism, American historian David

Hollinger (1995) added what he called a *postethnic* perspective. Pointing out that cosmopolitans have been "proudly rootless" (p. 6), Hollinger called for "the critical renewal of cosmopolitanism in the context of today's greater sensitivity to roots" (p. 6). Aligning his postethnic perspective with rooted cosmopolitanism, he favored voluntary over involuntary affiliations that develop cosmopolitan instincts by which most individuals develop many identities and live in many circles. According to him, it is this process of locating oneself amid various layers of "we's" that "most clearly distinguishes the postethnic from the unreconstructed universalist" (p. 106). Like other hybrid scholars, however, he acknowledged that "boundaries are necessary" (p. 172) but states that individuals "are all left with the responsibility for deciding where to try to draw what circles with whom, and around what" (p. 172).

It must be remembered that the hybrid revival of cosmopolitanism is not an invariant, unitary concept. Its "conceptual content and pragmatic character," declared Pollock, Bhabha, Breckenridge, and Chakrabarty, "are not only as yet unspecified but also must always escape positive and definite specification, precisely because specifying cosmopolitanism positively and definitely is an uncosmopolitan thing to do" (2002, p. 1). They urged that cosmopolitanism be considered in the plural, as cosmopolitanisms. According to them, the best way to understand cosmopolitanism in the plural is not to indulge in broad "philosophical reflection," which will only lead us to find "what we are looking for," but to "simply look at the world across time and space and see how people have thought and acted beyond the local." If we do that, then, we would "encounter an extravagant array of possibilities" (p. 10), suggesting "that we already are and have always been cosmopolitan, though we may not always have known it" (p. 12).

The phrase "an extravagant array of possibilities" fairly sums up a common promise that emanates from the colonial, postcolonial, and cosmopolitan versions of hybridity. They all describe hybridity as "an unending, unfinalizable process" that is "dynamic, mobile, less an achieved synthesis or prescribed formula than an unstable constellation of discourses" (Shohat and Stam, 1994, p. 42). They are all engaged in deconstructing the intermingling that is characteristic of intense cultural encounters and in demystifying the intricate process of hybridization. They all present a way of enunciating the dynamic nature of cultural identity that is constructed through continual negotiation and translation. They all attempt to make sense of complex and complicated themes ranging from violent as well as voluntary exchanges between the center and periphery to the lived experiences of diasporic communities. Given such a broad spectrum of interrogations, it is not surprising that hybridity "makes an elusive paradox" (Werbner, 1997, p. 1) resulting in widespread discontent.

7.2. Cultural Hybridity and Its Discontents

There are several shortcomings with the concept of hybridity as enunciated by Bhabha and others. First and foremost, critics have charged that the notion of hybridity wrongly places the margin at the center and, in doing so, it conflates the distinction between the oppressed and the oppressor. Recall Bhabha's claim that hybridity is just "another name for the strategic reversal of the process of domination" (1994, p. 112) and that it does not assume or impose hierarchy. It should be remembered that Bhabha's postcolonial insights emerge out of colonial encounters, particularly British colonialism in India. In the colonial context, he saw the potential for subversion and resistance on the part of the colonized, and for desire and denial on the part of the colonizer. One of the central aspects of colonialism is its ideological project of remaking the Other (the colonized) in the image of the Self (the colonizer). Given such an overarching objective, what hybridity does, according to Bhabha, is to effect a "strategic reversal" of the colonial agenda.

Illustrating such a "strategic reversal," Revathi Krishnaswamy (1998) pointed out how British colonialism in India produced culturally hybrid subjects among the colonizers as well as the colonized. The production of Anglicized Indians and Indianized Britons may be treated as a mark of disruption of the colonial authority. But, as Krishnaswamy observed, although both the colonizer and the colonized performed hybridity, "it was the Indian's hybridity that was systematically stressed and ridiculed, while the biculturality of the Anglo-India was silently suppressed" (1998, p. 39). The Anglicized Indians were caricatured, derided and stereotyped as *Babus*, pathologically effeminate, ridiculous, and inauthentic figures. Clearly, not all hybrids are equal.

Context, Krishnaswamy argued, "is decisive" in determining whether and when hybridity may be considered performative and subversive. Hybrid characteristics produced by colonial encounters between the British and the Indians were very different from those produced by colonial encounters between, say, the British and the Arabs. As she correctly pointed out, Lawrence of Arabia is considered to have adopted a "white skin, black mask" approach to colonial authority, a reference to the fact that he chose to wear the long Arabic robe and to have intimate relations with his colonial subjects while at the same time culturally and temperamentally remaining every inch a white man. A similar observation can be made from a linguistic perspective as well. That is, whereas the British colonial encounter in India produced Indian English, which is considered to be a systematic and standardized variety with its own phonological, syntactic, and pragmatic features, no variety called Arabic English ever emerged. It appears, then, that the production and practice of hybridity is not necessarily an automatic result of colonial cultural encounters, nor does it effectively lead to what Bhabha has called "colonial erasure" in all contexts.

Furthermore, Bhabha's celebration of "colonial erasure" neglects, if not negates, the notion of marginality. After all, apart from its "civilizing mission," the two distinct discursive practices that characterize colonialism are valorization of the Self and marginalization of the Other. By attributing more or less the same degree of cultural agency to the dominating and the dominated, hybridity theorists treat the power relations between these antagonistic groups unrealistically and unproblematically. Power, as the French sociologist Michel Foucault (1980) has persuasively argued, is exercised by people depending on how they are positioned in relation to each other. Clearly, the colonizer and the colonized are not positioned on an equal footing. In such an unequal encounter, hybridity is not only more often "compelled than chosen" (Fink, 1999, p. 250), but it can also "become simply another tool to dissolve difference, celebrate homogeneity, erase history" (Fink, 1999, p. 249)— all in the self-interest of the colonizer. The same is true, to a large extent, of the sociopolitical power differential that exists between mainstream and minority communities in a multilingual and multicultural society.

In fact, such a power differential is not confined to sociocultural practices alone. There is a similar power imbalance in language performance as well. "Just as, at the level of relations between groups, a language is worth those who speak it are worth," another

French sociologist, Pierre Bourdieu, observed perceptively, "so too, at the level of interactions between individuals, speech always owes a major part of its value to the value of the person who utters it" (1977, p. 652). Whether it is cultural translation or linguistic transaction, attributing equal power of controlling agency to both the dominating and the dominated flies in the face of historical and sociopolitical reality. Thus, the theory of hybridity fails to account for hegemonic structures that govern power relations in cultural processes (Ahmad, 1992).

In a similar vein, postcolonial critic Gayatri Spivak (1993) argued that it would be misleading to equate the hybridizing behavior of the diasporic communities in the developed world and that of the subaltern communities in the developing world. Hybridity theorists have largely focused on the diasporic communities that have, voluntarily or involuntarily, distanced themselves from their cultural roots. "The cultural hybridization of the global," as sociologist Zygmut Bauman (1998, p. 100) observed, "may be a creative, emancipating experience, but cultural disempowerment of the locals seldom is; it is an understandable, yet unfortunate inclination of the first to confuse the two and so to present their own variety of 'false consciousness' as a proof of the mental impairment to the second." In other words, not all hybridities are equal, and therefore, "it would be most disingenuous to use 'hybridity' as a theoretical sleight of hand to exorcise the reality of unequal histories and identities" (Radhakrishnan, 1993, p. 753).

Yet another discontent with the concept of hybridity is that it is a cultural phenomenon that is fairly limited to the globe-trotting citizens of the world, whether they are metropolitan intellectuals of academia or meticulous negotiators of transnational corporations. They are, as Pnina Werbner (1997, pp. 11–12) put it picturesquely, "multilingual gourmet tasters who travel among global cultures, savouring cultural differences as they flit with consummate ease between social worlds. Such gorgeous butterflies in the greenhouse of global cultures are a quite different social species from the transnational bees and ants who build new hives and nests in foreign lands." As such, the hybrid culture they represent "may be as elitist as that of the Imperial Chinese literati" (Davies, 1998, p. 129) and makes sense only in the context of transnational dimensions of cultural transmigration. "But for whom," as Jonathan Friedman asked (1997, p. 79), "is such cultural transmigration a reality? In the worlds of the post-colonial border-crossers, it is always the poet, the artist, the intellectual, who sustains this displacement and objectifies it in the printed word." In other words, the kind of transformation identified with cultural hybrids is confined to a particular cosmopolitan class of people and does not occur in the lower reaches of social reality.

In addition to being an elitist discourse, the concept of hybridity has also been a gendered one (Spivak, 1993; Yuval-Davis, 1997). That is, it has glossed over gender differences. As Yuval-Davis (1997) suggested, while cultural hybridity among a class of men has been welcomed and even celebrated as a mark of cosmopolitanism, it is frowned upon among women. Across time and space, women are constructed as bearers of a nation's collective cultural identity in its purest form. She pointed out that "a figure of a woman, often a mother, symbolizes in many cultures the spirit of the collectivity, whether it is Mother Russia, Mother Ireland or Mother India. In the French Revolution its symbol was 'La Patrie,' a figure of a woman giving birth to a baby; and in Cyprus, a crying woman refugee on roadside posters was the embodiment of the pain and anger of the Greek Cypriot collectivity after the Turkish invasion. In peasant societies, the dependence of the people on the fertility of 'Mother Earth' has no doubt contributed to this close association between collective territory, collective identity and womanhood" (Yuval-Davis, 1997, p. 45). Such representations of women as cultural custodians are quite common in other cultures as well.

Despite such widespread discontent, the concept of hybridity retains an intuitive, even a seductive, appeal because of its ability to capture the continual process of intermingling of cultures and peoples that produces new forms of cultural beliefs and practices. It also remains a concept of strategic value that has the potential to help individuals in navigating their path toward cultural transformation. It is not surprising, therefore, that language educators have attempted to make use of the theoretical underpinnings of the concept in order to derive pedagogic insights.

7.3. Cultural Hybridity and Language Education

The concepts of transculturation and hybridity gained ground in the field of foreign language education during the 1990s. Mary Louise Pratt, a Stanford University professor, is prominent among those who have drawn language educators' attention to the pedagogic implications of transculturation. She has explored life in what she called *contact zones* "where cultures meet, clash, and grapple with each other, often in contexts of highly asymmetrical relations of power, such as colonialism, slavery, or their aftermaths as they are lived out in many parts of the world today" (1991, p. 34). Maintaining that transculturation is a phenomenon of the contact zone, Pratt found the concept relevant not only for her anthropological explorations but also for her pedagogic exercises. Drawing from the concept, she fashioned a transcultural approach to teach courses on "Cultures, Ideas, Values" at Stanford. Moving away from the traditional academic discourse about language, communication, and culture that assumes a unified and homogeneous social world in which language exists, she guided her students to be *autoethnographers* capable of examining their own lives as cultural beings. "All the students in the class had the experience," she wrote, "of hearing their culture discussed and objectified in ways that horrified them; all the students saw their roots traced back to legacies of both glory and shame; all the students experienced face-to-face the ignorance and incomprehension, and occasionally the hostility, of others. . . . Virtually every student was having the experience of seeing the world described with him or her in it. Along with rage, incomprehension, and pain, there were exhilarating moments of wonder and revelation, mutual understanding, and new wisdom—the joys of the contact zone" (1991, p. 39). In such a situation, "no one was excluded, no one was safe." The fact that no one was safe, she reckoned, resulted in high degrees of trust and shared understandings among students and their teachers.

A concerted and commendable effort to apply the theoretical insights of cultural hybridity to foreign language education comes from Claire Kramsch, professor of German at the University of California, Berkeley. In a series of publications (e.g., 1993, 1998, 2003), Kramsch has persistently stressed the need for language learners to cross cultural borders. In order to begin to do that, they should learn to establish *a sphere of interculturality* that would enable them to take both an insider's and an outsider's view on both their first culture (C1) and their second (C2). The sphere of interculturality constitutes the third place, or third culture, which is located at the intersection between C1 and C2. At this intersection, "the major task of language learners is to define for themselves what this 'third place' that they have engaged in seeking will look like, whether they are conscious of it or not. Nobody, least of all the teacher, can tell them where that very personal place is; for each learner it will be differently located, and will make different sense at different times" (Kramsch, 1993, p. 257).

Although teachers cannot tell their learners where their third place is, Kramsch proposed strategies that they can employ in order to help them define and design it. One such strategy involves directing them toward a consideration of cultural boundaries rather than toward the construction of cultural bridges, for "we can teach the boundary, we cannot teach the bridge" (p. 228). In other words, a deep understanding of cultural boundaries will help learners discover that "each of these cultures is much less monolithic than was originally perceived" (p. 234) and strive to become border crossers. As a specific teaching strategy, Kramsch suggested role plays in contrasting and comparing two cultural phenomena. For instance: *"You are an American salesperson in Germany. Knowing what you know about the way many young Germans feel about nature and ecology,* compose a sales pitch for fruit, natural produce, or a beauty product for German 'green' buyers" (p. 229, italics as in original). What this kind of activity has the potential to do is to facilitate a "clash between the familiar meanings of the native culture and the unexpected meanings of the target culture, meanings that were taken for granted are suddenly questioned, challenged, problematized" (p. 238), leading to a better understanding of interculturality.

Kramsch has since expanded her work to include the notion of intercultural competence developed by Michael Byram (e.g., 1997), who defined an intercultural speaker as "someone who can operate their linguistic competence and their sociolinguistic awareness of the relationship between language and the context in which it is used, in order to manage interaction across cultural boundaries, to anticipate misunderstandings caused by difference in values, meanings and beliefs, and thirdly, to cope with the affective as well as cognitive demands of engagement with otherness" (1995, p. 25). Echoing Byram, Kramsch (1998) questioned the traditional culture teaching that is predicated upon the distinction between native speakers and nonnative speakers, a distinction that puts a premium on native-speaker norms of language use and cultural practice (see section 6.3). Arguing that "the dichotomy between native versus non-native speakers has outlived its use" (1998, p. 27), she sought to devise a pedagogy that privileges intercultural speakers—both native and nonnative—since they both "potentially belong to several speech communities of which they are more or less recognised, more or less unrecognised members" (p. 27). Such a pedagogy empowers not only the learner but also the teacher because in the process of questioning, challenging, and problematizing intercultural meaning, learners "are likely to engage their teachers in a voyage of discovery that they had not always anticipated and for which they don't always feel prepared. Allowing students to become intercultural speakers, therefore, means encouraging teachers to see themselves, too, as brokers between cultures of all kinds" (1998, p. 30).

Following the lead given by Byram, Kramsch, and others, a group of Australian scholars have further explored how the concept of hybridity can be applied to language learning and teaching. In a volume entitled *Striving for the Third Place: Intercultural Competence Through Language Education* (Lo Bianco, Liddicoat, and Crozet, eds., 1999), they presented the third place as a meeting place between different forces, different cultures, and different worldviews. Like Kramsch, they worked under the assumption that "an intercultural interaction is neither a question of maintaining one's own cultural frame nor of assimilating to one's interactant's cultural frame. It is rather a question of finding an intermediary place between these two positions—of adopting a third place. In so doing the participant in the interaction is an experiencer, not an observer, of difference. The ability to find this third place is at the core of intercultural competence" (Crozet, Liddicoat, and Lo Bianco, 1999, p. 5).

In order to prepare learners to know how to negotiate comfortable third places between the Self and the Other, the Australian scholars followed what they called Intercultural Language Teaching (ILT). According to Crozet and Liddicoat (1999, p. 117), "ILT implies that language teaching is no longer exclusively teaching about another linguaculture, it is also teaching language learners about their native linguaculture by contrasting it to the target linguaculture. ILT expands the traditional boundaries of language teaching by positioning language learning as a dual endeavour whereby learners not only learn the invisible cultural features of a foreign language but they also learn how to distance themselves from their native language/culture environment to see it for the first time as what it really is, as just one possible world view and not the only world view."

The ILT approach shifts the central aim of language teaching from communicative competence to intercultural competence and, as such, basically follows the same three-dimensional approach to culture teaching proposed by the American Council on the Teaching of Foreign Languages (ACTFL) in 1995. It consists of (a) learning about cultures, (b) comparing them, and (c) exploring them interculturally. Crozet and Liddicoat (1999) gave a three-dimensional teaching of "greetings" as an example of such an approach. Instead of limiting the teaching of "greetings" to the usual vocabulary (such as "Good morning," "Goodbye," etc.), they extend it to nonverbal codes in greeting (for instance, kissing rituals in France or bowing rituals in Japan), and to what people say to each other apart from "Hello" and "Goodbye" and in what order they say it (e.g., inquiring about health or need for food, asking about relatives to show intimacy, etc.). This is followed (or is done concomitantly) by contrasting greetings between learners' first and second cultures, which can, in turn, lead to intercultural exploration. They further stated:

> In our example this would for instance involve discussing to what extent learners might feel comfortable kissing or bowing during a greeting sequence, learners would learn to establish a personal balance between what feels natural in their native culture and the need not to offend the native speaker with whom they are relating. A resolution of the conflictual situation in this case could be a statement in which the non-native speaker recognises the cultural differences overtly as well as their response to it which could be expressed in the following sentence: "I know kissing (or bowing) in your culture is important but I am not quite comfortable with it." This statement is more likely to attract empathy than rejection from the native speaker and hence make both parties comfortable. (1999, p. 119)

They believed that the three-dimensional approach will lead to an awareness of what the cultural boundaries are, so that they can be profitably crossed.

While the field of foreign language education has been experimenting with the concepts of transculturation and hybridity for more than a decade, English as a second/foreign language teaching appears to be a fairly recent entrant into the arena. In his book *An Intercultural Approach to English Language Teaching*, John Corbett (2003) highlighted an ethnography-based, reflective component of the intercultural approach through which "successful learners become 'intercultural diplomats,' negotiating between the contrasting world views of home and target culture" rather than "becoming 'minority elites' who have absorbed enough of the target culture to replicate its beliefs, social structures, and inequalities" (p. 208).

An illustrative classroom activity he suggested pertains to forming cultural associations aimed at fostering intercultural awareness. One such cluster of associations might involve food with particular cultural significance. An "association chart" such as Table 7.1 is given to students. Corbett believed that "seeking, learning and knowing this kind of information can help one to understand cultural allusions and jokes in the target culture" (p. 109). It also casts light on cross-cultural similarities, such as "the rise of lowly haggis and feijoada from the status of peasant staple" to "national dish." In the case of haggis, for instance, "elevation of this form of offal in Scotland's affections is linked to a desire to present the nation as honest, straightforward, down-to-earth and free of pretensions" (p. 110). Corbett observed that activities such as this one "can be a useful first step in perceiving ordinary phenomena as culturally significant" (p. 110).

At a higher level of sophistication, Corbett suggested drawing from existing literature the use of critical incidents that can arise from differences in communication patterns. Students get an opportunity to consider incidents in which a conflict about values, goals, or meaning arises or the solution to the conflict is not immediately apparent or is controversial. An example: "An American teacher on a short multicultural summer course decided to give a party to her students, so she invited them to her house. The Japanese arrived at 8 p.m. and ate much of the food; however, they left at 10 p.m. just as the Italians were arriving. At around midnight the Latin Americans arrived, by which time the food was finished, but they stayed, singing and dancing, until about four. The Saudis did not turn up at all. Should she ever hold a party again?" (Corbett, 2003, p. 112). In spite of the inherent dangers of stereotyping, critical incidents such as this, Corbett believed, are "often effective ways of investigating cultural differences which cause communicational misfires" (p. 112).

As the above discussion indicates, compared to the earlier concepts of cultural assimilation and cultural pluralism, cultural hybridity has the potential to offer language learners and teachers a deeper understanding of the nature of cross-cultural encounters.

Table 7.1 Foods of cultural significance.

	Brazil	Scotland	United States
Food name	Feijoada	Haggis	Hot dogs
Ingredients	Salt port, pork sausage, ham, salted tongue, pig's knuckle and trotters, black beans, onion, parsley, tomatoes, garlic	Sheep's stomach, heart, liver, lungs, and windpipe, plus onions, suet, oatmeal, salt, herbs	Frankfurter sausage (beef or beef and pork), long, oval-shaped bun, optional mustard, ketchup, pickle
Meal/snack	Meal	Meal	Snack
Where or when eaten?	Wednesdays and Saturdays	Approximately Jan. 25	Sports games
Accompanied by	Rice, mandioca flour, sliced kale, sliced orange, hot pepper sauce	Mashed potatoes and turnips	Nothing
Origins	Peasant food	Peasant food	Convenient food at sports, games, etc.
Things to do afterward	Lie down; doze, Chat sleepily	Dance; listen to speeches, songs, poems	Go back to watching the game

Source: Corbett, 2003, p. 109.

By highlighting the interwoven character of culture as well as the intricate process of transcultural engagement, the concept "pushes us to raise questions about our pedagogical goals and research orientations and to probe unexamined assumptions" (Zamel, 1997, p. 350). A close examination of our pedagogic assumption can easily lead to a greater awareness among language educators about the need to help learners to forge productive linkages between the school curriculum and their lived experience. If taken seriously, it can also offer language teachers the opportunity to modify their classroom input and interaction so as to bring into the classroom many different cultural worlds in all their complexity.

It is the complex nature of transcultural transactions that poses serious challenges to any meaningful implementation of a hybridity-based transcultural approach to language education. "Although hybrid and hybridity are buzzwords in current discussions of literacy and education," Kamberlis (2001, p. 88) cautioned us, "these discussions are almost exclusively theoretical. Very few studies have described or explained how discursive hybridity can actually transform and enhance teaching-learning interactions in classrooms." It has also been pointed out that power differentials between teacher and learner and between native culture and target culture can easily affect the transcultural aspect of language learning and use (Liddicoat, Crozet, and Lo Bianco, 1999). Furthermore, the formation of a third place or third culture can be an unsettling experience for participants particularly in classroom communities, as it precipitates collisions with the established norms and parameters that characterize the potential within which we act and enact our cultural being (Carr, 1999). Some of these concerns are clearly related to the fundamental theoretical flaws discussed in the previous section.

Yet another challenge, one that is even more intractable, relates to questions of cultural identity in the era of globalization. As we discussed in Chapter 3, cultures are in closer contact now than ever before and are influencing each other in complex and complicated ways. Under these circumstances, border-crossing is not "a free-for-all. There is free cheese only in the mousetrap. As some boundaries wane, others remain or are introduced. Thus, as national borders and governmental authority erode, ethnic or religious boundaries or boundaries of consumption patterns and brand names emerge in their place" (Pieterse, 2001, p. 239). This global development is plunging the world in a creative as well as chaotic tension that both unites and divides people on cultural fault lines.

One of the results of such a global development has been the aggravation of identity politics that has prompted people to see a threat, real or perceived, to their own cultural way of life, compelling them to take active measures to preserve and protect their traditional cultural identities. The complex identity formation resulting from cultural globalization is a challenge that, I believe, neither hybridity theorists nor hybridity-inspired language educators have seriously considered. This challenge has a particular resonance to language policy planners around the world because, as Liddicoat, Crozet, and Lo Bianco (1999, p. 184) rightly observed, "language is a powerful symbol of identity and the ways in which identities are tied to language can either advance or impede language learning, depending on the symbolic role languages play in the ethnic identities of both the learner and the target language community."

By definition, the concept of hybridity seeks to promote the search for a third space in between one's inherited culture and one's learned culture by essentially diluting the character of one's identity that is based on one's native culture. In a globalizing world that is wary of cultural homogenization, such a stance has caused understandable anxieties among educators in many countries. Byram (1999, p. 94) cited governmental educational documents from certain Islamic states to highlight "an evident fear of foreign language learning having an undesired influence on learners' cultural identity." Fearing that the learning of English may turn out to be a source of rejection of one's own culture, some Gulf states have explicitly stated the following as their foreign language objective: "acquire a good understanding of English speaking people on the condition that the above will not lead to the creation of a hostile or indifferent attitude to the students' Arab/Islamic culture" (cited in Byram, 1999, p. 94).

There has also emerged a group of English language teaching professionals in the Middle East who have formed an organization called TESOL Islamia. The chief mission of this Abu Dhabi–based professional organization is to promote ELT in ways that best serve the sociopolitical, sociocultural, and socioeconomic interests of the Islamic world. According to their Website (www.tesolislamia.org), one of their goals is "promoting and safeguarding Islamic values in the teaching of English as a second or foreign language in the Muslim World." To achieve their goals, they wish to take "a critical stance towards 'mainstream' TESOL activity particularly in the area of language policy, curriculum design, materials development, language testing, teaching methodology, program evaluation, and second language research." Even a cursory reading of files in their "Discussion Forum" reveals that they are all seized upon the impact of cultural globalization on their linguistic and cultural identity.

7.4. In Closing

The purpose of this chapter has been to discuss the concept of cultural hybridity, its theoretical stance, its discontent, and its implications for language education. Hybridity is a concept that is at once conventional and contemporary. It is conventional in the sense that it connotes a long-established anthropological belief that all cultures are basically hybrid cultures. It is contemporary in the sense that it presents a postmodern, postcolonial twist to a traditional concept by incorporating a key feature of present-day life among a particular, cosmopolitan segment of the population, a life lived in a third space, a life characterized by border-crossing.

While acknowledging its seductive appeal and its strategic value, I discussed several shortcomings of the concept. I also maintained that hybridity does not have the capacity to deal with the recent phenomena of cultural globalization with its centripetal, as well as centrifugal, homogenizing as well as heterogenizing tendencies. Nor does it account for the intensification of nationalism that has resulted in the resurgence of linguistic, cultural, and ethnic chauvinism around the world. In short, it fails to address certain hard realities that characterize the practice of everyday life in this era of globalization. What are those realities? How do they shape the formation of individual identity in this age of cultural globalization? I turn to these and other related issues in the next chapter.

CHAPTER 8

Cultural Realism
and Its Demands

The 1998 Gold Cup soccer game between Mexico and the United States was played before a record crowd of 91,255 fans, who packed the Los Angeles Memorial Coliseum. An overflow group of another 6,941 watched the event on closed-circuit television at the nearby Los Angeles Sports Arena. The Trico-lores, the nickname for the Mexican team, scored the only goal of the game when the American defender Alexi Lalas lost control of the ball just in front of the American goalpost, and Mexico's Luis Hernandez promptly headed the loose ball into the goal.

The following day, most newspapers reported not so much on the game itself but on the crowd, which consisted largely of Latinos. The reports decried the behavior of a section of the crowd that turned raucous and rowdy. They pointed out that the American players were pelted with debris and cups of water or beer. "It was," wrote a *Los Angeles Times* reporter, "an ugly sight" (Jones, 1998, p. C1).

More than the ugly sight, what became a bone of contention is the report that the crowd was "delighted" by the outcome, and that the American players quickly found out that "playing in Los Angeles is not a home game for the United States national team" (Jones, 1998, p. C1). After the match, Lalas complained (cited in Jones, 1998, p. C7): "You don't get used to it. It stinks every time. I'm all for roots and understanding where you come from and having a respect for your homeland, but tomorrow morning all of those people are going to get up and work in the United States and live in the United States and have all the benefits of living in the United States. I would never be caught dead rooting for any other team than the United States because I know what it's given me." Political commentators as well as academic experts joined the fray. The memory of the event failed to fade away. Much later, Samuel Huntington (2004, p. 5) used it as an example to deplore the tendency among ethnic communities in the United States to develop "subnational identities," which pose, he warned, "challenges to America's national identity."

Interestingly, competitive sports were also used to express similar sentiments about ethnic and national identities in Britain. In 1990, Lord Norman Tebbit, a member of Parliament who went on to become chairman of the leading Conservative Party in Britain, devised what was called "the cricket test" as a way of measuring cultural integration. He declared that whenever England hosted a cricket match against its former colonies such as India, Pakistan, or the West Indies, only those who backed England over their ancestral homes could genuinely be described as British. Fifteen years later, referring to the attacks on the London subway stations by British-born suicide bombers on July 7, 2005, Tebbit claimed that if his advice on the cricket test had been acted on, "those attacks would have been less likely" (www.epolitix.com, dated 19 August 2005). He added: "What I was saying about the so-called cricket test is that it was a test of whether a community has integrated." Tebbit's earlier exhortation about the cricket test, though widely condemned in Britain, resulted in contentious and continuing debates about what constitutes "Britishness," or British national identity.

In both the American and British instances, the issue revolves around identity. What exactly is identity? How is national identity linked to individual identity? What might be the characteristics of individual or ethnic identity that does not pose any threat to national unity? How does cultural globalization contribute to the complexity of identity formation as well as identity politics? What might be a realistic response to the challenges and opportunities arising out of cultural globalization? In this chapter, I address these and other related issues under the rubric of cultural realism. Let us begin with identity and identity politics.

8.1. Identity and Identity Politics

Identity, according to its etymological root, is about *sameness*. It is an overarching term that has traditionally entailed membership in one or more social categories such as nation, ethnicity, race, religion, class, profession, or gender. Being an American black Christian woman, for instance, connects one with aspects of American-ness, Blackness, Christianness and womanhood—however they are all defined. Some of these typological identities are inherited (e.g., racial identity) and some are acquired (e.g., professional identity). So ubiquitous are identity markers that we all use them as convenient labels to position and project ourselves in the practice of our everyday life.

In spite of it being an everyday phenomenon, identity has been a problematic concept for a long time. One way of understanding it is to look at it from modern, postmodern, and postcolonial perspectives, as has been done by various scholars (e.g., Appadurai, 1996; Giddens, 1991; Hall, 1996; Jameson, 1991; Spivak, 1993). The issue is complex, but a defining core has been the relationship between the individual and the community, and how the individual navigates self and society. To put it briefly and simply, during the days of modernity (referring generally to a period established in postfeudal Europe, and extending well into the early twentieth century) the individual was largely expected to constitute his/her identities in tune with preexistent and relatively unchanging national or societal norms. More than anything else, the individual's identity was tied almost inextricably to affiliation to family and community. While some maneuvering was indeed possible, individuals encountered an essentialized and totalized concept of identity within which they had to find personal meaning.

With socially accepted boundaries of an objectified external world imposed on them, individuals had very little meaningful choice outside of clearly delineated characteristics of birth and ethnic origin. Thus, modern identity was "destined to find its expression in distinct social roles and relationships within the productive structures of modern life. These structures have provided for an identity premised on relatively fixed boundaries of the self based on distinctions between interior and exterior, self and other. These boundaries, however, defined lines of both separation and connection between the individual and the outer world" (Dunn, 1998, p. 64). In other words, modern identity was more externally imposed than self-constructed.

If modern identity is seen as essentialist, postmodern identity may be considered constructivist. That is to say, postmodernism treats identity as something that is actively constructed on an ongoing basis. It sees identity as fragmented, not unified; multiple, not singular; expansive, not bounded. Postmodern identity is marked by what Giddens (1991) has called a "disembedding" process whereby the individual takes over a modicum of agency in determining a sense of self. Hall (1996) has described such a postmodernist stance as "a strategic and positional one" (p. 3). According to him, the postmodern concept of identity "does *not* signal that stable core of the self, unfolding from beginning to end through all the vicissitudes of history without change; the bit of the self which remains always–already 'the same,' identical to itself across time" (p. 3, italics as in original). Identity formation, then, is conditioned not merely by inherited traditions such as culture, or by external exigencies such as history, or by ideological constructs such as power, but also by the individual's ability and willingness to exercise independent decision-making.

A crucial aspect of postmodern identity is the notion of *difference*. Although the emphasis on difference became prominent in the postmodern era, the intricate connection between sameness and difference has been a matter of philosophical speculation for a long time. Citing the work of German philosopher Friedrich Hegel (1770–1831), Jameson (1998, pp. 75–76) observed: "Hegel tells us how to handle such potentially troublesome categories as those of Identity and Difference. You begin with Identity, he says, only to find that it is always defined in terms of its Difference with something else; you turn to Difference and find out that any thoughts about that involve thoughts about the 'Identity' of this particular category. As you begin to watch Identity turn into Difference and Difference back into Identity, you grasp both as an inseparable Opposition, you learn that they must always be thought together."

A similar line of argument has been pursued by American philosopher Charles Taylor (1989, p. 36), who argued that self-identity exists only within what he calls a *web of interlocution*. "I am a self," he asserted, "only in relation to certain interlocutors: in one way in relation to conversation partners who were essential to my achieving self-definition; in another in relation to those who are now crucial to my continuing grasp of language of self-understanding—and, of course, these classes may overlap."

Although identity and difference co-exist, it is difference that most often stands out in marking one's identity. There is no identity without difference because one's identity is largely characterized in terms of how different somebody is from somebody else. Each of us can justifiably say that "I am who I am because I am not you," or, in the words of Amin Maalouf (2000, p. 10): "my identity is what prevents me from being identical to anybody else." Even if we closely align ourselves to a particular community based on ethnic, religious, or other affiliations, we still strive to maintain our own individual identity by positioning ourselves in opposition to others within that community. Therefore, postmodern identity is better seen as "a structured representation which only achieves its positive through the narrow eye of the negative. It has to go through the eye of the needle of the other before it can construct itself" (Hall, 1991, p. 21). What this crucially entails is that identity can be understood in a meaningful way only by understanding others and by recognizing and highlighting one's difference in relation to others.

Because of its unfailing emphasis on difference, postmodernity, unlike modernity, is less preoccupied with the formation of a durable identity. Instead, it embraces the idea that identity is fluid and discontinuous, one that is constantly invented and reinvented. As Bauman differentiated succinctly, "if the *modern* 'problem of identity' was how to construct an identity and keep it solid and stable, the *postmodern* 'problem of identity' is primarily how to avoid fixation and keep the options open. In the case of an identity, as in other cases, the catchword of modernity was creation; the catchword for postmodernity is recycling" (1995, p. 18).

The postmodern perspective on identity is largely shared by postcolonial scholars as well. They, however, provided an additional dimension to the discussion on difference by pointing out that colonialism of the past and, one might add, neocolonialism of the present, distort and denigrate the identity of the Other with the view to projecting a superior Self. As we discussed in Chapter 2, postcolonial critic Said (1978) showed how the discourse of orientalism has successfully built a binary opposition between Us and Them, producing an essentialized and static identity of the Other. The basic argument of the postcolonial approach to identity is that the Other identity is imposed by hegemonic power structures. Spivak, too (1993, p. 63), acknowledged the Saidian thought on false representation of the Other and called for "emancipatory social intervention" to redress it. For her it is not just "a question of redressing victimage by the assertion of (class—or gender—or ethnocultural) identity. It is a question of developing a vigilance of systematic appropriations of the unacknowledged social production of a *differential* that is one basis of exchange into the networks of the cultural politics of class—or gender—*identification*" (p. 63, italics as in original).

The postmodern, as well as the postcolonial, critique of identity has fed directly into the politics of identity. As can be expected, there have been conscious and concerted attempts by all sides of the political spectrum to press identity markers into the service of regional, national, and international politics. Initially, *identity politics* was used as a term to characterize sociopolitical movements spearheaded by marginalized groups in order to fight for equality and justice. It is in this context that Dunn (1998, p. 20) described it as "a strategy whereby individuals define themselves through identification with or membership in groups or categories regarded as the source of distinct feelings and experiences of marginalization and subordination." But in reality, identity politics is by no means confined to marginalized groups; it is practiced by mainstream communities as well. In fact, the American and British responses to sports events narrated in the lead episode of this chapter are a clear indication that identity politics is indeed everybody's game. Yet another prime example is Huntington's (2004) recent thesis that ethnic communities with their subnational identities pose a serious challenge to America's national identity. There is no doubt that identity politics has been used by vested interests to polarize people to create a political wedge between Us and Them.

As this brief account suggests, identity has historically been a difficult concept. Recent postmodern and postcolonial developments have made it more problematic. Now, even a greater and more intractable strain is being placed on it by the fast-unfolding process of globalization and the presence of contemporary realities.

8.2. Contemporary Realities and Identity Formation

As I see them, there are at least four realities that contribute to identity formation at the present time: global reality, national reality, social reality, and individual reality.

8.2.1. Global Reality

The global reality today manifests itself in the twin processes of economic globalization and cultural globalization, both fueled by the revolution in information technology. The causes and consequences of these two processes have been narrated in detail in Chapter 3; therefore, I shall not go into them at length here. But to recall briefly, we learned how the contemporary world is marked by dwindling space, shrinking time, and disappearing borders, resulting in an unprecedented flow not only of economic capital and consumer goods but also of cultural values across the world. As historian Francis Fukuyama (1999) pointed out, cultural change is clearly being driven by economic change. However, it is the former more than the latter that seems to destabilize nations and communities in unexpected and unwanted ways. With their hold on economic and trade matters weakened by economic globalization, nations across the world are energetically addressing the challenge of protecting and preserving their national cultural heritage.

We also learned in Chapter 3 that there is an ongoing tension between the forces of cultural homogenization and cultural heterogenization, the former seeking to weaken local cultural and religious identities and the latter seeking to strengthen them. This tension is generating a creative process of "glocalization," where the global is localized and the local is globalized. What this process indicates is that although there is a free flow of cultural products and information services around the world, people seem to be receiving them and using them for their own purposes. Accordingly, the purveyors of cultural goods are compelled to negotiate their way into foreign lands. For instance, Google, the preeminent American search engine, has agreed to censor its services in China in order to gain greater access to its fast-growing market. According to a BBC report ("Google censors itself for China," dated January 25, 2006), Google could "restrict access to thousands of sensitive terms and web sites. Such topics are likely to include independence for Taiwan and the 1989 Tiananmen Square massacre." Defending its stance, Google's chief executive, Eric Schmidt, said, "we've made a decision that we have to respect local law and culture. So it's not an option for us to broadly make information available that is illegal or inappropriate or immoral or what have you" (*San Jose Mercury News*, dated April 13, 2006, p. 3C). Similarly, the American media giant Viacom had to make serious compromises in its programs before it was allowed to introduce youth networks such as MTV and Nickelodeon into China. In fact, the Chinese government forbade the use of the Nickelodeon logo itself. Besides, as the Chinese scholar Liu Kang (1998, p. 166) pointed out, in China, MTV has been quickly absorbed and adapted into an effective tool for propagating Confucian values as well as communist doctrines.

The new information technology that carries cultural images around the world also carries much-needed knowledge. In fact, it is irrevocably linked to the global race for knowledge, including cultural knowledge. In his book *The World Is Flat: A Brief History of the Twenty-First Century,* Thomas Friedman, *New York Times* columnist, presents the idea that the world has gone from round to flat. "What the flattening of the world means," he explained, "is that we are now connecting all the knowledge centers on the planet together into a single global network, which—if politics and terrorism do not get in the way—could usher in an amazing era of prosperity and innovation" (2005, p. 8). The global network with its open-access system makes available for millions of people around the world many tools that they can use to flatten hierarchies in their areas. Friedman cited approvingly Google co-founder (and Russian-born) Sergey Brin's statement, "If someone has broadband, dial-up, or access to an Internet café, whether a kid in Cambodia, the university professor, or me who runs this search engine, all have the same basic access to overall research information that anyone has. It is a total equalizer" (p. 152).

Knitting together a tapestry of global episodes, Friedman attempted to show how old hierarchies are being flattened and the playing field is being leveled. Although such an optimistic observation can be legitimately questioned by millions who are deprived of access to political power and economic prosperity, what he said is partly true about access to cultural knowledge among certain segments of the world population. There is no doubt that nations, societies, and communities are in closer cultural contact with one another than ever before. People now have a greater chance of knowing about others' cultural way of life—the good, the bad, and the ugly. They also have a greater chance of directly or indirectly influencing cultural change beyond their cultural community. Consequently, people in many parts of the world see unparalleled opportunities for cultural growth, and equally unparalleled threats to their cultural identity.

The remarkable spread of cultural knowledge and the response to it accelerates the process of glocalization, and, as Friedman wrote (2005, p. 325),

The more you have a culture that naturally glocalizes—that is, the more your culture easily absorbs foreign ideas and best practices and melds those with its own traditions—the greater advantage you will have in a flat world. The natural ability to glocalize has been one of the strengths of Indian culture, American culture, Japanese culture, and, lately, Chinese culture. The Indians, for instance, take the view that the Moguls come, the Moguls go, the British come, the British go, we take the best and leave the rest—but we still eat curry, our women still wear saris, and we still live in tightly bound extended family units. That's glocalizing at its best.

Clearly, the task facing individuals and communities in such a glocalizing environment is to understand the fast-changing nature of global reality and adapt themselves quickly to its demands. In doing so, they are faced with the task of reconciling their perception of global reality with the pressures of national reality.

8.2.2. National Reality

The idea of a nation as we know it today is fairly recent, historically speaking. It was formulated during the late eighteenth century, when the European feudal system with its localized political power was successfully challenged in order to institute the principle of sovereignty and territoriality of self-governed states. The notion that the world should consist of, and should be divided into, independent sovereign states with clear geographical boundaries, and possibly with distinct national identities, was consolidated when the League of Nations was established after the First World War and was again reinforced with the formation of the United Nations after the Second World War. The end of colonialism in several African and Asian countries in the 1950s and 1960s, and the collapse of the Soviet Union in the 1980s, substantially increased the number of nations in the world. By sheer coincidence, I am writing this paragraph on the sixtieth anniversary of the United Nations (24 October 2005), whose membership has swollen from a mere 50 in 1945 to 191 today.

Ever since the formation of nation-states, the idea of a nation has had a magical hold on all of us. We all *belong* to a nation. We take pride in it. We salute its flag. We sing its anthem. We serve in its army. We guard its borders. We preserve its identity. We strive to instill in our children a supreme sense of patriotism. Educational and governmental institutions are constantly engaged in the task of nation-building. We surely recognize that the idea of a nation carries with it a liberating capacity and an ennobling ability. But we seldom realize that it also harbors vicious forms of oppression, genocide, and ethnic cleansing. It is, indeed, a powerful, controlling force.

And yet, a nation, as historian Benedict Anderson famously described, is an *imagined community*. According to him, "It is *imagined* because the members of even the smallest nation will never know most of their fellow-members, meet them, or even hear of them, yet in the minds of each lives the image of their communion. . . . It is imagined as a *community*, because, regardless of the actual inequality and exploitation that may prevail in each, the nation is always conceived as a deep, horizontal comradeship. Ultimately it is this fraternity that makes it possible, over the past two centuries, for so many millions of people, not so much to kill as willingly to die for such limited imaginings" (1983/2005, pp. 49–50). Clearly, a nation has the capacity to unify people across religion, race, class, gender, and other differences that can otherwise tear them apart.

Although a nation is considered an *imagined* community, it does have undeniable facets of reality. It intrudes into the practice of our everyday life. Coins and bank notes that we use on a daily basis typically bear national emblems. We hear our national anthem sung on festive occasions. National flags that are unmistakable symbols of statehood are ubiquitous. The display of flags on the windowsills and at front doors of ordinary homes in the United States after the 9/11 terrorist attack is a demonstration of how people spontaneously embrace national symbols to express their solidarity with their nation. Passports, visa regulations, and restricted entry permits are yet another reminder of national reality. Highlighting such common experiences, historian Michael Billig questioned the idea of the nation as an imagined community and argued that the imagining of the nation is almost mindlessly produced and reproduced by citizens through daily habits of which they are unaware or barely aware. He used the term *banal nationalism* to refer to the ubiquitous nature of nationalism, describing it as an "ideology by which the world of nations has come to see the natural world—as if there could not possibly be a world without nations" (Billig, 1995/2005, p. 184).

A world without nations may now be inconceivable, but a world without borders is not. The global reality outlined in the previous section has called into question the vibrancy of nation-states and national identities. It has reduced the image of a nation-state to a shaky skyscraper with a rickety foundation, prompting historians, sociologists, political scientists, and others to renew their debate on nation and nationalism. There are those who believe that globalization has weakened the sovereignty of nation-states so much that it is now a mere ghost of what it once was. Prominent among them are historians David Held, Eric Hobsbawm, and Robbie Robertson. According to Held (1998), "any conception of sovereignty as an indivisible, illimitable, exclusive and perpetual form of public power—embodied within an individual state is defunct." Sovereign states, he argued, have become "decision-takers" as much as "decision-makers." The decision-making authority vested in supranational institutions such as the United Nations and the World Trade Organization bears testimony to his assertion. Earlier, Hobsbawm (1990, p. 192) declared that the phenomenon of nation-states has reached its peak and that its decline has already started. He proclaimed rather joyously: "The Owl of Minerva which brings wisdom, said Hegel, flies out at dusk. It is a good sign that it is now circling round nations and nationalism" (p. 192). Equally celebratory is the view expressed by Robbie Robertson, who rejoiced in the possibility that "a rebirth of small local cultures will give back to humanity that rich multiplicity of behavioral expression that the nation state annihilated in order to create so-called national cultural identities towards the end of the eighteenth and particularly in the nineteenth century. As nation states weaken, forgotten marginalized local cultures will re-emerge" (Robertson, 2003, p. 251).

There is no doubt that globalization is playing a pivotal role in the weakening of nation-states. Its impact is reflected in the fact that more and more regional groups within a nation-state are getting emboldened to seek autonomous status. As Giddens (2000, p. 31) rightly observed, globalization "is the reason for the revival of local cultural identities in different parts of the world. If one asks, for example, why the Scots want more independence in the U.K. or why there is a strong separatist movement in Quebec, the answer is not to be found only in their cultural history. Local nationalisms spring up as a response to globalising tendencies, as the hold of older nation-states weakens." As a consequence, there now seems to be a greater awareness for the need to recognize subnational identities within a national framework. Separatists who were fighting for outright independence, such as the Tamils in Sri Lanka and the French in the Quebec region of Canada, have shown willingness to negotiate and settle for a greater political, economic, and cultural autonomy within the purview of the national constitution. Conversely, national governments are enacting laws to grant more and more autonomy to regional entities as revealed in the establishment of Scottish Parliament and the Welsh Assembly in the United Kingdom, and in the more recent move by Spain's parliament to grant greater autonomy to the northeastern region of Catalonia. According to on-line BBC News, a slogan repeatedly heard during the Spanish parliamentary debate on Catalonia was: "times change, so change the statute" (BBC News, 6 November 2005).

In spite of these and other developments, there are prominent historians and sociologists who believe that the concept of nation-states is still valid and vibrant. Michael Mann (1993), for instance, pointed out that nation-states are not dying; they are only diversifying. They are still maturing. In a similar vein, Will Kymlicka (2001) noted that "nation-states still possess considerable autonomy; their citizens still exercise this autonomy in distinctive ways, reflective of their national political cultures; and citizens still want to confront the challenges of globalization as national collectivities, reflective of their historic solidarities, and desire to share each other's fate" (p. 320). These facts, according to him, provide abiding meaning and renewed significance to the concept of nations and nationalism.

It is apparent from the above discussion that, regardless of the political, economic, and cultural imperatives brought on by the forces of globalization, nationalism remains too strong a reality to be wished away. It is equally apparent that it has come under severe stress not just from above (i.e., global reality) but also from below (i.e., social and individual realities).

8.2.3. Social Reality

A nation is a community of communities. At a broad level, a community may constitute a group of individuals who share the same ethnicity, religion, culture, or language that keeps them connected in an interlocking social web. Out of these affiliations emerge a community's shared values and beliefs, as well as shared norms of interpretation that help its members derive meaning out of myths, reason out of rituals, sense out of symbols. Bounded by a feeling of belonging and by a need for unity, the members of a community take on a social persona with varying roles, relationships, and reputations. In other words, each community creates its own social reality. As social psychologist Giuseppe Montovani (2000, p. 16) observed, this social reality extends far beyond mere interpersonal relationships. It "establishes bonds between individuals, sets them within a framework; and this framework creates between them special links concerning particular values which are codified in those particular maps which people use to explore reality" (p. 16).

The exploration of social reality is often facilitated by broad labels that are used to characterize people. One such label is ethnicity. From a sociological point of view, we all belong to one ethnic community or another, in the sense that we share with our community a common origin, a common history, a common culture. In popular usage, however, the term *ethnicity* is often used to refer to a minority or *marked* category of people that is different from the mainstream or *unmarked* category. In the Western world, for instance, anything that is non-Western, or anybody who is non-white, is often characterized as ethnic. That is why we hear about ethnic food, ethnic dress, ethnic music, ethnic festivals—all referring to minority objects or events.

Ethnic labels such as Latinos or Chinese in the United States, Scots or Irish in the United Kingdom, and Singhalese or Tamils in Sri Lanka, not only describe an order of things within a community but also ascribe a series of traits to the members of that community. These labels prompt us to recognize and to expect each ethnic community to have its own way of life, its own places of worship, its own social organizations, etc. "Once labels are applied to people," as cultural critic Kwame Anthony Appiah observed, "ideas about people who fit the label come to have social and psychological effects" (2005, p. 66). In other words, people use these labels not only to shape how they view others but also how they view themselves. "I shape my life," continued Appiah, "by the thought that something is an appropriate aim or an appropriate way of acting for an American, a black man, a philosopher" (p. 66). In other words, members of a group are very much influenced by the labels that are ascribed to them when they negotiate their social reality.

Yet another social marker that identifies people is language.

Every ethnic community usually shares a common language. In fact, it has been argued that "the entire phenomenon of identity can be understood as a linguistic one" (Joseph, 2004, p. 12). Several reputed social scientists (e.g., Anderson, 1983/2005; Hobsbawm, 1966) routinely associate language with national identity, arguing that language is a foundation upon which nationalist ideology is constructed. For instance, in France "it is widely believed that to speak French badly, to break the rules of French grammar or to make frequent use of foreign words is to be in some way unpatriotic" (Lodge 1998, p. 30). This point was sharply driven home recently when French president Jacques Chirac stormed out of a summit meeting of European Union leaders because a French business leader addressed the delegates in English. BBC News ("Chirac Upset by English Address," dated March 24, 2006) reported that he was "deeply shocked" that a Frenchman chose to address the summit in English.

As the English-only movement in the United States shows, nationalists everywhere attempt to identify and foster one national language. In reality, though, most nations are bi- or multilingual, and different social networks within a nation operate primarily on a linguistic basis. At times, when politico-economic tensions between communities reach a peak, language becomes a prime source of separatist movements, as witnessed in the long struggle waged by French speakers in the Quebec province of Canada or Tamil speakers in the northern part of Sri Lanka. While these are special cases, it is evident that language functions as a strong distinguishing element even when other commonalities are present within a nation. The Indian diasporic communities in the United States, for instance, have organized themselves, in spite of their common cultural and religious heritage, into language-based social organizations such as Gujarati Association, Kannada Association, Tamil Association, Telugu Association, etc.

While factors such as ethnicity, language, or religion operate at broader levels of social reality, there are other factors that operate at lower levels. People may come together as a social group based on their political views (conservatives, liberals), sexual orientation (gays, lesbians), sports interests (soccer moms, NASCAR dads), etc. Social scientists use the term *community of practice* to refer to such ideology-based or interest-based social networks, defining it as "an aggregate of people who come together around mutual engagement in an endeavor" (Eckert and McConnel-Ginet, 1992, p. 464). Etienne Wenger (1999) noted that a community of practice forges coherence by means of mutual engagement, joint enterprise, and shared repertoire. The first refers to the way meaning and purpose are negotiated among participants; the second to activities that bring members together; and the third to the common resources that are made available for successful practice.

It should be remembered that, whether operating at the broader or narrower levels, communities are not stable, fixed entities. They, in fact, have overlapping boundaries. Besides, no community can insulate its members from contacts with, and influences from, the outside. Even within a community there may be deep disagreements among members. As Wenger succinctly put it, "In real life, mutual relations among participants are complex mixtures of power and dependence, pleasure and pain, expertise and helplessness, success and failure, achievement and deprivation, alliance and competition, ease and struggle, authority and collegiality, anger and tenderness, attraction and repugnance, fun and boredom, trust and suspicion, friendship and hatred" (Wenger, 1999, p. 77). It is this complex and complicating social reality that an individual has to deal with in order to create and maintain his or her individuality.

8.2.4. Individual Reality

Every individual is deemed to have a sense of the self. As described in section 8.1, modernism has presupposed that the individual has a fixed, coherent core of the self. Postmodernism, however, has depicted the individual as diverse, contradictory, dynamic, and changing over historical time and social space. The postmodern perspective presumes that making sense of the self entails "reflexive awareness," something a person is conscious *of* in the term *self-conscious* (Giddens, 1991, p. 52). It is this reflexive awareness that prompts a person to ask the question *Who am I?* and to respond to it differently at different times and in different situations. The individual constructs a sense of the self through sustained reflexive activities that entail considerable rational choice. Although the individual possesses a significant degree of choice in the construction of self-identity, national and social realities have always played a facilitating as well as a constraining role in that effort.

In this era of globalization, the individual is beset with a bewildering array of challenges and opportunities. "For the first time in human history," declared Giddens (1991, p. 32), "self and society are interrelated in a global milieu." Economic and cultural globalization along with electronic media have vastly increased the interactional opportunities worldwide, thus opening up unlimited possibilities for individual growth and development. In addition, the boundaries of difference and sameness are greatly challenged. Identity politics has now been extended to what Giddens called *life politics*. Seen to have the potential to emancipate the individual from cultural fixities and hierarchical domination, life politics "concerns political issues which flow from processes of self-actualisation in post-traditional contexts, where globalising influences intrude deeply into the reflexive project of the self, and conversely where processes of self-realisation influence global strategies" (Giddens, 1991, p. 214).

The intricate connection between self, society, and the global milieu is fast turning the identity of the individual into that of a consumer. In an unrelenting transnational corporate process that has been described as "the becoming cultural of the economic, and the becoming economic of the cultural" (Jameson, 1998, p. 60), consumers are ceaselessly bombarded with alluringly deceptive sound bites that entreat them to shape their self-image in the image of their favorite cultural icons. As a consequence, the very process of identity formation is said to undergo transformation, and it does so in four basic ways:

> First, the individual is turned into a *consumer,* and increasingly a consumer of signs and images. While social identities persist (for example, employee, parent, student), these identities are now subsumed by the role of consumption, which increasingly shapes and conditions the individual's social orientations and relationships. Second, the *sources* of identity formation change as tangible, role-based relationships are subordinated to the disembodied visual images of mass culture. Third, identity formation is *exteriorized* in the sense that its locus shifts from the inner self to the outer world of objects and images comprising commodified culture. . . . Fourth, and as a consequence, the self loses its sense of autonomy from the outside world. (Dunn, 1998, p. 66, italics as in original)

The commodification of culture has been accelerated because of the collapse of communism and the spread of free-market economy around the world.

Global marketing methods pursued by free-market economy are

so subtle and seductive that they produce and deliver what I call *manufactured identities*. Even in societies such as the United States, where individualism is supposed to reign, what seems to be thriving is the kind of individualism that markets promote. Advertising firms are adept at giving individuals the illusion of agency and control when in fact a substantive part of identity formation is influenced by profit-driven consumer industry. "Market-governed freedom of individual choice," observed Giddens (1991, p. 197), "becomes an enveloping framework of individual self-expression."

Although individuals have to deal with global, national, and social realities in the formation of their identity, it would be wrong to assume that they have no option but to surrender their agency to higher forces. As Pavlenko and Blackledge (2004, p. 27) pointed out, "individuals are agentive beings who are constantly in search of new social and linguistic resources which allow them to resist identities that position them in undesirable ways." Global electronic communication systems such as the Internet make critical knowledge available to those who seek it. These systems also open up new windows to ideas and ideals of people who are different from us. Using such a facility, individuals can try to make sense of their own and others' way of life. After all, "making sense of ourselves is what produces identity" (Spivak, 1993, p. 179).

To sum up this section, the global, the national, the social, and the individual are closely connected. They shape and reshape each other in a synergic relationship where the whole is greater than the sum of the parts. The relationship is seen as interactive, the impact of which may vary widely within an individual at different times, places, and situations. It is this dialectical relationship that is now guiding identity formation in most parts of the world. What is needed in today's circumstances, therefore, is a logic of realism inspired by robust common sense that will help us navigate the complex cultural trajectories.

8.3. The Concept of Cultural Realism

To start with a formal definition, cultural realism is the notion that any meaningful cultural growth in this globalized and globalizing world is possible only if individuals, communities, and nations adopt a pragmatic approach to identity formation that entails a true understanding of the competing forces of global, national, social, and individual realities, and make a genuine attempt to translate that understanding into actionable plans. The premise of cultural realism is based on a simple and straightforward proposition that globalization, with its incessant and increased flow of peoples, goods, and ideas across the world, is creating a novel "web of interlocution" that is effectively challenging the traditional notions of identity formation of an individual or of a nation. This development is plunging the world in a creative as well as chaotic tension that both unites and divides people. It is also resulting in an unintended and unexpected movement toward tribalization that contributes to an increase in ethnic, racial, religious, and national consciousness.

How the concept of cultural realism is playing out in the life of an individual or a nation can be seen in the triumphs and tribulations of supranational entities such as the European Union (EU). The idea of a united Europe has deep historical origins as, for instance, reflected in the stirring words of the nineteenth-century French novelist Victor Hugo: "A day will come when you, France, you, Russia, you, Germany, you, all nations of the continent, without losing your distinctive qualities and glorious individuality, will be merged within a superior unit" (cited in *The Economist,* dated December 30, 2003). Europe had to wait for a long time to realize even a fragment of that dream. It was able to rapidly move forward with political and economic integration in a substantial way only after World War II. In fact, it was the ratification of the Treaty of Maastricht in 1992 that fully formalized the institutional framework for the EU in terms of a European Parliament, a European Council of Ministers, a European Court of Justice, and a European currency (euro). These institutions are structured to guarantee national sovereignty of member states while at the same time requiring them to adhere to certain common principles governing the political, economic, and social life of all Europeans.

The triumph of political and economic integration is very much reflected in the fact that the EU, which originally had fifteen members, has since been expanded to twenty-five, with more eagerly waiting to join, stretching its territory from the Atlantic to the borders of Russia and west Asia. The successful establishment of liberal democracies and free-market economy has facilitated the easy movement of capital and services across the continent. It has also ensured greater educational as well as employment opportunities for European citizens and, as a result, has enhanced their chances for upward economic mobility. As the *Economist* (dated Dec. 8, 2005) reported, Europe's "commendable" migration has triggered a "brain-drain cycle" in which skilled workers are leaving their country looking for "higher pay and a better life," while highly qualified professionals are returning to their country after gaining much needed experience in other countries. Through it all, budget flights make travel affordable and efficient so that people can keep in touch with their family, language, and culture, and "can choose easily how long they go for, and where." Juxtaposed to these unifying developments are voices of concern. For instance, in the referendum held during the summer of 2005, the people of France and the Netherlands rejected the draft European Constitution slowing down the unification process. Similarly, while a majority of nations have adopted the euro as their currency, Britain, Denmark, and Sweden have not done so.

A greater challenge the EU faces is in the realm of socio-cultural integration. It was hoped that politico-economic unification would ultimately lead to socio-cultural integration as well. The Maastricht Treaty has a provision for a *Union citizenship*, under which citizens of all member states are also citizens of the EU, a clause that is intended to promote an active civic identity, a European identity. In fact, the treaty has given each member state a mandate to promote European identity by fostering among its citizens an awareness of a common European identity. Article 128 of the treaty provides a precise statement about its cultural mission: "The Community contributes to the cultural development of the member States while respecting their national and regional diversity, and at the same time highlighting the common cultural heritage" (cited in Zarate, 1999, p. 44). This definition makes it abundantly clear that each state, while free to preserve its own cultural identity, has to facilitate the formation of a European identity as well.

Unlike its relatively successful political and economic agenda, the idea of a common European identity seems to flounder as it hits the solid rock of cultural and religious beliefs. Blessed with a predominantly Christian population (though of various denominations), Europe does share certain cultural commonalities associated with the Judeo-Christian faith. However, each nation proudly projects its own culture including specific language, literature, music, art, and philosophy. There has, however, been a concerted effort to promote cultural diversity within the EU. One such effort is the organization of an annual cultural forum, at which artists, intellectuals, and government ministers in charge of cultural affairs meet to formulate strategies for promoting cultural understanding within Europe. The forum held its first meeting in Berlin in 2004, followed by meetings in Paris and Budapest in 2005, with more scheduled for Madrid and Lisbon in 2006. The EU has also instituted its Global Diversity Award to highlight its stance that diversity issues cover not just Europe but the entire world. Accordingly, for the 2005 award the EU selected two non-European celebrities as symbols of global diversity: Indian actress Aishwarya Rai and Chinese actor Jackie Chan, both of whom have become cultural icons in Europe.

In spite of its celebration of global diversity, the EU is currently faced with a twin challenge that highlights the contemporary realities of identity formation. One is the tricky issue of full membership for Turkey. With its mainly Muslim population of seventy million, Turkey became an associate member in 1963 and applied for full membership in 1987. Although it has for a long time belonged to other Western institutions, such as the North Atlantic Treaty Organization (NATO), and has been sensitive to EU's legal norms governing certain social issues (e.g., the death penalty), it is facing stiff opposition, mainly because of its Islamic identity. The second issue, a related one, is the growing Muslim presence in other European countries. According to a recent estimate, there are 15.5 million Muslims living in Europe—including 5 million in France, 4 million in Germany, 1.5 million in the United Kingdom, and 1 million each in Italy and Spain. For cultural as well as for other reasons that are beyond the scope of this book, the Islamic presence in Europe and the mainstream response to it are creating a volatile situation that has turned the spotlight on identity formation. A case in point is the November 2005 riots by Muslim youth in France, which, according to French president Jacques Chirac, demonstrates no less than "an identity crisis."

The identity crisis faced by France and by other European nations is not confined to internal developments alone. The Europeans reckon that a serious threat to their cultural identity comes from a global player: American pop culture. They point out that Hollywood controls 72 percent of the European film market; 50

percent of drama programming on European television is American; and nine out of ten fiction best-sellers worldwide are by English language writers. Mainly because of this threat, all of Europe recently supported a French-led move at the United Nations Educational, Scientific, and Cultural Organization (UNESCO) to approve a convention on cultural diversity to facilitate subsidies for countries worldwide to support their own culture and to shield most cultural exchanges from free-trade rules adopted by international agencies such as the World Trade Organization (WTO). Incidentally, that this convention was approved by UNESCO with an overwhelming majority (148 for and 2 against, with the United States being one of the two voting against) demonstrates how other Asian, African, and Latin American countries too are concerned about cultural globalization and its threat to their cultural heritage.

It is instructive to compare the politico-economic achievement and the relative socio-cultural unease triggered by the European transnational project with an Asian counterpart, the Association of Southeast Asian Nations (ASEAN). Started nearly four decades ago, this ten-nation union, like that of the EU, has as its main objective the task of accelerating economic growth, social progress, and cultural development in the region through joint ventures. However, it is not the explicitly stated objective of ASEAN to forge an "Asian identity," although terms like "Asian values" have been used to justify and explain certain governmental plans. The lack of emphasis on any common cultural identity is perhaps deliberate considering the fact that, unlike the EU, which is a conglomeration of largely Christian countries, ASEAN consists of nations that include Buddhist (Cambodia, Thailand), Confucian (Singapore), Christian (the Philippines), and Islamic (Brunei, Indonesia, and Malaysia) cultures. Politically too, the EU nations are democratic whereas the ASEAN consists of communist states (Vietnam and Laos), a military regime (Myanmar), an Islamic monarchy (Brunei), and parliamentary democracies of various kinds.

It may be safe to assume that because ASEAN is glued together more by economic and educational ties than by a common cultural agenda, the kind of cultural turbulence one witnesses in the EU unification project is markedly less among the ASEAN countries. Even within a multilingual and multicultural state like Singapore, the emphasis on the Singaporean national identity does not diminish the value of Chinese, Malay, or Indian ethnic identities and their way of life, nor are these subnational identities seen as a threat to national identity. Each of these ethnic communities has its own social reality, which is mediated through social institutions such as families, literary and cultural associations, places of worship, etc. Within their discourse domains, these communities use their mother tongue to ensure identification with and maintenance of traditional cultures and their values. It is this social reality, with its cohesive, closely-knit safety net, that offers a cushioning effect for individuals in their attempt to face the challenges posed by global and national realities, and to create and maintain their individual identity.

The ongoing EU and ASEAN experiments offer us illustrative lessons in the logic of cultural realism. It appears that the idealistic project involving the formation of a common European identity is causing serious tensions between transnational, national, social, and individual interests in spite of political, economic, and even larger religious commonalities. On the contrary, the more pragmatic and less ambitious ASEAN project, in which nations of varying political, cultural, and religious persuasions have shown the ability to stay together for economic and social mobility of their citizens, seems to strengthen national, social, and individual identities while posing no threat to constituents and their cultural values.

The complexities of culturally realistic identity formation are illustrated not just by the supranational entities such as the EU or the ASEAN, but also, as the Singaporean example shows, by national entities that are multilingual and multicultural. In countries like the United States and the United Kingdom, where a considerable number of immigrants and their descendants live, the global, national, social, and individual realities are broadening the very concept of citizenship, which was until recently tightly linked to nation-states. Transborder citizenry is becoming a reality and is getting solidified in law. Nations such as Brazil, Mexico, India, and Israel permit immigrants who have become naturalized citizens in countries such as the United States to retain dual nationality. Some have even given them voting rights in their country of origin. The form and meaning of citizenship is changing so fundamentally that Aihwa Ong (1998) used the term *flexible citizenship* to refer to the strategies and effects of people who benefit from different nation-state regimes by selecting different sites for investments, work, and family relocation.

Contrary to common belief, the challenge of cultural complexity is not confined to nations with immigrant populations alone. According to the United Nations–sponsored Human Development Report (2004), almost no country in the world is culturally homogeneous. The report pointed out that the nearly two hundred countries of the world contain some five thousand ethnic groups. Two-thirds of the nations have at least one substantial minority—an ethnic or religious group that makes up at least 10 percent of the population. In these societies, too, "we are looking at the birth of a variety of complex, postnational social formations. These formations are now organized around principles of finance, recruitment, coordination, communication, and reproduction that are fundamentally postnational and not just multinational or international" (Appadurai, 1996, p. 167). What the above examples show is that whatever the level—supranational, national, or subnational—cultural realism is exerting extraordinary demands on all the participants.

By all accounts, individuals seem to be making an effort to negotiate the complex, postnational social formations in a way that enriches their practice of everyday life. It is becoming increasingly clear that the global spread of American media and entertainment outlets that carry cultural images does not necessarily result in unquestioned acceptance of Western cultural values. The same is true of food and fashion. Non-Westerners can hardly be considered culturally Westernized simply because they wear Western fancy clothes or enjoy Western fast foods. By the same token, Americans who regularly frequent Chinese, Indian, and Japanese restaurants, or British who enjoy the popular dish chicken tikka masala (which, by the way, has been called a *British* national dish), can hardly be suspected of embracing Asian cultural values. Conversely, as the U.N. Human Development Report (2004, p. 88) pointed out, simply because members of ethnic communities may want to retain their cultural identities, this "does not mean that they do not develop loyalties to their new country. People of Turkish ancestry in Germany may speak Turkish at home well into the second generation, but they also speak German. Mexicans in the United States may cheer for the Mexican football team but serve in the US Army." These examples give us reason to believe that, regardless of the identity politics practiced by vested interests, individuals themselves may jump in and out of several cultural domains at the same time. There is, however, no gainsaying the fact that cultural realism makes extraordinary demands on the individual.

8.4. Cultural Realism and Its Demands

Cultural realism demands the creation of a heightened awareness among educated citizenry about the forces of globalization that have brought with them what cultural critic Arif Dirlik (2003) called "global modernity." Paradoxically, the contemporary world has to contend not only with the persistence of transnational interests that seek to preserve hegemonic control, but consequently also with reactionary revivals of religious fundamentalism and cultural traditions, as well as with the transnational alliances of global capitalism. What is special about global modernity "is precisely the element of transnationality: while there is no doubt about the weight of the United States in the world economy or politics, ruling class interests in the United States may be realized best not in antagonism to but in cooperation with ruling class interests elsewhere, through transnational organizations which now include representatives from all societies, with their different and conflicting but common claims on global modernity—with a globalized capital at its core" (Dirlik, 2003, p. 213). Unlike modernity and postmodernity, both of which are Eurocentric, global modernity is truly transnational.

What the individual needs more than anything else to make sense of cultural realism and its impact on identity formation is global cultural consciousness. Cultural realism has the potential to offer strategies and tactics that may lie in the development of global cultural consciousness. Such a consciousness requires the cultivation of a critically reflective mind that can tell the difference between real and unreal, between information and disinformation, between ideas and ideologies. Only such a critical mind can help the individual develop the knowledge, skill, and disposition necessary to deal with the challenges of contemporary realities.

Developing global cultural consciousness is a complex process that requires constant and continual self-reflection. What guides an individual in such a critical self-reflection is his or her own value system based on his or her own cultural heritage. One's learned knowledge and experience of other cultural contexts not only expands one's cultural horizon but also clarifies and solidifies one's own cultural heritage. This critical self-reflection helps one to identify and understand what is good and bad about one's own culture, and what is good and bad about other cultures. It eventually leads to a deeper cultural transformation, not just superficial cultural information. In understanding other cultures, we understand our own better; in understanding our own, we understand other cultures better. We then use this deeper understanding to enrich our lives and the lives of those whom we love. When we do that, and do that right, we are not culturally melting. We are not culturally hybridizing. We are, in fact, culturally growing.

The real cultural growth, in its critical sense, does not come easily or quickly. It has to be constructed consciously and systematically by individuals through a meaningful negotiation of differences between the culture they inherited by birth and the culture they learned through experience. The inherited culture should be freely allowed to interact with the learned culture so that there is mutual enrichment. The key to this enrichment is the lived experiences of individuals. Global cultural consciousness demands that all individuals function as self-regulating human beings capable of receiving, understanding, exchanging, and judging cultural information. Such a consciousness becomes a tool both for self-reflection and for self-renewal.

Between the modernist position that undervalues the agency of the individual and the postmodern stance that overvalues it, cultural realism signifies contradictory and competing allegiance by recognizing that cultural identity is socially conventionalized and yet individually constructed. Between an arrogant valorization of the Self and an abject marginalization of the Other, cultural realism invokes the reality of historical exigency that no one culture embodies all and only the best or the worst of human cultural experience. Every cultural community has virtues that one can be proud of, and every cultural community has vices that one should be ashamed of. To state this is not to embrace cultural relativism, but to accept cultural realism. The difference is that whereas cultural relativism blindly believes that there are no universal standards of human behavior or social morality, and that no value judgment can be made about the beliefs and practices of other cultures, cultural realism stubbornly reckons that no individual or community is an island unto itself, either in cultural sufficiency or in human survivability, particularly in this era of globalization. "Each culture," as theologian Jonathan Sacks noted, "has something to contribute to the totality of human wisdom" (2003, p. 64).

To put it briefly and briskly, far from a contentious assimila-

tionism, or a conciliatory pluralism or a convenient transcultural-
ism, cultural realism seeks to grasp the cultural moment in the
multiplicity of its realities and to give the individual the agency toward cultural transformation. By calling for such a pragmatic approach, cultural realism emphasizes formation and re-formation of
one's identity through continual negotiation between conflicting
belief systems.

8.5. In Closing

The prevailing concepts of cultural assimilation, cultural pluralism,
and cultural hybridity discussed in previous chapters do not have
adequate explanatory power to elucidate how the relationship between global, national, social, and individual realities are closely
connected or how the relationship has problematized the traditional
concept of identity formation. How to cope with the challenges
posed by contemporary realities is a vexing question that has not
yet been fully addressed. In this chapter, I attempted to address that
issue by positing the concept of cultural realism. I argued that a
true understanding of how the complex and competing forces of
cultural globalization contribute to identity formation in the contemporary world will help us to cope with the chaotic tension that
these forces have brought about. I put forward the proposition that
creating global cultural consciousness is one way to come to grips
with challenges of cultural realism. In the next chapter, I'll present
certain educational possibilities that might open up viable avenues
for creating global cultural consciousness in our learners.

CHAPTER 9

Cultural Realism and Pedagogic Principles

> I have become a queer mixture of the East and West, out of place everywhere, at home nowhere.
>
> —JAWAHARLAL NEHRU, 1936, p. 596

> I don't want my house to be walled in on all sides and my windows to be stuffed. I want the cultures of all lands to be blown about my house as freely as possible. But I refuse to be blown off my feet by any.
>
> —MOHANDAS GANDHI, 1921, p. 170

A tale of two leaders.

One was born into a wealthy, cosmopolitan family. His father was a successful barrister and an influential political figure in colonial India. Educated in the most prestigious Indian schools of the time, he went on to study in England at one of its finest institutions—Cambridge University. After spending nearly seven years in England, and after successfully completing his bar exam, he returned to India to practice law before following his father's footsteps into politics. His sojourn in England made him vastly Westernized in thought, in speech, and in action. Not that the Western way of life was anything alien to him. He was, in fact, born and brought up, as he wrote in his autobiography, in a household that "became more and more westernized" (Nehru, 1936/1980, p. 5).

The other was born into a middle class, orthodox family in India. His father, as he stated in his autobiography, "had no education, save that of experience" (Gandhi, 1927/1997, p. 4) and "never had any ambition to accumulate riches" (p. 3). Through long years of work, his father rose to the level of a *Diwan*, a provincial bureaucrat. Gandhi himself was not an outstanding student during his early schooling, and yet he managed to go to England to train as a barrister. After successfully completing his three-year study at University College of London, he returned to India to practice law. A couple of years later, he went to South Africa to appear in a court case. There, his life underwent a tremendous change as he decided to initiate and lead a civil rights movement to fight for the dignity of the individual. There he experimented with his powerful ideas of *Satyagraha* (pursuit of truth) and *Ahimsa* (nonviolence), which he perfected later in India. His life experiences in foreign lands, however, only solidified his Indiannness.

Gandhi and Nehru strove together for nearly three decades in a historic nonviolent struggle to free their country from British colonial rule. When India finally achieved independence in 1947, Nehru became its first prime minister and continued to serve in that capacity until his death in 1964. He laid the foundation for independent India's socioeconomic development. He was also an accomplished writer and historian. Unlike Nehru, Gandhi renounced politics, vowing to devote his time and energy to ensure peace and harmony among warring religious communities in the subcontinent. However, within a few months after independence, he fell to an assassin's bullet. His life, as he often said, was his message. A grateful nation affectionately called him *Babuji* (Father of the Nation) and called Nehru *Panditji* (Erudite One), and celebrates their birthdays as national holidays.

What has this tale of two leaders to do with the topic of this chapter? The tale tells us in part how close encounters of the cultural kind can influence the life of even thoughtful individuals in fundamentally different ways. It sheds some light on how individuals who otherwise share an apparently common religious, historical, national, and political milieu negotiate the contours of cultural contacts in a manner that is diametrically opposed to that of the others. More importantly, it highlights the role of individual agency in the formation of cultural identity.

Nehru's personal dealings with the Indian and the Western cultural traditions produced in him an ambivalent, hybrid identity very much like the one we discussed in Chapter 7. "I cannot," he bemoaned, "get rid of either that past inheritance or my recent acquisitions. They are both part of me, and, though they help me in both the East and the West, they also create in me a feeling of spiritual loneliness not only in public activities but in life itself" (Nehru, 1936/ 1980, p. 596). Spiritual loneliness. Cultural in-betweenness. Psychological ambivalence. These characteristics of cultural hybridity haunted Nehru all his life, with the result that this erudite, cosmopolitan intellectual found himself in a cultural limbo—neither here nor there. "In my own country," the leader of the millions of the masses acknowledged, "I have an exile's feeling" (p. 596).

No such feeling of alienation for Gandhi. He had no cultural ambivalence of the type Nehru experienced. He knew where his cultural roots were. He also knew where those roots were branching off. More importantly, he knew where the roots were drawing their sustenance. His encounters with his native and foreign cultures produced in him an enriched and enlightened cultural persona. While he gladly opened his windows to let alien cultural winds to flow freely into his house, and while he used them to shape his own thought and action, his feet were firmly planted on the cultural core that he inherited. He repeatedly emphasized the importance of embracing the best of one's own cultural heritage, which does not have to be forsaken in order to imbibe what is best in other cultures. "Nothing can be farther from my thought," he observed, "than that we should become exclusive or erect barriers. But I do respectfully contend that an appreciation of other cultures can fitly follow, never precede, an appreciation and assimilation of our own" (Gandhi, 1921, p. 277). As Oxford University scholar Robert Young noted, "Gandhi theorized his diasporic receptivity to other ideas and cultural forms as a combination of rootedness and openness—rooted in the ancient heritage of his native Hinduism, but opened to the spiritual inheritance of all the great religions of the world" (Young, 2001, pp. 366–67). Declaring loudly that "my religion forbids me to belittle or disregard other cultures" (Gandhi, 1921, p. 277), Gandhi rejected cultural isolationism and freely acknowledged his debt to Western culture in his own identity formation.

It is the Gandhian view of cultural growth, with its twin pillars of rootedness and openness, that, I believe, offers a strong foundation for the construction of global cultural consciousness in the contemporary world. In fact, because of the complex and competing realities we discussed in the previous chapter, Gandhi's thoughts on cultural consciousness have a greater relevance today than they had in his time. One of the difficult tasks facing language educators is how to develop global cultural consciousness in their learners. In order to facilitate critical reflections on the task, I present in this chapter certain educational possibilities in terms of fundamental factors and pedagogic priorities.

9.1. Fundamental Factors

By fundamental factors, I refer to a set of broad insights that can be derived from the critical review of anthropological, sociological, historical, and cultural studies presented in the previous chapters. I list five major factors below with a brief description of each (for details, see the chapters cited):

Cultural connectivity: Cultures do not exist in splendid isolation. They are interconnected. They influence others they come into contact with and are, in turn, influenced by others. Hence, they are seldom found in their purest form. Rigid cultural boundaries are more an illusion than a reality. Cultural borders, to the extent they are artificially drawn, have always been porous, and we have all been constantly crossing them whether we are aware of it or not. Although culture is normally associated with a superordinate national entity ("American culture," "British culture," "Chinese culture," etc.), it functions at various subcultural levels such as race, religion, ethnicity, class, and gender. Individuals within a family, families within a community, and communities within a nation—all exhibit specific cultural characteristics along with common cultural traits they share. Thus, culture has multiple facets embedded in multiple layers. (Chapters 2 and 8)

Cultural complexity: Although culture plays an integral part in the practice of everyday life, it remains an elusive concept that defies a clear understanding, leading to cultural stereotyping and cultural Otherization. Cultural stereotyping is very common. We stereotype others, and others stereotype us. We generally accept and propagate stereotypes without proper reflection. Stereotyping is also related to Otherization in the sense that there is a natural tendency among individuals and communities to portray their own culture as one that is superior while presenting the culture of people who are religiously, racially, ethnically, or linguistically different as one that is inferior. The reductive processes of stereotyping and Otherization ascribe a simple and simplistic profile both to the celebrated Self and to the marginalized Other. (Chapters 2 and 4)

Cultural globality: The current wave of globalization, which is very different from the earlier ones, is shaping the global flows of cultural capital and interested knowledge with unprecedented speed and scope. It has caused a globality that is marked by simultaneous and opposing processes of cultural homogenization and cultural heterogenization, plunging the world into an uncomfortable tension between the forces that are seen to weaken local cultures and those that are seen to strengthen them. Global information systems, along with the easily accessible World Wide Web, have created an astounding degree of cultural awareness among people in many parts of the world. As a result, people see unparalleled opportunities for their cultural growth and equally unparalleled threats to their cultural heritage. This threat—perceived or real—has given rise to cultural politics where vested interests across the political spectrum exploit cultural markers for local, regional, national, and international political gains. (Chapters 2, 3, and 8)

Cultural reality: The fast-changing cultural life of the contemporary world is being influenced by four realities: the global reality that marks the advent of global neighborhood with shrinking space, time, and borders; the national reality that nurtures robust nationalism partly as a reaction to the onslaught of perceived global cultural homogenization; the social reality that is created and sustained through social institutions such as families and communities; and the individual reality that depicts the individual as complex, contradictory, and dynamic. These realities are locked up in a synergic relationship where the whole is much more than the sum of the parts. One of the consequences of this relationship has been an increase in ethnic, racial, religious, and national consciousness as well as tensions among the people of the world. All this is making cultural connectivity and cultural complexity even more pronounced and problematic. (Chapters 2, 3, 7, and 8)

Cultural identity: The realities mentioned above are also having an impact on the formation of cultural identity. The impact varies from individual to individual, and also within an individual at different times, places, and situations. The commodification of culture with a global free-market economy that is bent upon manufacturing and marketing artificial identities adds yet another dimension to the process of identity formation. In these circumstances, the individual is both a sufferer and a doer, sometimes succumbing to the pressures brought on by controlling realities and sometimes succeeding to exercise a degree of agency in the formation of self-identity.

Maintaining a modicum of personal agency, the individual strives to accumulate cultural capital that can contribute not only to one's own cultural growth but also to cultural change in the larger community. (Chapters 2, 3, 7, and 8)

Taken together, the five fundamental factors have the potential to provide necessary theoretical bases for the learning and teaching of culture in the current globalizing environment. They also send a cautionary note that the field of language education cannot remain insulated and isolated from the impact globalization forces have on the cultural identity of the individual or the nation. They have unmistakable implications for pedagogic priorities as well as for instructional strategies, particularly if we are serious about developing global cultural consciousness in our learners.

9.2. Pedagogic Priorities

The foundational factors sketched above warrant a serious reconsideration of pedagogic priorities that govern the theory and practice of learning and teaching culture. They also demand a serious exploration of what kind of transition is required in order to put in place a teaching program that is sensitive to the chances and challenges posed by cultural globalization. Such a transition, as I visualize it, stipulates several shifts in our pedagogic priorities. I shall highlight five of the shifts: (a) from target language community to targeted cultural community, (b) from linguistic articulation to cultural affiliation, (c) from cultural information to cultural transformation, (d) from passive reception to critical reflection, and (e) from interested text to informed context. As will become clear below, these shifts encompass various aspects of language education, including policies and planning, and methods and materials.

9.2.1. From Target Language Community to Targeted Cultural Community

The first and foremost priority shift the language teaching profession has to consider pertains to a change of focus from target language community to targeted cultural community. So far, in most formal systems of language education, the learning and teaching of culture have been confined to the learning and teaching of the cultural beliefs and practices associated with the members of the target language (TL) community, that is, the community of people speaking the second or foreign language (L2) that the learners are studying. The underlying assumptions here include: (a) languages and cultures are closely connected, (b) learning an L2 also means learning a C2 (second culture), and (c) L2 learners should develop necessary knowledge and skills in C2 for interactive (e.g., travel), integrative (e.g., relationship), or instrumental (e.g., career) purposes.

The focus on the target language community and its underlying assumptions are very much reflected in the "axiomatic" belief that "cultural learning has to take place as an integral part of language learning, and vice versa" (Byram and Morgan, 1994, p. 5). They have also informed some of the teaching practices linked to the three major cultural concepts—cultural assimilation, cultural pluralism, and cultural hybridity—discussed in previous chapters. To recall briefly, teaching practices inspired by the concept of cultural assimilation impressed upon L2 learners to learn linguistic and cultural nuances necessary to assimilate the behaviors, values, beliefs, and lifestyles of the TL community (cf. Chapter 5). Teaching practices influenced by the concept of cultural pluralism encouraged L2 learners to preserve and protect C1 (native culture) and also to recognize and respect the virtues of C2 and other cultures (cf. Chapter 6). Teaching practices inclined toward the concept of cultural hybridity exhorted L2 learners to create an in-between third culture drawing from both C1 and C2 (cf. Chapter 7). Thus, all three of them, in one way or another, have been preoccupied with helping L2 learners negotiate the cultural contours of C1 and C2 in order to achieve specific pedagogic objectives.

It is my contention that in the context of cultural realism and its imperative to develop global cultural consciousness in our learners, the learning and teaching of culture cannot and should not be confined to the culture of the target language community alone. The exclusive focus on the culture of the TL community not only treats contemporary cultural challenges inadequately but it also neglects the L2 learners' need for developing global cultural consciousness. It leads them to believe, rather falsely, that their choice of L2 and their knowledge of C2 are enough to prepare them to face the challenges posed by economic and cultural globalization. It fails to help them recognize that intercultural competence restricted to C2 opens them up only to one other cultural reality as against the multiplicity of realities that are out there in the world. What needs to be done, therefore, is to extend the pedagogic focus of culture teaching from target language community to targeted cultural community.

By *targeted cultural community,* I refer to a cluster of cultural communities in the world that can become the prime target for teaching culture in the language classroom. Why target a *cluster* of cultures? The paramount reason is that, in the current globalized environment, even if L2 learners do not go to the world, the world will come to them. Therefore, it is beneficial for them to be aware of the beliefs and practices of a broader network of cultural communities, not just those of the TL community. Such an extended focus beyond the TL community is clearly necessary in order to help them develop global cultural consciousness. Let me hasten to add that the emphasis on *global* cultural consciousness does not mean that L2 learners should be introduced to the cultural beliefs and practices of all the people living on this planet. In the interest of feasibility and usability, it would be necessary to target a cluster of communities, the cultural norms of which may have an impact on the practice of everyday life of a given group of learners.

Taking into consideration national, regional, and international developments as well as individual and institutional interests, policy planners and teacher educators may formulate a set of criteria for selecting the cluster of communities on which any given language program may focus. Based on the criteria, practicing teachers and their learners may make the final selection of the cluster of cultural communities that they wish to target. To offer a couple of illustrative scenarios with particular reference to two supranational entities and their identity problems discussed in Chapter 8, L2 learners from member countries of the European Union may choose to include in their cluster cultural beliefs and practices of a few fellow European communities. Likewise, L2 learners from the Association of South East Asian Nations may like to focus on certain communities from the region. In addition, both groups may find it useful to learn about cultural communities in America (because of its global importance), China (because of its emerging prominence), or the Islamic world in general (because of its current relevance). Within the purview of such a scheme, a number of permutations and combinations are possible. Clearly, the resulting cluster will vary from country to country and from context to context.

What the proposed shift of focus from target language community to targeted cultural community does is to decouple the exclusive link between the teaching of the target language and the teaching of the culture associated with it. No doubt that any cluster of cultural communities jointly put together by teachers and learners will necessarily and prominently figure the culture of the TL community, but the pedagogic focus will not be limited to it. In fact, if this idea is stretched to its logical end, it can no longer be assumed that culture learning and teaching should be restricted to *language* classrooms and to *language* learners. Given the interdisciplinary nature of cultural globalization and its studies, it makes eminent sense to talk about culture across the curriculum, just as we talk about language across the curriculum. School and college classes in several subject areas, particularly within the field of humanities and social sciences such as anthropology, sociology, psychology, history, and politics, can easily benefit from an informed discussion on cultural matters.

The possibility of culture across the curriculum, even if it is adequately explored, does not in any way free language teachers from taking on the prime responsibility for culture teaching. More than any other educators, language teachers face distinct challenges and opportunities to help learners construct their cultural identity because it is mostly in the language classroom that learners come into contact with unfamiliar languages and cultures. In such a contact zone, language operates not merely as a mode of linguistic transaction, but also as a medium for cultural expression; and hence the importance of the next shift of focus.

9.2.2. From Linguistic Articulation to Cultural Affiliation

Drawing insights from mainstream second language acquisition research that learning a second language means learning to use new phonological, grammatical, lexical, and pragmatic features, the language teaching profession has long focused on helping learners successfully encode and decode linguistic features. Following a similar orientation, the teaching of second culture was also concerned with linguistic realizations of cultural expressions. When, in the 1980s, communicative approaches to language teaching became popular, the teaching of culture was seen mostly as an endeavor to help L2 learners develop the linguistic ability necessary to use the TL in culturally appropriate ways for the specific purpose of performing certain speech acts in certain specified contexts. Thus, the teaching of pragmatic conventions tied to the grammatical and lexical structures of communicative acts such as greetings, requests, refusals, apologies, complaints, etc., became an important feature of the teaching of culture. A number of cross-cultural studies (see, for instance, the volumes edited by Blum-Kulka, House, and Kasper, 1989; and Kasper and Blum-Kulka, 1993) investigated in detail how native speakers of particular languages perform speech acts, and projected their performance patterns as models for L2 learners to follow. These studies have generated an impressive body of cross-linguistic data, some of which could easily be incorporated into lessons on discourse grammar.

The limited focus on linguistic mechanisms and native speaker articulations has been questioned by those who advocate the importance of sociocultural theories to second language acquisition research, learning, and teaching (for a recent volume on the subject see Lantolf, ed., 2000). They see "second language learning not as the acquisition of a new set of grammatical, lexical, and phonological forms but as a struggle of concrete socially constituted and always situated beings to participate in the symbolically mediated lifeworld" of another culture (Pavlenko and Lantolf, 2000, p. 155). Second language learning, therefore, involves "an intentional renegotiation of one's multiple identities, which are reconstructed in communications with members of another discourse" (p. 172). It also involves a conception of identity that is based on social power relations between language learners and target language speakers (Norton, 2000). These developments have resulted in a growing awareness that culture teaching has to move beyond a preoccupation with native speakers' linguistic performance and their cultural perspectives.

Consequently, L2 educationists such as Michael Byram (1997), Claire Kramsch (1993), Anita Pavlenko (1998), Gail Robinson (1991), and others have emphasized how human beings interpret their cross-cultural experiences, how they construct meaning in cross-cultural encounters, and how they develop intercultural communicative competence. They have pointed out that cultural understanding is more than knowing about discrete objects; rather, it is a serious effort to come to grips with how people live and express their lives.

Therefore, culture teaching should treat the L2 classroom as a site of struggle between the learners' meanings and those of native speakers. Through this struggle "between the familiar meanings of the native culture and the unexpected meanings of the target culture, meanings that were taken for granted are suddenly questioned, challenged, problematized" (Kramsch, 1993, p. 238). This struggle helps L2 learners create their own personal meanings at the boundaries between the native speaker's meanings and their own. Therefore, it was suggested that one way of facilitating the negotiation of cultural meaning in the classroom is to use memoirs of bicultural and bilingual writers who have recounted their second language/ culture learning experiences (Pavlenko, 1998).

Notice that even this expanded notion of culture teaching that seeks to go beyond linguistic articulation of cultural experiences still focuses on the cultural norms of, and interactions with, the target language community. Although the shift from a narrow linguistic realization to broader cultural experiences is indeed an important move forward, its focus on the target language community alone may not be adequate to meet the challenges of cultural globalization. In order to help L2 learners develop global cultural consciousness, we may need to move even further—toward cultural affiliation.

I use the term *affiliation* the way historian David Hollinger (1995, p. 7) used it—to suggest "a greater measure of flexibility consistent with a postethnic eagerness to promote communities of consent." Through affiliation, people in their everyday lives are making concerted efforts to form associations and linkages with members of other cultural communities. In that sense, affiliation is not just a speculative exercise; it is, as Hollinger asserted, performative in nature, calling attention to the social dynamics of cultural identity formation. This notion of affiliation "appreciates multiple identities, pushes for communities of wide scope, recognizes the constructed character of ethno-racial groups, and accepts the formation of new groups as a part of the normal life of a democratic society" (p. 116). Affiliation as cultural performance is consistent with the demands of cultural realism aimed at developing global cultural consciousness in our learners. Such a consciousness, as we discussed in Chapter 8, requires the cultivation of a critically reflective mind that can help learners change their basic attitudes toward their own culture and toward other cultures. In order to facilitate such an attitudinal change in the learner, the language teaching profession is obligated to make yet another shift.

9.2.3. From Cultural Information to Cultural Transformation

It is fair to state that the predominant approach to the learning and teaching of culture in the language classroom has been mostly information-oriented. That is, learners were given information about the cultural beliefs and practices of their target language community through cultural tidbits about food and festivals, rites and rituals, and myths and manners. In this informational approach culture was treated as no more than static products or facts that may be collected, codified, objectified, and presented to learners in discrete items. The language teaching profession has indeed been aware of such limitations for quite some time. Crawford-Lange and Lange (1984), for instance, cautioned us that an information-oriented culture teaching implies that culture is a static, closed phenomenon, in contrast with the consensus view that it is dynamic and ever-changing. Besides, "an information-only culture-learning strategy may actually establish stereotypes, since it provides no means of accounting for cultural variation across individuals or regions at the same point in time" (Crawford-Lange and McLaren, 2003, p. 134). As a way of addressing the inadequacy of this approach, it was felt necessary to move away from teaching culture as product to teaching culture as process.

One of the popular books that presents several classroom strategies for achieving the desired transfer from culture as product to culture as process is *New Ways in Teaching Culture*, published by the Washington-based TESOL organization. In it, editor Alvino Fantini (1997, pp. 40–41) presented what is called "a process approach framework." It consists of a seven-stage guideline to ensure that "language work is always complemented by explicit attention to sociolinguistic aspects, cultural aspects, and the comparing and contrasting of target and native linguacultures" (p. 41). The stages are: (1) presentation of new material, (2) practice of new material in controlled contexts, (3) explanation of the grammar rules behind the material, (4) transposition and use of new material in less controlled contexts, (5) sociolinguistic explanation of the interrelationships of social context and language use, (6) culture exploration for determining appropriate interactional strategies and behaviors, and (7) intercultural exploration for comparing and contrasting the target culture with the student's native culture. Although these stages of classroom implementation are a helpful guide for teachers to follow, they can be seen as continuing the emphasis on linguistic features and cultural products.

It is worthwhile to pause and ponder whether or not the forces of cultural globalization and information revolution are actually offsetting the limitations of culture teaching that is commonly practiced. Obviously, language classrooms are not the only place where learners are prompted to take cognizance of cultural connectivity. As we have seen in previous chapters (mainly Chapters 3 and 8), life in this globalizing world carries with it a significant level of cultural flow. Most adolescent and adult students in urban areas, who are conversant with information technology and entertainment media, do not come to the classroom with a blank mental slate that can be characterized as cultural tabula rasa. On the contrary, there are clear indications that students themselves are far ahead in their efforts to come to grips with how people live and express their lives in cultural contact zones. As a result, they may be bringing to the classroom a much greater cultural awareness and adaptability than the language teaching profession has given them credit for.

As a case in point, consider this: British applied linguist Ben Rampton (1995, 2006) conducted a detailed ethnographic study of social interactions in and outside the classroom among British peer group adolescents of Anglo, Caribbean, Indian, and Pakistani descent. He found that they used the languages associated with each other's ethnic, racial, and cultural identities in highly innovative and interesting ways. He called such uses *crossing*. The youths crossed the boundaries of cultural expressions in self-talk, in games, in cross-sex interaction, and in the context of performance art. Sometimes, they did it in the classroom in order to playfully resist teacher directives to participate in class activities. Drawing from his studies, Rampton concluded that if ethnic and cultural absolutism had been hegemonic, language crossing would have been unacceptable. Instead, "crossing arose out of solidarities and allegiances that were grounded in a range of non-ethnic identities—identities of neighbourhood, class, gender, age, sexual orientation, role, recreational interest and so on—and it was these that generated, among other things, the local multiracial vernacular" (Rampton, 1995, p. 312).

What the Rampton study shows is that students bring with them personal knowledge of the cultural world gained from their lived experience. They actively process this prior knowledge in their interaction within different social networks in and out of the classroom, thereby demonstrating a capacity to negotiate very effectively the intricate relationship between language, culture, and group membership. As Rampton emphasized, their cultural understanding "emerged from a plurality of identity relations" (1995, p. 313), of which they seem to be fully aware. In such a circumstance, the responsibility of the teaching profession is to use students' thought, speech, knowledge, and experience as the foundation for developing global cultural consciousness. In other words, the profession has a responsibility to shift its focus from cultural information to cultural transformation.

Cultural information merely provides us with a superficial rendering of fragments of the cultural beliefs and practices of a cultural community, most often leading to cultural stereotypes and even to a false sense of superiority. Cultural transformation, on the other hand, entails a long journey into a rediscovery, and a consequent redesigning, of one's own identity. This self-exploratory journey helps us get a realistic view of our place and our community's place in the cultural universe. And, as Montovani put it, "when a journey leads us to expand the boundaries of our identity to the point at which we include in the 'we' what was previously simply 'other,' our journey is a return home, we come full circle" (2000, p. 41). When we return home with a global cultural consciousness, we are able to see our own cultural roots with a different, critical eye. This transformative process opens up new pathways to the exploration of new meaning to our world of experience. This way of cultural exploration, from a learning/teaching point of view, is undoubtedly far more valuable than the one envisioned in the informational approach.

A number of scholars, including sociologist Montovani (2000), historian Robbie Robertson (2003), educationist Luke (2003), postcolonial critic Mignolo (1998), and teacher educator Lange (2003), have stressed the importance of effecting cultural transformation in our learners through educational means. The current stage of globalization is adding urgency to that task because the globalizing process contains the potential to be a transformative process. What is required in this context is a pedagogic program that will be able to "recruit, rather than attempt to ignore and erase, the different subjectivities, interests, intentions, commitments and purposes that students bring to learning. Curriculum now needs to mesh with different subjectivities, and with their attendant languages, discourses, and registers, and use these as a resource for learning" (The New London Group, 2000, p. 18). Such a pedagogic program should seriously consider how to create the conditions necessary for encouraging learners to participate in the negotiation and articulation of cultural meanings and values, and how to open up new avenues of cultural exploration that will enable them to transform their individual identity through critical engagement.

9.2.4. From Passive Reception to Critical Reflection

A true self-exploratory journey toward cultural transformation cannot be undertaken by passively receiving and accepting cultural information that emanates from various vested interests. It requires critical cultural reflectivity that can tell the difference between information and disinformation, and also between the trivial and the consequential. It requires the knowledge, skill, and disposition necessary to understand, analyze, and assess

- how global, national, social, and individual realities shape personal identity formation in complex and sometimes contradictory ways;
- how affective and cognitive demands of critical mind engagement will challenge one's conception of self and society;
- how multiple subject positionings according to gender, age, class, ethnicity, etc., are shaped by the social, political, and cultural environment one is accustomed to;
- how cultural stereotypes determine the way people perceive themselves and others; and
- how difficult and sometimes disturbing dialogues can bring about a change of basic attitudes toward one's own culture and toward other cultures.

These and other related aspects of critical cultural reflectivity promise the emergence of an overall academic ability, intellectual competence, and mental fortitude necessary for learners to develop global cultural consciousness.

Clearly, such a far-reaching goal cannot be attained by learners working alone. They need the willing cooperation of all those who play a prominent part in their educational endeavor, especially that of their teachers. To begin with, teachers have to take into account the prior cultural knowledge that their learners bring with them to the classroom, and start treating them as cultural informants. When that happens, the learners "are likely to engage their teachers in a voyage of discovery that they had not always anticipated and for which they don't always feel prepared" (Kramsch, 1998, p. 30). Teachers—whether they are native speakers or nonnative speakers—will find themselves challenged, and should be willing to accept the challenge, to reflect on their own cultural selves as deeply as they expect their learners to do. As a consequence, both learners and teachers become contributing partners in the mutually beneficial quest for true cultural understanding in this globalized world. In the effort to create global cultural consciousness in the language classroom, then, there can be no center; there can only be peripheries.

In their joint endeavor to explore global cultural consciousness, teachers and learners can make use of several critically reflective techniques, most important of which comes from ethnography. Originated in anthropology, ethnography, which literally means a written account of peoples/cultures, has become an established way of studying cultures. It is an investigative process by which one can learn about the culture of other people by, in part, systematically and directly asking them about it. It mainly involves observing cultural behavior, identifying researchable questions, interviewing cultural informants, analyzing the data, interpreting the results, and writing about it. An interesting aspect of ethnographic studies is that researchers have the option of getting involved and of becoming "participant observers," that is, they can immerse themselves in the cultural community that they wish to study in order to bring to bear on the study their own experiential knowledge.

As John Corbett (2003, p. 94) rightly pointed out, "ethnographic practices, in a variety of forms, are becoming increasingly central to intercultural approaches to language teaching and learning." Several scholars (see, for instance, the volumes edited by Byram and Fleming, 1998; Fantini, 1997) have found a basic training in ethnographic practices to be beneficial to the language learner. Following the traditional approach to ethnography, Corbett suggested clusters of activities under the rubric of concept training, cultural associations, critical incidents, and others. Concept training is aimed at helping learners develop systematic observation of everyday situations such as buying books in a bookstore. Since "cultural frames" associated with bookstores vary from place to place, he suggested that learners can be trained to contemplate about them. Drawing from his experience in Brazil, Russia, and the United Kingdom, Corbett explained how bookstores in Russia arrange books so as to physically separate the customers from the books, while those in the United Kingdom and the United States cultivate a social atmosphere, offering coffee shops and comfortable reading areas. He connected these practices respectively to communism, which strictly regulates the flow of information, and to capitalism, which promotes consumption as a leisure and social activity. He reckoned that "detailed observation and contemplation of an ordinary 'concept,' such as a bookshop, can lead to cultural insights and speculations" (Corbett, p. 108). The same is considered true of other ethnographic activities pertaining to cultural associations and critical incidents (see Chapter 7, section 7.3, for more of his examples). It should, however, be remembered that these are conventional ethnographic practices that are more likely to lead to information than to transformation.

What might be of greater importance to cultural transformation based on global cultural consciousness are critical ethnography and autoethnography. Unlike conventional ethnography, which is considered to be mostly descriptive, critical ethnography is deemed to be mainly reflective. Critical ethnographers take into account historical, political, sociological, and other macrocontextual factors that influence a person's cultural life. They seek to pose probing questions at the boundaries of ideology, power, knowledge, class, race, and gender. They recognize, along with anthropologist George Marcus (1998, p. 51), that "any cultural identity or activity is constructed by multiple agents in varying contexts, or places," and, consequently, their task is not merely to discover and describe cultural life as it exists, but to interrogate and interpret it critically in order to bring out the multiplicity of meaning associated with it.

Critical ethnography involves gathering of spoken and/or written data from multiple sources, including interactional episodes, participant-observation, and interviews and discussions with participants at different levels and at different times. It also involves *thick* description and *thick* explanation. To do thick description, popularized by anthropologist Clifford Geertz, the critical ethnographer returns to the same piece of data again and again and adds layers of analysis as seen through the participant as well as the observer. To do thick explanation, the critical ethnographer takes into account "relevant, theoretically salient micro- and macrocontextual influences, whether horizontal or vertical, that stand in a systematic relationship . . . to the behavior or event(s) one is attempting to explain" (Watson-Gegeo and Gegeo, 1996, p. 62). Such an approach recognizes the complexity of the relationship between broader contextual factors and the researchers' own socially determined position within the reality that they are attempting to describe, interpret, and explain.

How the use of critical ethnography in the language classroom can help teachers and learners penetrate hidden meanings and underlying connections has been addressed before (e.g., Kumaravadivelu, 1999). In a study that used interactive data from student conferences done through electronic media, Suresh Canagarajah (1997) demonstrated, using how African-American students in his Texas classroom negotiated the ideological challenges of the academic culture, and how they critically interrogated their classroom discourses. He showed how they exhibited a heightened consciousness of their ethnic identity by exploring many issues not raised by the prescribed textbook, thus giving additional depth to the subject. He pointed out that starting from "the what and how of distortions in history they go on to explore the why, and eventually probe the political-economy of textbook production that functions against minorities and sustains the hegemony of the majority groups. The written word is thus creatively given new ramifications in reference to the larger social contexts and discourses of the students" (Canagarajah, 1997, p. 184). In another study on English language learning and teaching in Sri Lanka, he noted how critical ethnography can introduce "an element of ideological critique into cultural description," thereby helping the researcher, the teacher, and the learner "explicate the cultural strands that may facilitate community empowerment and self-determination" (Canagarajah, 1999, p. 49).

Yet another critical ethnographic method that is of relevance to culture learning and teaching is autoethnography. It is "an autobiographical genre of writing that displays multiple layers of consciousness, connecting the personal to the cultural" (Ellis and Bochner, 2000, p. 739). It is an analytical account of one's cultural self. It is a critical review of one's sense of affiliation to, or differentiation from, a group or culture. It is considered to have better explanatory power than the traditional ethnography because, as anthropologist Deborah Reed-Danahay (1997, p. 2) observed, it "synthesizes both a postmodern ethnography, in which the realist conventions and objective observer position of standard ethnography have been called into question, and a postmodern autobiography, in which the notion of a coherent, individual self has been similarly called into question." As a self-analytical tool, autoethnography is concerned more with interpretable knowledge than with irrefutable facts. This does not mean "anything goes"; rather, it means that a meaningful balance has to be struck between objective evidence and subjective meaning.

Autoethnography is also considered a valuable tool to explain the complex and contentious relationship between the Self and the Other, to explain Self to the Other, and to explain how one is, or feels, "Othered." It is in this sense that Mary Louise Pratt has popularized the term autoethnography in her work on colonialism. She used it "to refer to instances in which colonized subjects undertake to represent themselves in ways which engage with the colonizer's own terms. If ethnographic texts are a means in which Europeans represent to themselves their (usually subjugated) others, autoethnographic texts are those the others construct in response to or in dialogue with those metropolitan representations" (Pratt, 1992, p. 7). Such a perspective is useful in the context of cultural Otherization or the (mis)representation of the Other that we discussed in Chapters 2 and 7. It is also useful in the context of cultural globalization which, as we saw in Chapter 3, is seen by some as an imposition of the culture of the West on that of the rest.

By familiarizing our learners with the fundamentals of critical ethnography and autoethnography, and by giving them basic training in those methods of inquiry, we can help them share their individual perspectives with the teacher as well as other learners whose lived experiences differ from theirs. We can also engage them in the process of critical reflection and what the New London Group (1996, p. 87) has called *critical framing*, through which "learners can gain the necessary personal and theoretical distance from what they have learned, constructively critique it, [and] account for its cultural location." Investigative tools such as critical ethnography and autoethnography have the potential to give our learners the cultural consciousness necessary to challenge taken-for-granted notions about culture, and also the critical judgment needed to not readily accept the finality of cultural information presented in interested texts.

9.2.5. From Interested Text to Informed Context

If we are serious about developing global cultural consciousness in the learner, it is imperative that we pay greater attention to the designing of teaching materials that are genuinely authentic and appropriate. There are at least three reasons for such an imperative. First, not only textbooks have a ubiquitous presence in the language classroom, but they also seem to have a magical hold over teachers and students. Second, teachers "tend to pass on the cultural information included in the textbook, irrespective of whether or not this information is of interest to the pupils or has the potential of changing distorted pupil images" (Sercu, 2005, p. 165). Third, as has been widely acknowledged, textbooks are not a neutral medium (Byram, 1993; Cortazzi and Jin, 1999; Luke, 1989; Kramsch, 1993; Kumaravadivelu, 2003b). They reflect a particular worldview that is directly or indirectly imposed on teachers and learners. They carry hidden cultural values embedded in them in subtle ways. They are truly cultural Trojan horses.

Even materials and methods that are put together with great care and with good intentions often contain subtle messages that may lead to unintended outcomes. A recently published book (Brown and Eisterhold, 2004) meant for upper-division undergraduates and beginning graduate students who aspire to become schoolteachers explores, according to the blurb, "the interrelationships between language and culture that have the most significant implications for the classroom and for the global community." It has a short section on "Distinguishing Cultures." The authors, drawing from anthropological literature, briefly presented "dichotomous models, which distinguish two groups based on an opposition or difference between them" (p. 6)—dichotomies such as universalism-particularism, individualism-communitarianism, achieved status-ascribed status, etc. They are very careful in informing their students that "these constructs do not exist separately but instead combine with each other to describe the attributes and styles of different cultures" (p. 8), and that "these are not value judgments but descriptions" (p. 8).

Consider, however, what the students are asked to do in a follow-up exercise reproduced below:

Apply your knowledge

Look at the pairs of words below. Do you associate them with U.S. culture or with another culture or cultures? Do you associate the words with particular cultures? Work with a partner. Put the words into one of the two columns below:

individualism/community

fate/freedom

tradition/innovation

ascribed status/achieved status

inner directed/outer directed

cooperation/competition

idealistic/practical

religious/secular

hierarchy/equality

sequential time/synchronous time

U.S. culture	Another culture or cultures

(Brown and Eisterhold, 2004, p. 11)

It is not unreasonable to assume that most students, based on what they may have read or heard, will be driven by this exercise to put words such as individualism, freedom, innovation, achieved status, equality, etc., in the U.S. column, and the opposing words from each pair in the second column. In this context, it is worth remembering Allan Luke's (1989) cautionary note about what he called *closed texts*, that is, texts that present an unproblematic world that confirms or reinforces learners' preconceived notions of culture. Clearly, texts that are not properly selected and tasks that are not carefully designed have the potential to create and sustain the very kind of stereotypical cultural representations that educators wish to avoid.

There is a plethora of textbooks on culture that are available for language teachers and learners to choose from. Most of them offer basic information about the mainstream cultural practices contrasted with those of specific cultural groups with the view to helping learners understand cultural patterns (e.g., Oxford, 1995) or examine cultural contrasts (e.g., Shulman, 1998). There are others that focus mainly on the target language culture, such as the ones that seek to help learners discover America (e.g., Delk, 1997), or rethink America (e.g., Sokolik, 1999).

In order to create greater motivation in the language classroom, it has been suggested that teaching materials be designed in a "culturally neutral way so that they reflect the native culture of the learners, rather than of the target language's native speakers" (Allwright and Bailey, 1991, p. 159). In response, it has been argued that "the goal of cultural neutrality is profoundly misguided, representing a lack of understanding of the anthropological concept of culture. If material from the target language is stripped of its culture (even assuming such a possibility) and skewed toward the native language, the result is a conscious separation of language learning from culture learning" (Brody, 2003, pp. 44–45). Yet another pattern that has been found in the context of EFL teaching is textbooks that reflect the source culture, the target culture, or cultures set in countries where English is used as an international language (Cortazzi and Jin, 1999). More recent textbooks have included, perhaps as a response to globalization, a wide range of activities on global issues such as racism, human rights, AIDS, homelessness, environment, etc. (e.g., Sampedro and Hillyard, 2004).

Textbooks of the kind mentioned above, whether they focus on the culture of L1 or L2 community, or on global issues, may offer useful and usable information that has the potential to stretch the learner's general knowledge on cultural matters. But, in my view, they are only of limited relevance to culture teaching in the era of cultural globalization. What are sorely needed are materials that can deeply and critically engage the learners' minds about the intricacies of cultural realism that are shaping identity formation and identity politics in today's globalizing world (cf. Chapter 8). The task of promoting global cultural consciousness in the classroom can hardly be accomplished unless a concerted effort is made to use materials that will prompt learners to confront some of the taken-for-granted cultural beliefs about the Self and the Other. An important step in that direction has been taken by Adrian Holliday, Martin Hyde and John Kullman (2004), whose textbook focuses on three major cultural issues: identity, Otherization, and representation.

One of the compelling sources that can provide an endless supply of materials for instructional purposes is global communication networks such as the Internet. Here is a digital medium that is not only rich in informational resources but is also one that contemporary students are very familiar and comfortable with. It already appears to be leading the younger generation toward desired attitudinal changes necessary for developing global cultural consciousness. As Nicholas Negroponte of Massachusetts Institute of Technology has observed, "while the politicians struggle with the baggage of history, a new generation is emerging from the digital landscape free of many of the old prejudices. These kids are released from the limitations of geographic proximity as the sole basis of friendship, collaboration, play, and neighborhood. Digital technology can be a natural force drawing people into greater world harmony" (Negroponte, 1995, p. 230). Given the influence of such a force and the greater degree of cultural awareness it has generated, there are very few students today who will unhesitatingly and unquestioningly accept whatever is presented in interested textbooks or by interested teachers.

In addition to on-line newspapers and magazines, which often carry narratives of the practice of everyday cultural lives, students have access to encyclopedias as well as, if Google's announced plan materializes, to the rich resources of the libraries of the University of Michigan, Stanford University, and the University of California. A judicious collection, and proper use, of materials generated via the World Wide Web and gathered from targeted cultural communities around the world can easily help teachers and learners transcend the limitations of interested texts. By shifting from interested texts to informed contexts in which various shades of cultural meanings play out, they will be able to explore, in detail and from a critical perspective, topics that interest them, and gain a deeper understanding of how they are treated in different cultural contexts (see the next chapter for sample texts and tasks).

9.3. In Closing

In this chapter, I have attempted to present a set of organizing principles for teaching culture in the language classroom. I have argued for the proposition that the chief objective of culture teaching in this era of globalization must be the development of global cultural consciousness in our learners. I have also argued that any viable global cultural consciousness must be based on cultural realism, and on a critical understanding of one's own culture as well as on others'. Such a global cultural consciousness constructed on the twin pillars of rootedness and openness is likely to help our learners not only to cope with the chances and challenges posed by forces unleashed by the current phase of cultural globalization but also to utilize the learning opportunities they have created.

In order to begin to achieve the central goals and objectives, I outlined certain fundamental factors and pedagogic priorities that have the potential to function as organizing principles governing various operations of language education, including policies and planning, and methods and materials. I believe an educational agenda such as the one outlined above will effectively address the intricacies of cultural realism and help us foster global cultural consciousness in our learners. Whether the objectives and goals can be effectively achieved or not depends to a large extent on the instructional strategies used in the classroom.

CHAPTER 10

Cultural Realism and Instructional Strategies

A few years ago, I was teaching in the MATESOL program of a University in the southeastern part of the United States. In addition to courses in TESOL, the program at that time was offering classes for advanced international students aimed at improving their reading/writing skills. It was part of my administrative responsibility, as director of the program, to periodically review the teaching effectiveness of instructors teaching those classes. One day, at about the mid-point in a semester, I observed a class taught by Debbie (pseudonym). The class consisted of 20 students mostly from the Middle East and Southeast Asia. Debbie had put together a course pack of readings under the theme "American Heroes." It consisted of selected texts about outstanding American politicians, scientists, artists, and the like. The readings, I thought, were well chosen and well organized. On the day of my observation, Debbie chose to use a text called "Mission to the Moon." She started with pre-reading questions which elicited no more than monosyllabic responses from her students. She explained the heroic contribution made by Apollo 11 astronauts to advance the frontiers of knowledge. She then asked several comprehension questions to which her students, again reluctantly, answered in monosyllables. She continued in the same vein, and ended the class after giving a writing assignment. As pre-arranged, she left the classroom to enable me to talk to the students to get their perspective of classroom events.

As I was observing that class, it was fairly apparent to me that (a) this was a teacher-fronted class; (b) the students had not read the text; and, (c) they were not able to participate in class discussions, in spite of their advanced level proficiency in English. Given what I thought was a dismal lack of preparation and participation on the part of the students, I was wondering what Debbie could have done differently to make the class more productive. It was therefore with sympathy and support for her that I started talking to the students. I had barely finished introducing myself when several of them vociferously started complaining about Debbie. It was as if their silence in class was just a matter of the proverbial calm before the storm. They said that she was not at all helping them improve their reading/writing skills. "She is all the time talking about American culture and American heroes and nothing else," they complained bitterly. It soon became clear to me that the tension arose not because of the content of the text, but partly because of Debbie's method of teaching and partly because of the students' perception of her ethnocentricity. They felt that their identities were not being recognized and that their voices were not being respected. Their unwillingness to prepare for the class and to participate in class discussion appeared to me to be a form of passive resistance.

It is reasonable to assume that this episode or a variation of it may be playing out in many ESL classrooms. It emphasizes how "classrooms are decontextualised from the learners' point of view when the learners' feelings, their beliefs about what is important, their reasoning and their experience are not part of the assumed context of the teacher's communication" (Young, 1992, p. 59). It reminds us as TESOL professionals that classroom is the crucible where the prime elements of education—ideas and ideologies, policies and plans, materials and methods, teachers and the taught—all mix together to produce exclusive and at times explosive environments that might help or hinder the creation and utilization of learning opportunities. . . .

(Debbie) paid little or no respect for students' voice, and they responded with their own subversive tactics. I believed then as I do now that the tension that prevailed in her class has more to do with her instructional strategy than to do with the textual content. I subtly drew Debbie's attention to this in my feedback to her. I pointed out that the theme she selected for the course was well suited for an instructional strategy that not only respected her students' sociocultural sensibilities and their sociopolitical awareness but tapped their experiential knowledge as well. I suggested that, for instance, she could start a discussion about the concept of hero and hero-worship in different cultures represented in the class, ask her students to say who their heroes were and why they considered their heroes to be their heroes, compare their cultural concepts of hero and hero-worship with the American perspective represented in the prescribed texts. In other words, I suggested ways for Debbie to pay attention to the cultural capital students bring with them.

The above classroom episode was taken from one of my earlier writings (Kumaravadivelu, 1999, pp. 453–54, 480). It indicates how some of the established classroom strategies fail to use students as cultural informants and thus fail to capitalize on the cultural capital they bring to the classroom. They are clearly inadequate for the purpose of promoting global cultural consciousness in the learner. What we need are alternative classroom strategies that are consistent with the fundamental factors and pedagogic priorities discussed in the previous chapter.

One way of formulating effective classroom strategies for raising global cultural consciousness is to design reflective tasks and exploratory projects centered on familiar dichotomies and popular themes. Traditional anthropological models have given us cultural dichotomies such as individualism versus collectivism, innovation versus tradition, equality versus hierarchy, active involvement versus passive participation, critical evaluation versus uncritical acceptance—just to name a few. And these are normally presented within yet another overarching oppositional dichotomy—the West and the East, with the positive-sounding first word in each of the pairs normally associated with the West. Most of us are aware that these are overly simplistic conceptualizations and yet we continue to use them. Of course, we take care to use them with the usual caveats: these are tendencies not absolutes, these are valuable descriptions not value judgments, these are beginning gambits not endgames, etc. Yet these dichotomies have in them the power to (mis)lead people to an entrenched Us-versus-Them mindset. Therefore, making use of the same familiar dichotomies in order to help our learners critically interrogate their soundness should be a major part of our instructional strategy.

Yet another area of concentration is popular cultural themes that capture the imagination of the younger generation. Possible themes include sports, music, friendship, dating, rites of passage, family values, etc. A natural tendency on the part of students is to treat these themes as something they already know about. The task of the teacher is to show how these familiar themes have unfamiliar dimensions when looked at from a global perspective. In this regard, the advice given by Shirley Brice Heath and Leslie Mangiola (1991, p. 37) is worth listening to: "we want to urge teachers to make schooling equally strange for all students and thus to expand the ways of thinking, knowing and expressing knowledge of all students through incorporating many cultural tendencies." When teachers do that, they will be able to help their students accumulate valuable global cultural capital.

In this chapter I present samples of reflective tasks and exploratory projects that are aimed at helping learners develop global cultural consciousness. It can be seen that the possibilities for designing reflective tasks and exploratory projects are endless. There are, however, certain design criteria worth keeping in mind. They include (a) keeping the focus on familiar dichotomies, favorite stereotypes, and popular themes, (b) paying attention to the topics that really interest our students, (c) involving them in the selection of topics and in the collection of background information necessary for a fruitful discussion, and (d) making sure the activities bring out cross-cultural perspectives, and facilitate collegial and critical dialogue even if the dialogue is at times difficult and disturbing.

10.1. Reflective Tasks

The following tasks are no more than illustrative examples, and so teachers will find it necessary to modify/simplify them to suit the needs and wants of a given group of learners, keeping in mind their learners' cognitive, communicative, and linguistic abilities.

10.1.1. Dating Practices

In many parts of the world, young adults in schools, colleges, and workplaces begin searching for a romantic partner, and as a result they find themselves preoccupied with the thought of flirting and dating. How and why they choose a particular partner is influenced as much by personal preferences as by social sanctions. With the greater mobility the process of globalization has brought about, people have greater opportunities to come into contact with an array of cultures, races, and religions. Although students may be aware of certain common dating practices in their own cultural community, they may not have given much thought to the idea and practice of dating across cultures, races, and faiths. This reflective task is designed to assist them to articulate their cultural knowledge of dating, and also to improve their cross-cultural understanding. It is important to remember that the term *cultural* is used here to refer to cultural as well as subcultural characteristics.

> Step 1: Start by asking your learners what dating actually means to them. If necessary, prompt them with questions such as: What ex-

actly is the purpose of dating? Is it just a mechanism to flirt, to have fun, or to get to know a person better? Or . . .

Step 2: Form small groups and ask them to discuss what, according to them, are general norms they are supposed to be guided by when they are dating. How often do they follow these norms? What are the conditions that make them defy these norms? Have each group share their thoughts with the whole class.

Step 3: Again in small groups, ask them to talk about the desirability and the possibility of intragroup, intergroup, interracial and interfaith dating. Let them share their initial thoughts with the class.

Step 4: Focusing first on interracial dating, use an overhead projector (OHP) to show the following passage taken from Mukhopadhyay, Henze, and Moses (2007, p. 235):

In the U.S., the prevention of interracial dating, mating, and marriage was one way that the visible differences we call "race" were preserved, both by legal measures and by social pressures. By marrying and having children with someone of your own ethnic/racial group, it is likely that your children will look somewhat like you and your spouse, and you and your family will thereby fit the physical features that make people of your ethnic/racial group look similar. In this respect, we can say that culture creates race. In other words, the culture of mating and marriage, by imposing restrictions on whom you can mate with or marry, preserves a group's physical similarity and screens out people of a different ethnicity or race whose genes would introduce some minor and superficial physical differences.

After helping them with their reading comprehension, ask them whether they agree that cultures regulate dating, mating, and marriage. Do they agree with the reasons presented in the passage for opposition to interracial dating in the American context? Can they think of other possible reasons?

Step 5: Citing a number of studies, Mukhopadhyay, Henze, and Moses (2007, p. 240) point out that currently about 13 percent of U.S. marriages involve persons of different races. However, U.S. racial groups differ in their rates of intermarriage across racial lines. The authors go on to say (references deleted): "Some have a higher rate of intermarriage than others. For example, white and black people are the most likely to marry within their racial group, with about 93% of marriages being endogamous. Asians and Latinos marry within their racial group about 70% of the time, and

American Indians do so only 33% of the time. . . . Furthermore, when Asians and Latinos marry outside their group, they usually do so with whites. Trends among younger Asians and Latinos indicate that intermarriage rates are increasing."

Ask your students to think about possible reasons for this differential attitude toward interracial marriage among various ethnic communities in the United States. If necessary, hint at historical, sociological, political, or personal factors.

Step 6: Moving on to norms of dating, mating, and marriage among different religious communities, ask your learners to pick a particular religious community and search the Internet to find out about that particular community's views on the idea of dating/marriage in general and interfaith dating/marriage in particular. Let them bring the information to class to share with other students. Organize and moderate a class discussion on this topic.

Step 7: Depending on class level and interest, project the following extracts taken from Yvonne Haddad and Jane Smith (1996, pp. 22–24) about Islamic values about dating/marriage and how American Muslims practice them:

At the heart of the concerns is the matter of male-female relationships, before and during marriage. There is obviously much in the American culture that runs counter to traditional Muslim views of the propriety of these relationships. . . . The strictest interpretation of Islamic law would say that Muslim men and women (defined as postpuberty) should not be alone together with persons with whom marriage is a legal possibility for any reason. When a man and woman sit alone together, says an often quoted *hadith* attributed to the Prophet Muhammad, the third party is Satan. A Muslim boy interested in seeing a Muslim girl is allowed to visit her at her home, provided that other members of her family are present. . . . The presence of a family member is understood to preclude the possibility of any untoward behavior such as kissing or fondling. It goes without saying that any kind of explicit sexual encounter before marriage is strictly forbidden. . . . Some Arab Muslim communities have found that the mosque provides a helpful context in which to encourage young men and women to meet and socialize. There, under the watchful eyes of other members of the congregation, teens and young adults can interact with each other and enjoy the pleasures of sociability without explicitly countering the wishes of their parents or crossing the boundaries of culture or the strictures of the faith.

Ask your students to think and talk about the ways in which the American culture "runs counter to traditional Muslims views." Also, ask them whether or not the authors are using the term *American culture* in an unproblematic, totalizing way. Is *American culture* such a monolithic, homogeneous entity? Are there subcultural variations within *American culture* with regard to dating/marriage practices?

> Step 8: In continuing their discussion, Haddad and Smith (1996, p. 23) quote a Lebanese father who has lived in America for several decades: "dating is not our way of life. The way it is done is ridiculous. I see some people who date one person for three days, then drop them. . . . I am not against finding yourself a partner, but I am against the way they abuse this 'dating.' I don't have as much problem with boys dating girls as I do with girls dating."

Ask your students to discuss whether they think there is room for "abuse" in dating practices. Encourage them to talk about what constitutes abuse and how they address it.

> Step 9: Draw your students' attention to the Lebanese father's statement "I don't have as much problem with boys dating girls as I do with girls dating." What do they (particularly your female students) think about it? You may also wish to help them connect this statement to larger gender issues within a society.

> Step 10: Continuing your focus on the issue of gender in the specific context of dating, project the following extracts from a news item by the United Press International dated March 14, 2003. It was titled "2000 Census Shows Interracial Marriage Gender Gaps Remain Large":

The Census Bureau confirmed black women's complaints that white women were more likely to marry black men than white men were to marry black women. In 2000, African-American men had white wives 2.65 times more often than black women had white husbands. In other words, in 73 percent of black-white couples, the husband was black and wife was white. . . .

Like most guys, Asian-American men are fairly reticent about admitting any frustrations in the mating game. But the news for them was even worse. Asian women had white husbands 3.08 times more often than Asian men had white wives. That means 75 percent of white-Asian couples featured a white husband and Asian wife. . . .

The inevitable flip side of the lack of interracial marital opportunities felt by black women and Asian men is that black men and Asian women find themselves more in demand as spouses.

Again, ask your students to discuss probable causes for this gender disparity in American interracial relations, and ask them what they think about it.

Step 11: Project the following text (or make hard copies to distribute) taken from on-line BBC News (dated December 26, 2005) written by David Willey, BBC correspondent in Rome:

Cardinals Issue Marriage Warning

A number of Catholic cardinals have warned Italian women against mixed marriages with the rising number of Muslims in the country.

Church officials say that as Italy's Muslim population touches the one million mark, some 20,000 mixed marriages took place this year alone.

That is an increase of around 10% on last year.

The Catholic Church's official position is to encourage dialogue between Rome and other religions, including Islam.

The late Pope John Paul II was the first pope in history to pray in a mosque, when he visited Damascus. His successor, Benedict XVI, has insisted that he is also keen to promote religious and cultural dialogue with the Islamic world.

But two documents published in Rome have called for extreme caution by Catholic women contemplating marriage to a Muslim.

Criticism

In one, issued by the Vatican last year, a Vatican cardinal, Stephen Hamao, wrote about what he called the "bitter experiences" that European women have had in marrying Muslims. The difficulties are compounded if the couple then goes to live in a Muslim country, the cardinal warned.

The tone was unusually strong in an age when interfaith dialogue seems the predominant buzz word. Then last month, Cardinal Ruini, the head of the Italian bishops, added his voice.

In addition to the problems any couple faces setting up a family, he said, Catholics marrying Muslims have to reckon with extra difficulties arising from deep cultural differences. Some Muslim scholars have expressed surprise at the Vatican documents and Italian liberal groups have also criticised them.

The passage raises several issues that can be used to critically engage the minds of your students. For instance, why do they think that women are "warned against mixed marriages" and not men? What, in the context of interfaith dating/marriage, might be the "difficulties arising from deep cultural differences"? How does a warning like this contribute to the overall objective of promoting "religious and cultural dialogue"? Pick any of these or other related questions depending on the level and interests of your students.

> Step 12: Recently, Larissa Remennick of Bar-Ilan University in Israel conducted a study about the cross-cultural dating patterns on an Israeli campus involving Russian immigrants and Israeli natives, all of whom, incidentally, belong to the same religious faith. Using an OHP, project the following abstract from her research paper (Remennick, 2005):

> This study focused on reported dating patterns between Israeli-born and immigrant students from the former Soviet Union. Earlier survey findings indicated that twice as many Russian immigrant women reported having had a romantic relationship with an Israeli-born partner than did their male counterparts. Six focus groups were conducted on two Israeli campuses with third-year BA students. Results suggest that Russian women are "popular" in part because of their perceived compliance with gender role expectations (i.e., passive and accepting), whereas Russian men are not as popular precisely for the same reason (i.e., adhering to the traditional masculine role in courtship). Across participants, however, those who were most prone to dating Israeli peers were those who felt more integrated and secure in Israeli society, had better Hebrew proficiency, and reported having a greater number of same-sex Israeli-born friends.

In light of the earlier student discussion about gender issues in relation to dating/marriage, ask them what they think about the findings of this study. Let them also discuss whether the findings can explain any aspect of dating they are familiar with.

> Step 13: At the end of this series of activities, give them a writing assignment in which they pull together various strands of thought and write a critical report or a short essay on the topic. Ask them to include a brief narrative on how the class discussions and the activities did (or did not) help them enhance their understanding of the topic. Also, encourage them to reflect on any new cultural understanding that may have led them to a change in their own attitude toward a particular cultural belief/practice.

10.1.2. Musical Border Crossings

Music of one kind or another captures the imagination of people everywhere. Students are no exception. Many of them walk around campus unfailingly plugged into their iPods—when they are not using their cell phones, that is. They all have their favorite musicians, yet they may not be fully aware of the cross-cultural nature of the music they typically play. This task is designed to help them reflect on it.

Step 1: Start by asking your students who their favorite musicians/ songs are, and why they like them.

Step 2: In the fall of 2001, *Time* magazine published a special thematic issue titled "Music Goes Global." The reference is not merely to the commercial nature of the transnational music industry but, more importantly, to the global flavor of modern music—how melodies mix and beats blend. The thematic issue contains a four-page spread that describes border crossings in world music. If you can, take a look at this issue; you may wish to use some of the colorful pictures in class. Write "Music Goes Global" on the board and ask your students what it means to them, without prompting them in any particular direction. Let the students exchange their views on it.

Step 3: Either copy on the blackboard, or display using an OHP, the following extract from the *Time* editorial, which begins:

Globalization may be a fighting word in politics and business, but in the realm of music it has a nice ring to it—and a funky beat, and a tantalizing groove. Today musicians and listeners the world over are plugged into one another via the Internet, TV and ubiquitous recordings. The result is a vast electronic bazaar through which South African *kwaito* music can make pulses pound in Sweden or Brazilian post-mambo can set feet dancing in Tokyo. Cultures are borrowing the sounds of other cultures, creating vibrant hybrids that are then instantly disseminated around the globe to begin the blending process all over again [*Time*, Fall 2001, p. 2].

After helping them with any difficult vocabulary, ask them to think and talk about "cultures borrowing the sounds of other cultures." What do they know about it?

Step 4: Pursue their responses. If they are unable to come up with specific examples, prompt them with some information you may have collected, for instance, how Paul Simon mixed the rhythms and spirited harmonies of South African music in his *Graceland* album, which won the 1986 Grammy award for best album, or how Madonna or Britney Spears mix and blend global flavors to great acclaim from their fans.

Step 5: Next, write "Fusion Music" on the board. Ask your students what this is all about. They may not know much about it. Start with the meaning of the word *fusion*. Expand on what they may have to say about fusion music. Tell them how it is an artistically stimulating music created by integrating ideas from more than one musical tradition. In the American musical context, the term *fusion* was used in the 1950s and 1960s to describe the melding of jazz with rock. Now it stands for cross-cultural musical varieties that range from an easy blend of pop music with world music to a synthesis of seemingly irreconcilable traditions, such as the *melody* of Indian classical music and the *harmony* of Western classical music, thus producing a new music genre called *melharmony*.

Step 6: As an out-of-class activity, have your students surf the Internet and collect more information about fusion music (when I did a Google search of "fusion music" in January 2006 I came up with about 13,826,000 results). Ask them to prepare a brief write-up.

Step 7: Continuing their work from the previous step, ask your students to narrow their search to one musician/singer who has successfully drawn ideas from various cultural traditions. They should collect details of how this particular individual (or a group) chose and synthesized different musical traditions, etc. Encourage them to reflect on what has been the final product of such a synthesis, and how this may or may not contribute to cross-cultural understanding.

Step 8: In class, form small groups and allow the students to share the information and views with other group members, and later with the whole class.

Step 9: Moderate a discussion in class in which you try to help your students talk about what is cultural and what is cross-cultural about music in general and fusion music in particular, and what cultural transformation may take place because of such creative endeavors of global scale.

10.1.3. Collective Individual

This task is aimed at prompting learners to think critically about one of the enduring cultural dichotomies: Individualism versus collectivism.

Step 1: Write the terms *individualism* and *collectivism* on the board and ask students to think about them and share their thoughts with the class. Encourage them to give specific examples to substantiate what they may have to say.

Step 2: Drawing from introductory anthropological literature or from any search engine, gather and present brief background information. Or, use my rendering by typing the following text on a transparency and display it using an OHP. Ask your students to read it carefully.

According to sociologist Harry Triandis (1995), collectivism refers to a social pattern consisting of closely linked individuals who see themselves as parts of one or more collectives such as family, tribe, or nation. The individuals are primarily motivated by the norms of, and duties imposed by, those collectives. They are willing to subordinate their own personal interests in order to emphasize their connectedness to members of these collectives. Individualism, on the other hand, refers to a social pattern that consists of loosely linked individuals who view themselves as independent of collectives. They are primarily motivated by their own preferences, needs, and rights, and give priority to their personal goals over the goals of others in the collectives.

Such a dichotomous model has led to the traditional belief that people in a particular society are uniformly individualistic or uniformly collectivistic, in spite of the fact that social scientists have cautioned against it. It has also given rise to the impression that collectivism is an Eastern cultural trait and individualism a Western cultural trait. However, empirical research shows that individualistic and collectivistic tendencies co-exist within individuals and cultures (e.g., Realo, 2003). Furthermore, it has been shown that, within the same cultural community, women as primary caregivers tend to be more collectivistic than men, who tend to be more individualistic (Triandis, 1995).

Step 3: Help your learners comprehend the text first. Then, form small groups and have the group members discuss the text. Encourage them to draw from their own personal experience. If necessary, give the following two examples from Triandis (1995) along with my paraphrase of his explanation:

(a) In India, a senior engineer is asked to move to New York, at a salary that is twenty-five times his salary in New Delhi, but he declines the opportunity.

(b) In California, a senior engineer is asked to move to New York, at a salary that is 50 percent higher than his salary in Los Angeles, and he accepts.

According to Triandis, the Indian engineer, the product of a collectivistic society, must stay with his aging parents to attend to their needs, while the American engineer, the product of an individualistic society, would place his parents in a nursing home.

Encourage learners to think about whether these are really comparable situations and whether they truly represent the contrasting concept assigned to them. How does this, for instance, explain the predominance of Indian software engineers in the IT (information technology) industry in California's Silicon Valley?

Step 4: Ask one member from each group to share the group's views with the class, followed by class discussion.

Step 5: Next, use an OHP to show the students the following text. Ask your students to read it carefully. The text is taken from the work of Aihwa Ong, a professor at the University of California, Berkeley. She has studied the ethnic Chinese community from Hong Kong and Southeast Asia who have parked their families in safe havens in Australia, Canada, the United States, and Great Britain. Her description of Chinese professionals shows the limits of closely linking the familial, collective cultural trait with the Asian community. She pointed out that Hong Kong newspapers call the traveling Chinese professionals *astronauts*, whose parents live in Hong Kong while their spouses and children are located in Australia, Canada, or the United States.

Presenting the above as background information, ask the students to read the following extracts from Ong (1998, pp. 149–50):

The astronaut as a trope of Chinese postmodern displacement also expresses the costs of the flexible accumulation logic and the toil it takes on an overly flexible family system. The astronaut wife in the United States is euphemistically referred to as "inner beauty" (*neizaimei*), a term that suggests two other meanings for "inner person," that is, "wife" (*neiren*) as well as "my wife in the Beautiful Country (i.e., America)" (*neiren zai Meiguo*). Wives thus localized to manage suburban homes and take care of the children—lessons in ballet, classical music, Chinese language—sarcastically refer to themselves as "widows" (and computer widows), expressing their feeling that family life is now thoroughly mediated and fragmented by the technology of travel and business. . . .

In the Bay Area, wives bored by being "imprisoned" in America parlay their well-honed sense of real estate property into a business sideline. Down the peninsula, the majority of real estate agents are immigrant Chinese women selling expensive homes to other newly arrived widows. Here also, flexibility reigns as wives keep trading up their own homes in the hot residential market. . . .

In some cases, the flexible logic deprives children of both parents. The teenagers dropped off in Southern California suburbs by their Hong Kong and Taiwan parents are referred to as "parachute kids." One such child left to fend for herself and her brother refers to her father as the "ATM machine," because he issues money but little else from some extraterrestrial space.

Step 6: Again, help the students understand the text. There are some vocabulary items that may be unfamiliar to them. Then, form small groups and have the group members discuss the text. Specifically, ask them to think about how they would characterize the practice followed by Chinese professionals and their wives in terms of collectivistic responsibilities of raising a family normally associated with Asian cultures. Does the individualism/collectivism dichotomy explain the situation narrated by Ong?

Step 7: Assign homework appropriate to the level of your students. For instance, ask them to talk to their parents or grandparents to find out whether they view themselves as individualistic or collectivistic, or under what circumstances would they exhibit traits of individualism or collectivism. You may also advise them to go to a search engine such as Google, enter "individualism, collectivism," and gather information about how these twin notions play out in a couple of other foreign cultural communities. Ask them to write a brief report and bring it to class. Tell them not to ignore factors such as age, gender, class, educational status, etc.

Step 8: Have a select number of students read their reports to the class, followed by Q&A.

Step 9: Finally, ask them to what extent this assignment has or has not helped them to increase their understanding of the concepts of individualism/collectivism or to change their initial views on these concepts.

The three reflective tasks provide illustrative examples of brief classroom activities that can easily be modified to suit the cognitive, communicative, and linguistic level of a given group of students. The following exploratory projects are meant to be extended investigative tasks that can be spread out over a semester or done as a term project.

10.2. Exploratory Projects

Like the reflective tasks, the following projects are also given as illustrative examples. Teachers need to adapt them to make them appropriate for their learners.

10.2.1. *Know Thyself*

This project is designed as an exercise in autoethnography. Briefly explain to your learners what autoethnography is (see Chapter 9). Let them know that the project objective is to help them explore a slice of their own cultural self, and to write a critical account of the process of their identity formation with regard to that particular autobiographical fragment. Here is a project proposal; adapt it to suit the demands of your class.

> Step 1: Give a brief rationale for the study informing your students how we all have multiple identities, how we play multiple roles in the practice of our daily life, how we all belong to several groups at the same time, and how our membership in each group gives us a particular identity. And then provide a detailed, properly sequenced set of guidelines such as the following (addressed to the students):
>
> (a) Think of any new identities you may have taken on recently: as a member of a school club, a fraternity or sorority, a social association, a sports team, a recreational club, a volunteer organization, a religious sect, a political party, and so on. For the purpose of this study, select any one group you belong to.
>
> (b) Each group has its own subculture. That is, each group has members who share certain beliefs and values, goals, and activities. Describe, with specific examples, the subculture of the group you selected.
>
> (c) Although all the members of a group have something in common, they are not really identical human beings. Think about, and write down, how you are similar to as well as different from other members of the group. You might, for instance, wish to choose one other member of your group and compare and contrast yourself with that person in terms of group behavior, attitude, interest, and participation.
>
> (d) What do you ascribe the identified similarities and differences to—age, gender, class, race, or anything else? Explain with specific examples.
>
> (e) How has your membership in that group shaped you as an individual? How has it affected your sense of your Self? Consider the changes you may have made to your own beliefs, attitudes, appearances, and activities because of your association with this group.
>
> (f) What personal and psychological aspects of your identity have you been willing/able to change in order to fit in with that group? In other words, what aspect of your identity is rooted in tradition

and therefore relatively fixed, and what aspect is open to change and therefore flexible?

(g) What larger sociocultural factors or forces (your family, your ethnic community, etc.) influenced your identity formation in one way or another? Has there been any tension between your own personality and these forces?

(h) Now, using a first-person narrative style, write an analytical, autoethnographic account of yourself. Draw true episodes and examples from your life. You may also include information about the group gathered through research. Your objective here is to present yourself to an outsider who is not a member of your group, explaining how you see yourself and others in relation to the subculture of the group you selected. Feel free to share with your reader any cultural conflicts you may have gone through and any cultural understanding you may have gained because of this process of identity formation and cultural transformation.

Step 2: You (i.e., the teacher) may employ some parts of this project as in-class activity. At appropriate stages, you may form small groups and have each group discuss the experience of other classmates. At the end of the project, you may consider asking a select number of students to give a brief oral presentation followed by class discussion.

10.2.2. Know Thy Neighbor

This is an exercise in critical ethnography. The primary aim of this project is to give advanced learners hands-on experience in collecting, analyzing, and interpreting ethnographic data. This is especially designed for those students who live amid immigrant populations. However, the project may be adapted for use with students who live in nonimmigrant cultural contact zones, that is, in a culturally and religiously pluralistic society. They can focus on subcultural issues. Adapt the points of inquiry in order to address the needs of a given group of learners. It may be beneficial to allow students to do the project in pairs, if they wish.

Step 1: Provide a brief rationale for the study. Here are some cues: because of economic globalization, there has been a significant degree of mobility among the people of different countries. Many of them immigrate to other countries (or to other parts of their own country) on a permanent basis or live there for a considerable period of time before returning to their homeland. Many come from countries where cultural, social, religious practices and value systems are very different from those of their adopted land. In order to lead a successful life in the new land, they have to make several cultural adjustments, both individually and collectively. This project focuses on the kinds of cultural adjustments an individual or a family makes in their adopted land.

Step 2: Give your students a detailed set of procedures to follow. Here again is a possible version (items a–c are addressed to students). Modify it to suit your needs:

(a) Select an individual or a family you know (or people of different cultural/religious background living in your neighborhood). The family members or individuals you choose to study are called *subjects*. Your subjects must (i) belong to an ethnic or religious community that is different from yours; (ii) have immigrated to their adopted land and be living there for at least five years; and (iii) intend to work and live in the country for an extended period, if not permanently.

(b) Plan to have an extended conversation/interview with your subjects (it may take more than one session). If that is not feasible, try to elicit information through a series of e-mails or phone calls. It is a good idea to talk to members of a family belonging to different generations (e.g., grandparents, parents, children). Plan also to have a follow-up session to seek clarification after your initial analysis of data, if necessary. With the permission of your subjects, you may also audio- (or video-) tape the conversation.

(c) Frame specific questions in order to elicit the following information from your subjects:

- Are there any native (C1) cultural beliefs and practices that they value so much that they would steadfastly cling to them? If so, what and why?

- Are there any native (C1) cultural beliefs and practices they would be willing to give up? If so, what and why?

- Are there any nonnative (C2, C3, C4 . . .) cultural beliefs and practices they would be willing to adopt fully without significant modification? If so, what and why?

- Are there any nonnative (C2, C3, C4 . . .) cultural beliefs and practices they would be willing to adapt and modify to suit their C1 cultural value system? If so, what and why?

- Are there any nonnative (C2, C3, C4 . . .) cultural beliefs and practices that they find most difficult/easiest to adjust to? If so, what and why?

- Ask any follow-up question(s) arising from their answers.

Step 3: Once the data collection is over, ask your students to analyze the data and write up their findings, making references to the relevant readings they may have done for your class and to any independent study they may have done. Encourage them to bring out in their report the personal and psychological tensions and conflicts that their subjects may have encountered on their way to cultural adjustment.

Step 4: Ask them to prepare to give an oral report to class, briefly explaining their project findings and what they may have learned from doing the project. If they themselves have gone through the process of cultural adjustment, let them offer a comparative perspective incorporating their experiences where appropriate.

Step 5: Conduct a class discussion with a view to bringing out the complex nature of cultural adjustment and identity formation.

10.3. In Closing

This chapter has been concerned with specific instructional strategies that might help language educators design their own classroom activities to help raise global cultural consciousness in their learners. The strategies presented in the form of reflective tasks and exploratory projects are consistent with the organizing principles discussed in the previous chapter. I suggested that one way of creating and sustaining student interest and at the same time promoting global cultural consciousness in them is to design tasks and projects centered on familiar dichotomies and popular themes. Over time, teachers should be able to design, test, revise, and build a bank of tasks and projects that they can use as source materials.

An understanding of global cultural perspectives will, hopefully, contribute not only to dispel cultural stereotypes but also to enhance the chances of communicating with the Other in a meaningful way. Given the importance of intercultural communication in this globalized world, I turn to the topic in the next chapter.

CHAPTER 11

Cultural Realism and Intercultural Communication

Body Ritual Among the Nacirema

HORACE MINER

University of Michigan

The anthropologist has become so familiar with the diversity of ways in which different peoples behave in similar situations that he is not apt to be surprised by even the most exotic customs. In fact, if all of the logically possible combinations of behavior have not been found somewhere in the world, he is apt to suspect that they must be present in some yet undescribed tribe. This point, has, in fact, been expressed with respect to clan organization by Murdock (1949:71). In this light, the magical beliefs and practices of the Nacirema present such unusual aspects that it seems desirable to describe them as an example of the extremes to which human behavior can go. . . .

Professor Linton first brought the ritual of the Nacirema to the attention of anthropologists twenty years ago (1936:326), but the culture of this people is still very poorly understood. . . .

Nacirema culture is characterized by a highly developed market economy which has evolved in a rich natural habitat. While much of the people's time is devoted to economic pursuits, a large part of the fruits of these labors and a considerable portion of the day are spent in ritual activity. The focus of this activity is the human body. . . .

The fundamental belief underlying the whole system appears to be that the human body is ugly and that its natural tendency is to debility and disease. Incarcerated in such a body, man's only hope is to avert these characteristics through the use of the powerful influences of ritual and ceremony. Every household has one or more shrines devoted to this purpose. The more powerful individuals in the society have several shrines in their houses and, in fact, the opulence of a house is often referred to in terms of the number of such ritual centers it possesses. . . .

While each family has at least one such shrine, the rituals associated with it are not family ceremonies but are private and secret. The rites are normally only discussed with children, and then only during the period when they are being initiated into these mysteries. I was able, however, to establish sufficient rapport with the natives to examine these shrines and to have the rituals described to me.

The focal point of the shrine is a box or chest which is built into the wall. In this chest are kept the many charms and magical potions without which no native believes he could live. The preparations are secured from a variety of specialized practitioners. The most powerful of these are medicine men, whose assistance must be rewarded with substantial gifts. . . .

Beneath the charm-box is small font. Each day every member of the family, in succession, enters the shrine room, bows his head before the charm-box, mingles different sorts of holy water in the font, and proceeds with a brief rite of ablution. The holy waters are secured from the Water Temple of the community, where the priests conduct elaborate ceremonies to make liquid ritually pure.

In the hierarchy of magical practitioners, and below the medicine men in prestige, are specialists whose designation is best translated "holy-mouth-men." The Nacirema have an almost pathological horror of and fascination with the mouth, the condition of which is believed to have a supernatural influence on all social relationships. Were it not for the rituals of the mouth, they believe that their teeth would fall out, their gums bleed, their jaws shrink, their friends desert them, and their lovers reject them. . . .

The daily body ritual performed by everyone includes a mouth-rite. Despite the fact that these people are so punctilious about care of the mouth, this rite involves a practice which strikes the uninitiated stranger as revolting. It was reported to me that that ritual consists of inserting a small bundle of hog hairs into the mouth, along with certain magical powders, and then moving the bundle in a highly formalized series of gestures.

In addition to the private mouth-rite, the people seek out a holy-mouth-man once or twice a year. These practitioners have an impressive set of paraphernalia, consisting of a variety of augers, awls, probes, and prods. The use of these objects in the exorcism of the evils of the mouth involves almost unbelievable ritual torture of the client. The holy-mouth-man opens the client's mouth and, using the above mentioned tools, enlarges any holes which decay may have created in the teeth. Magical materials are put into these holes. If there are naturally occurring holes in the teeth, large sections of one or more teeth are gouged out so that the supernatural substance can be applied. In the client's view, the purpose of these ministrations is to arrest decay and to draw friends. The extremely sacred and traditional character of the rite is evident in the fact that the natives return to the holy-mouth-men year and after year, despite the fact that their teeth continue to decay.

It is to be hoped that, when a thorough study of the Nacirema is made, there will be careful inquiry into the personality structure of these people.

Given above are excerpts (pp. 503–7) from an article written by Horace Miner, who was professor of sociology and anthropology at the University of Michigan. It was published in 1956 in *American Anthropologist*, a reputed journal of the American Anthropological Association. In this article, Miner reported on a study of the "magic-ridden" tribe of "Nacirema" to show "the extremes to which human behavior can go." In accordance with the traditional anthropological research paradigm, he established "sufficient rapport with the natives" in order to have their rituals described to him. He found that, among other behavioral patterns, the natives "have an almost pathological horror of and fascination with the mouth" which "strikes the uninitiated stranger as revolting."

Miner presented this paper as a scholarly work providing anthropological evidence, citing dates and page numbers of his sources, and attaching a list of the references cited. However, he was not really describing the daily rituals of any exotic tribal community that he visited and studied. He was, in fact, talking about the American people. Nacirema is "American" spelled backward. He wrote this tongue-in-cheek parody to demonstrate how normal activities such as tooth-brushing or visiting the dentist can be seen as an exotic, even "revolting," behavior by "the uninitiated stranger." In addition, he was also presenting a not so subtle critique of the traditional anthropological and sociological approaches to intercultural understanding and intercultural communication.

The message is clear: interpreting the beliefs and practices of another cultural community from the perspective of one's own is bound to result in misunderstanding and miscommunication. Successful intercultural communication is premised upon a true understanding of the cultural communities in contact. This is even more so in these days of cultural globalization when cultural identity—national or individual—is becoming ever so complex. In this chapter, I start with a discussion on the traditional approaches to intercultural communication, followed by a presentation of post-structural/postcolonial perspectives. I will then consider the global imperatives that need to be taken into account for studying effective intercultural communication. Finally, I will outline certain educational possibilities that might open up if we broaden the scope of intercultural communication.

11.1. Traditional Approaches

Intercultural communication is a fairly new field of academic activity. It was born from the rubble of World War II when, as the leader of the winning Allied forces, the United States found its international diplomacy, commerce, and trade expand to unprecedented heights. Government officials, diplomats, business leaders, and other Americans sent to work overseas realized that their lack of knowledge of foreigners' cultural practices and communication styles impeded their effective functioning. To address this problem, Congress passed the Foreign Service Act in 1946, which facilitated the establishment of the Foreign Service Institute. The Institute hired a team of anthropologists, psychologists, and linguists to develop methods and materials for training government officials in intercultural communication. It was this team that laid the foundation for the field of intercultural communication, thus making the field a truly American invention.

Among the scholars the Institute hired were anthropologist Edward Hall and linguist George Trager. Drawing freely from their respective fields, they jointly produced a Foreign Service Institute training manual titled *The Analysis of Culture* (Hall and Trager, 1953). In it, they presented a matrix for mapping a foreign culture along certain dimensions the most important of which was communication, both verbal and nonverbal. A central anthropological linguistic concept that guided their work was the Sapir-Whorf hypothesis, which posited a close connection between language and reality, between language and cultural thought patterns (see Chapter 2). They also believed that since cultures are created and maintained mainly through language, language has an inherent capacity to provide a window into cultures, and therefore it should be possible to draw useful insights into intercultural communication by analyzing and understanding language communication. To a large extent, the importance they gave to the role of language in general and to the Sapir-Whorf hypothesis in particular continues to characterize the field of intercultural communication even today.

Hall expanded the initial insights presented in the training manual and wrote a book called *The Silent Language* (1959). This seminal work became so influential that it is considered to be "the founding document in the new field of intercultural communication" (Rogers, Hart, and Miike, 2002, p. 11). In it, he focused on interpersonal communication among people of different cultural backgrounds. Declaring unequivocally that "culture is communication and communication is culture" (Hall, 1959, p. 186), he highlighted the importance of factors such as personal space and the sense of time, and how they affect intercultural communication. He also emphasized nonverbal communication, such as gestures, and their role in intercultural understanding. In this and other works, he posited several dichotomous cultural parameters and drew sharp distinctions between, for instance, *low-context* societies (e.g., the United States), where communication is premised upon explicit verbal statements, and *high-context* societies (e.g., Japan), where communication relies crucially on nonverbal, contextual cues or even on silence; and, between *polychronic* cultures (e.g., west Asia), where time is conceptualized as flexible and circular, prompting individuals to attend to multiple events and tasks simultaneously, and *monochronic* cultures (e.g., the United States), where time is considered fixed and linear, encouraging individuals to handle events and tasks sequentially and on time.

Hall's emphasis on interpersonal communication, including nonverbal communication, was in part necessitated by his chief task of helping Foreign Service officers "to go overseas and get results" (Hall, 1959, p. 35). He realized that "what was needed was something bold and new, and not more of the same old history, economics, and politics" (p. 36). Therefore, he departed from the mainstream anthropological approach, which focused primarily on a culture's broader social, political, and religious systems, and instead concentrated on the microlevel dynamics of face-to-face interaction between individuals, such as tone of voice, gestures, time and spatial relationships, etc. Intercultural training based on such interpersonal factors helped the members of the Diplomatic Corps prepare to face their communicational challenges in alien nations.

Apart from the Diplomatic Corps, yet another government agency that found the studies on intercultural communication useful was the Peace Corps. Founded in 1961 by the Kennedy administration, the Peace Corps aimed at sending American volunteers to work with local communities in several newly independent, developing countries. From time to time the agency produced and updated manuals such as *Guidelines for Peace Corps Cross-Cultural Training* (Wright and Hammons, 1970), *Cross-Cultural Training for Peace Corps Volunteers* (Edwards and McCaffery, 1981), and *Culture Matters: The Peace Corps Cross-Cultural Workbook* (Storti and Bennhold-Samaan, 1997). Using mainly these materials, the agency trained, by the year 2003, an estimated 168,000 Americans, who served in more than 136 countries in Asia, Africa, Latin America, and eastern Europe. All these training manuals unfailingly bear the stamp of Hall's seminal work.

Insights derived from the studies on interpersonal communication across cultures conducted in the context of international diplomacy were also found to be immensely useful by the corporate sector. When trade and commerce with other countries expanded after the Second World War, the American business community found it necessary to train its overseas employees in several dimensions of intercultural communication, including negotiating, socializing, identifying communication breakdowns, avoiding cross-cultural misunderstanding, keeping proper eye contact and physical distance, minding body language and politeness formulas, and so on. Particular importance was given to American and Japanese intercultural communication because of extensive trade and personnel exchanges between the two largest economies of the world. As a result, "today there are more studies of Japanese/American communication than of intercultural communication between any two other cultures" (Rogers, Hart, and Miike, 2002, p. 15). These studies, following the lead given by Hall, stressed the American/Japanese cultural differences such as individualism/collectivism, and low-context/high-context behaviors and their impact on intercultural communication. Also stressed were nonverbal communication patterns such as hierarchy-based bowing practices, facial expressions, and physical touching, which were considered to differentiate the two cultures in contact.

In emphasizing the microlevel behaviors of face-to-face interactions between people of different cultures, Hall and other interculturalists departed significantly from traditional anthropological interests, and thus introduced a new and important component to the study of intercultural communication. But, in doing so, they generally adhered to the popular "cultural difference" paradigm, which directed anthropologists' attention to variations in cultural beliefs and practices, instead of an earlier "cultural deprivation" paradigm, which suggested that other cultures are somehow deficient and, therefore, disadvantaged and underdeveloped. Like other anthropologists, they too followed an ethnographic investigative technique that consisted mainly of participant observation, in which they systematically and directly observed cultural behaviors, and also of interviews with local cultural informants. Clearly, such a technique put a premium on the interculturalists' personal observation as well as on their critical interpretation of what they heard, observed, or experienced. The resulting accounts—mostly subjective and descriptive in nature—were then deemed to be the cultural construct of a particular cultural community.

During the 1980s, an empirical dimension was introduced to intercultural communication studies by Geert Hofstede, a social psychologist from the Netherlands. Using statistically oriented quantitative methods, he conducted a factor analysis of cultural values contained in survey responses from more than 116,000 IBM employees in forty countries and reported his findings in his influential book *Culture's Consequences* (Hofstede, 1980). Based on this empirical study, he identified four dimensions of corporate culture: (a) inequality acceptance, that is, how people accept authority embedded in hierarchical relationships, (b) uncertainty avoidance, that is, how people feel threatened by, and therefore avoid, ambiguity, (c) social role, that is, how the gendered role relationship between men and women is prevalent in the corporate sector, and (d) individualism versus collectivism, that is, how individuals relate to the company they work for or the community they belong to. Hofstede unhesitatingly extended these corporate cultural behaviors to larger society as well.

The fact that the interculturalists profiled intercultural communication differences generated out of data collected from governmental and corporate players and overgeneralized them to the entire population has resulted in justifiable criticism (see Martin and Nakayama, 2000, for a review). Even in cases where they approached cultural informants from nongovernment and noncorporate sources, the limited number of samples and the limited experience of informants responding to interview questions or to survey questionnaires easily rendered the findings unrepresentative of the cultures selected for study (Chuang, 2003; Miyahara, 2000). Moreover, the interculturalists also paid scant respect to the fact that human interaction, particularly intercultural interaction, embedded as it is in multiple layers across space and time, is a complex, ongoing process that cannot be reduced to expedient labels and convenient dichotomies. It cannot be captured in snapshots.

More than the methodological concerns, a crucial conceptual drawback of the intercultural communication studies popularized by Hall, Hofstede, and others is that it has been very much conditioned by Western perceptions of non-Western cultures. As George Renwick (2004, p. 450) has recently remarked: "most of the theorists we have drawn on are Western. This can be illuminating, of course, but it is certainly limited and can be limiting." It *is* limiting because most interculturalists treated European patterns of social and corporate communication styles as the norms against which those of other cultures were studied, analyzed, described, and judged. In doing so, they were following a long-cherished sociological and anthropological tradition in which, as Oxford University cultural critic Robert Young (1995, p. 94) pointed out, "civilization and culture were the names for the standard of measurement in the hierarchy of values through which European culture defined itself by placing itself at the top of a scale against which all other societies or groups within a society, were judged." Consequently, interculturalists seldom recognized that certain communication behavioral patterns of other, particularly Asian, cultures may not be satisfactorily explained by Western theories (Xiaoge, 2000). But still they persisted with a solely Western interpretation of Eastern cultures. This has led to the charge that the field of intercultural communication is beset by Eurocentrism.

Several Asian scholars have asserted that, because of widespread Eurocentrism, the intercultural field remains anything but *intercultural* (e.g., Chuang, 2003; Dissanayake, ed., 1988; Kim, 2002; Miike, 2003; Starosta and Chen, eds., 2003). In a comprehensive review, Yoshitaka Miike (2003, p. 244) explains that Eurocentrism in the intercultural field "refers to hegemonic Eurocentrism in which we structurally and systematically privilege certain theorizing and researching methods of Western origin over others and disadvantage alternative possibilities of theorizing and researching culture and communication phenomena. Eurocentrism in intercultural communication studies appears to manifest in our academic activities in at least three spheres: (1) theoretical concepts and constructs, (2) research material and methodology, and (3) otherization in theory and research." Since these three spheres cover major aspects of the field of intercultural communication, Asian scholars have stressed the need to radicalize the field's intellectual roots. They would, for instance, "like to see the classical texts associated with Confucianism, Daoism, and Buddhism as well as the treaties associated with classical Asian aesthetics brought into discussion" (Dissanayake, 1996, p. 10).

Western scholars too recognize the need to open up the field to non-Western thoughts. Toward that end, the prestigious *Journal of Cross-Cultural Psychology* dedicated an entire volume (#31, 2000) to discuss the problematic aspect of Western-oriented concepts and methods and to construct alternative paradigms of intercultural understanding and training. Attempts such as this have resulted in growing optimism that "as we continue our journey, we should be sure to explore carefully the perspectives of thinkers in other traditions and other regions of the world" (Renwick, 2004, p. 450). One such perspective comes from scholars working in the field of poststructural/postcolonial studies.

11.2. Poststructural/Postcolonial Perspectives

As the above discussion reveals, two major drawbacks that characterize the work of traditional interculturalists are the Whorfian connection they made between language and culture, and the ethnocentric orientation they adopted toward alien cultures. Any serious attempt to address these drawbacks has to necessarily take into account some of the contributions from the field of cultural studies, particularly from its poststructural/postcolonial critique of language, culture, and society.

Unlike interculturalists, who treat language as an autonomous system with its segmental (i.e., grammatical and lexical) and suprasegmental (i.e., stress and intonation) features, poststructuralists treat language as one aspect of a larger discourse. French sociologist Michel Foucault, a prominent poststructuralist, offered a three-dimensional definition of discourse, "treating it sometimes as the general domain of all statements, sometimes as an individualizable group of statements, and sometimes as a regulated practice that accounts for a number of statements" (Foucault, 1972, p. 80). The first definition relates to all actual utterances or texts. The second relates to specific formations or fields, as in "the discourse of racism" or "the discourse of feminism." The third relates to sociopolitical structures that create the conditions governing particular utterances or texts. Discourse thus designates the entire conceptual territory on which knowledge is produced and reproduced. It not only includes what is actually thought and articulated but also determines what can be said or heard and what is silenced, what is acceptable and what is tabooed. Discourse in this sense is a whole field or domain within which language is used in particular ways. This field or domain is produced in and through social practices, institutions, and actions.

In characterizing language as one, and only one, of the multitude of entities that constitute discourse, Foucault (1970 and elsewhere) significantly extended the notion of linguistic text, which includes both verbal utterances and written narratives. A text means what it means not because of any inherent objective linguistic features but because it is generated by discursive formations, each with its particular ideologies and particular ways of controlling power. No text is innocent, and every utterance reflects a fragment of the world we live in. In other words, texts are political because all discursive formations are political. Analyzing a text therefore means analyzing discursive formations, which are essentially political in character and ideological in content.

Foucault further argued that every individual and every text is embedded in and controlled by discursive fields of power/knowledge, which is expressed in terms of *regimes of truth*—sets of rules, statements, and understandings that define what is true or real at any given time; a body of established and fairly unquestioned thoughts through which we perceive the world. Thus, as Sara Mills (1997, p. 17) succinctly pointed out, "power, knowledge and truth—this configuration is essentially what constitutes discourse." This configuration is made up of what Foucault called *discursive practices*, which are used in certain typical patterns in order to form *discursive formations*. Discursive formations make it difficult for individuals to think outside of them; hence they are also exercises in power and control. A discursive change, whether social, political, or cultural, can therefore be effected only when an entire community, not just an individual, changes its ways of thinking, knowing, speaking, and doing.

Although Foucault does entertain the possibility of systemic social or discursive change through subversion and resistance in his later works (e.g., *The History of Sexuality: The Use of Pleasure*, 1984), much of his analysis tends to focus mainly on the workings of power and the powerful. A somewhat different focus on the relationship between dominance and resistance comes from another French sociologist, Michel de Certeau, who drew attention to the subversions embedded in the practices of everyday life. For him, the powerful institutions of our society are able to demand particular behaviors, thoughts, and responses from individuals. He described the coercive power of these institutions as a *calculus of force-relationships* or *strategy*. Individuals, however, do not always comply with the dictates of dominant institutions. Instead, for a variety of reasons, ranging from incompetence to unwillingness to outright resistance, they reject the demands placed on them institutionally and operate according to their own desires, in a way that presents itself to them as personally empowering. This oppositional response he called *tactic* (de Certeau, 1984, pp. xviii–xx).

A tactic "is an art of the weak . . . clever tricks of the weak within the order established by the 'strong,' an art of putting one over on the adversary on his own turf. . . . The space of a tactic is the space of the other. Thus it must play on and with a terrain imposed on it and organized by the law of a foreign power" (de Certeau, 1984, pp. 31–40). The weak know intuitively how to manipulate the strong, so much so that, under certain adverse circumstances, the tactics of the weak can take the form of systematic and sustained subversion. Tactics, de Certeau explained, can be seen in acts such as refusing to cooperate with authority or spreading disinformation. They "characterize the subtle, stubborn, resistant activity of groups which, since they lack their own space, have to get along in a network of already established forces and representations" (de Certeau, 1984, p. 18).

Since subtle, stubborn forms of subversion are part and parcel of the practice of everyday life, de Certeau emphasized the importance of investigating them along with subtle forms of dominance. And, one site of such investigation is the linguistic text. Like Foucault's discourse, de Certeau's text extends beyond language. "Today, the text is society itself. It takes urbanistic, industrial, commercial, or televised forms," which produce a system "that distinguishes and privileges authors, educators, revolutionaries, in a word, 'producers' in contrast with those who do not produce" (1984, pp. 166–67). But, unlike Foucault, who conceived discourse largely as power/knowledge, de Certeau, as Terry Threadgold (1997, p. 71) noted, "made clear the need to think about both the way disciplinary knowledges work to conceal the positions and interests of those who enunciate them and the way conceiving knowledge as discourse excludes an account of the power of enunciation to subvert or change it."

Poststructuralists of different hues thus relate particular texts and events to larger macrosocial structures by specifically connecting the relations among various discourse formations with notions of power and knowledge, and of dominance and resistance. Acknowledging and extending their contributions, postcolonial scholars such as Homi Bhabha (1984), Edward Said (1978), Gayatri Spivak (1984), and others demonstrate how colonialism legitimizes widespread discursive frameworks arising from unequal power relations. Their perspectives have been highlighted in previous chapters (see Chapters 2, 7, and 8) and, therefore, I shall not go into detail here. Recall that they mainly draw our attention to

- the binary opposition between the West and the East, between Us and Them that produces an essentialized and static Self and Other;

- the working of power and inequality that tends to grant hegemony to dominant systems of cultural representation;

- the heterogeneity and agency of colonized peoples that problematize any rigid dichotomy of colonial domination and subordination;

- the state of the ambivalence that results in the exercise of agency on the part of the dominated and their influence over the dominant; and

- the attempt by periphery scholars to decenter Western knowledge systems, resulting in the blunting of the power of orientalism and its cultural representation of the Other.

These and other postcolonial thoughts highlight the ways in which the West constitutes the rest as a homogeneous group in order to easily analyze and interpret its communicational behavior, without considering larger historical, social, and political power structures that operate between the West and the non-West. In short, postcolonialism has effectively questioned the wide acceptance of such totalizing, monolithic constructs such as the West, the East, the Self, and the Other.

Recognizing the importance of poststructural/postcolonial critique and its relevance to the domain of intercultural understanding, representation, and communication, several interculturalists (e.g., Hibler, 1998; Kelly, 1999; Kim, 2002; Martin and Nakayama, 1997) have recently emphasized the need to deconstruct and reconstruct Western approaches to intercultural communication. Kristin Hibler (1998), for instance, stated that a postcolonial approach to intercultural communication might provide novel analytical tools necessary for assisting people, particularly those who have never been forced to do so, to see themselves as Others. Without this broad-based approach, she reckoned, adventures in intercultural communication will result only in superficial knowledge and not in any real change.

In fact, an earnest and accelerated exploration of how poststructural and postcolonial thoughts can expand the nature and scope of the field of intercultural communication can also prepare it to meet some of the challenges posed by the forces of cultural globalization. The fast-acting global imperatives are such that they are bound to have a significant impact on the field.

11.3. Global Imperatives

In previous chapters we saw how the new cultural globality is creating a novel cultural reality that, in turn, warrants the development of global cultural consciousness. We learned how the global flows of cultural capital aided by a communication revolution are generating an unprecedented level of cultural awareness, leading to renewed attempts to safeguard the cultural identity of the individual or the nation. We also learned how the contemporary global, national, social, and individual realities are changing the very process of identity formation and, with it, intercultural relations.

In the context of cultural globalization, then, the field of intercultural communication is faced with new challenges as well as with new opportunities. It is, however, yet to seize the moment in a substantive manner. As sociologist Randy Kluver (2000) pointed out in an on-line journal article, "intercultural communication theorists have often noted the globalizing forces of economic integration, tourism, migration, etc., as important forces that provide a rationale for increased intercultural communication competency. Few, however, have attempted to discern the more fundamental questions of how these forces will change the very nature of intercultural contact." Noting that established intercultural communication concepts such as the distinction between high and low context cultures are becoming problematic in the new global context, he wondered whether the traditional study of intercultural communication is "even relevant to the new issues arising with globalization and informatization."

One of the issues that raise serious doubts about the relevance of established study of intercultural communication is what has been called the reification of national cultures. It refers to how interculturalists "located culture at the level of nation, believing that cultural difference runs uniformly throughout the nation, essentializing and reifying nation by cultural practice, and working at the level of dichotomies of high- or low-context cultures and monochronic or polychronic times" (Starosta and Chen, 2003a, p. 15). It is the reification of national cultures that has long facilitated the scant attention shown by American interculturalists to subnational and subcultural diversity within their own nation and in other nations they studied. Until recently interculturalists focused almost entirely on the cultural characteristics of the mainstream "US-American," and even more narrowly, "USAmerican male" (Bennett and Bennett, 2004; Hibler, 1998; Pusch, 2004). As we learned earlier, cultural identity formation in the globalized world is a complex process of the interrelationship between global, national, social, and individual realities, and, therefore, focusing on an essentialized, unchanging national culture cannot but yield a distorted picture of intercultural relations and intercultural communication styles.

Yet another reason why the relevance of current modes of intercultural communication for the globalized world has been called into question is the failure to recognize that cultural globalization and information technology have generated new trends in terms of cultural knowledge, skill, and disposition among a vocal and active segment of the world population in ways that never happened before. Importantly, this phenomenon is not only producing individuals whose cultural capital is fast expanding, but it is also empowering them to be assertive about their own cultural identity. Therefore, approaching intercultural encounters with an outdated ethnocentric worldview is bound to be futile. Consider the following reports.

In 2005 Karen Hughes, undersecretary for public diplomacy and public affairs in the U.S. Department of State, undertook an important trip to the Islamic countries of Egypt, Indonesia, Malaysia, Saudi Arabia, and Turkey. Her chief objective was to talk to people from different walks of life in order to promote cultural understanding, bridge gaps in perception, and burnish the American image, which has been under severe stress in the Islamic world in the wake of the Afghan and Iraqi wars and the perceived clash of civilizations. As a former communications director, she was mindful of the power of evocative images and simple one-liners, and so she purchased and wore a pearl necklace with a medallion inscribed with the Arabic words for *love, sincerity, friendship,* and introduced herself as a working mom to strike an emotional chord with her Muslim audience.

According to news reports (see, for instance, www.washingtonpost .com/wp-dyn/content/article/2005/09/29/AR2005092901290.html), in her meeting with a group of highly educated Saudi women she said the United States would support efforts to raise their status in the Saudi society. The women surprised her by responding that Americans misunderstand their embrace of traditions and that their status is quite fine. When she referred specifically to the fact that Saudi law prohibits women from driving, saying they should be able to drive in order to "fully participate in society," the women informed her that they were pleased to move around in chauffeur-driven cars. One of them is reported to have said amid applause from others: "The general image of the Arab woman is that she isn't happy. Well, we're all pretty happy." In addition to cultural assertiveness, what the episode reveals is that deep-level sociopolitical and historical conditions may shape surface-level communication style and substance.

Yet another episode from international diplomacy relates to Silvio Berlusconi, the then Italian prime minister. A political commentary published in the *Economist*, dated September 2, 2004, reports on a summit meeting of European leaders held in Brussels. The Italian prime minister was chairing an important committee that was trying to wrap up sensitive negotiations over a proposed constitution for the European Union. He startled the assembled leaders by suggesting that they discuss "football and women" and that Gerhard Schröder, the German chancellor, was best suited to initiate the talk on women, as he had been married four times. Some diplomats concluded that the Italian prime minister must be deliberately embarrassing the German chancellor because of his policy differences with him. Italian officials explained later that, according to Italian cultural traditions, it is perfectly normal to create a relaxed atmosphere before a difficult meeting either by discussing football or by teasing one's colleagues about their love lives.

That it is essential not to operate under the mistaken belief that there is only one cultural worldview—one's own—is brought out by another episode, this time from the corporate sector, and narrated by social psychologist Montovani (2000). A famous international computer company opened a branch in Saudi Arabia. As part of its intercultural training for local managers, it conducted a mandatory workshop on sexual harassment, considered to be a thorny interpersonal issue in the American workplace. Workshop participants were asked to role-play and discuss a situation in which a manager makes not-so-subtle advances to the new secretary while they have a drink together. The American instructors were surprised when the Saudi managers expressed displeasure and even amazement at the simulation game. The organizers "did not realize that the situation was offensive for pious Muslims, and ridiculous in a country where men and women are strictly segregated and alcohol is officially banned for religious reasons" (Montovani, 2000, p. 31).

No doubt that, in recent years, there has been a growing awareness among interculturalists about the need to render intercultural communication more sensitive to global cultural contexts and complexities. This awareness, however, has not yet been translated into viable theories or actionable plans in part because of a paradoxical situation that interculturalists find themselves in. Sociologist Roland Robertson (1992, p. 172) articulated the paradox thus: "The practitioners of this discipline are attempting to develop an applied science of communicative relations between 'unique' populational units. In order to claim academic, professional and advisory legitimacy they must display the universality of their insights, methodology, research results and advisory successes. But at the same time they have a vested professional interest in accentuating difference, at least in the middle run; for if there occurs an attenuation of the perception of difference their raison d'être is in doubt." This paradox might mitigate against the formulation of intercultural communication theories and practices that are truly sensitive to the complexities of cultural globalization.

Perhaps because of this disciplinary paradox, the field of intercultural communication continues to promote, as Deborah Cameron (2002, p. 68) rightly observed, "particular interactional norms, genres and speech-styles across languages, on the grounds that they are maximally 'effective' for purposes of 'communication.'" Consequently, the trajectory of the field continues to be predicated upon a Western (mostly American) orientation making it singularly unidirectional. It is apparent that, in spite of the forces of globalization, we "know no case in which the communicative norms of a non-Western, or indeed non-Anglophone society have been exported by expert consultants. Finns do not run workshops for British businesses on the virtues of talking less; Japanese are not invited to instruct Americans in speaking indirectly" (Cameron, 2002, p. 70). Under these circumstances, it is crucial for language educators to critically review current pedagogic practices governing the teaching of intercultural communication and to begin to explore appropriate educational application.

11.4. Educational Application

For the teaching of culture in general, the language teaching profession has derived its theoretical principles and classroom practices mainly from the cultural concepts of cultural assimilation, cultural pluralism, and cultural hybridity (see chapters 5, 6, and 7). But if we look narrowly at the teaching of intercultural communication, we find that the profession has drawn its basic pedagogic insights mainly from three related sources: a contrastive rhetoric approach proposed by Robert Kaplan, a sociolinguistic approach advocated by John Gumperz, and a discourse approach introduced by Ron and Suzanne Scollon. Kaplan's work pertains to written communication whereas Gumperz and the Scollons focus on verbal as well as nonverbal communication.

Kaplan's contrastive rhetoric approach to intercultural communication has been discussed in detail in the chapter on cultural assimilation (see Chapter 5, section 5.3.1). Therefore, I shall not go into details here. To recall briefly, Kaplan (1966) identified five lin-gua-cultural groups (such as Oriental, Semitic, etc.) and, relying chiefly on a particular interpretation of the Sapir-Whorf hypothe-sis, posited a simple and symmetric relationship between linguistic rhetorical patterns and cultural thought patterns. He argued, for in-stance, that the linear structure of the English paragraph that is preferred in academic circles also signifies logical thinking on the part of native speakers of English. Asian rhetorical pattern is spiral because Asians think in circles. Kaplan's contrastive rhetoric approach adheres to two fundamental tenets of Whorfian orienta-tion: (a) language and culture are inextricably interconnected, and (b) cultural difference is cultural deficiency. From an educational perspective, Kaplan suggested that it is not the language teacher's responsibility to change foreign students' thought patterns into American English thought patterns. In what appears to be a tone of ethnocentric condescension, he cautioned: "The English class must not aim too high" (Kaplan, 1966, p. 20). In spite of his caution, as has been pointed out in Chapter 5, his approach has been widely adopted by language educators.

John Gumperz, a professor of anthropology at the University of California, Berkeley, is considered to be an authority on cross-cultural communication. He explored the close connection between linguistic knowledge and cultural understanding, showing how subconscious cultural presuppositions can affect conversations be-tween individuals from different ethnic backgrounds. In a series of studies, Gumperz (1982) focused on prevailing tensions between residents of London and immigrants from India, Pakistan, and the Caribbean islands. He found that cross-cultural misunderstanding and mistrust prevalent among these communities arise because of faulty use of stress and intonation features by nonnative speakers of English. He has provided several interesting examples to support his claim.

One such example deals with a London bus driver, an immigrant from the West Indies. When a passenger got on the bus and gave a large bill to buy a ticket, the driver said, "Exact change, *please*," putting extra emphasis on *please* and with falling intonation. Walk-ing down the aisle, the passenger wondered aloud, "Why do these people have to be so rude and threatening" (Gumperz, 1982, p. 168). Gumperz explained that according to the conventions of British English, the polite way of marking this directive would be to put the stress on *change* and not on *please*, the reason being that *change* is the new information that needs to be highlighted. Or, the driver could have used *please* with a rising intonation, signaling a polite question. A strong stress on *please* with a falling intonation would be equivalent to giving an order—a convention that would be appropriate if the speaker is in a position of authority, as in the case of a parent who might firmly say to a child: "Clean up the mess . . . *please.*"

In yet another example, Gumperz (1982, p. 173) showed how Indian and Pakistani women serving in a cafeteria at a British airport were perceived as "surly and uncooperative" because they did not get their intonation right. According to the conventions of English, when customers who had chosen meat were asked whether they wanted gravy, the Asian assistants would say *gravy* using falling intonation, instead of saying it with rising intonation. Saying the word with a falling intonation is likely to be interpreted as a statement giving a piece of information as if to say, "hey, this stuff here is called gravy." Saying it with a rising intonation would indicate a polite offer.

Based on similar examples drawn from cross-cultural encounters in British workplaces such as banks, post offices, restaurants, and government offices, Gumperz argued that participants in a conversation provide what he has called *conversational cues* "by means of which participants in an exchange assess others' intentions, and on which they base their responses" (p. 153). According to him, these cues operate at different linguistic (such as words) and extra-linguistic (such as intonation) levels, different ways of structuring/sequencing information (e.g., general points first, details later, or vice versa), and different ways of interpreting verbal/nonverbal cues. Thus, cross-cultural communication may fail because of different cultural assumptions or different use of linguistic conventions. It may also fail because of any potential mismatch between speaker intention and hearer interpretation. Gumperz asserted that "while basic conversational principles are universal and apply to verbal exchanges of all kinds, the way they are articulated in situ is culturally and subculturally specific" (p. 96).

The way basic conversational principles are articulated in different cultural and subcultural groups became the focal points for teaching intercultural communication in the language classroom. Gumperz (1982) suggested several discourse strategies for reducing cross-cultural misunderstanding in face-to-face communication, which language teachers and teacher educators found very useful. They include

- check everyday assumptions,
- state assumptions explicitly and clearly,
- do not rely on intonation to carry meaning; it's easier to use explicit words,
- reformulate (not just repeat) important points,
- listen until client has finished; do not interrupt or switch off and jump to conclusions, and
- guard against hidden ways of discrimination and stereotyping.

Using these and other strategies, language teachers have attempted to raise the learners' awareness of subtle nuances of linguistic features and cultural assumptions that govern successful intercultural communication. Even though Gumperz's analysis of cross-cultural communication and his strategies for promoting it are nearly a quarter century old, they still are recommended for use in the language classroom. In fact, his work on cross-cultural communication is the only one on this subject that has been included in *The Language, Ethnicity and Race Reader*, recently compiled by British applied linguists Roxy Harris and Ben Rampton (2003).

Another substantive work that has influenced the language teaching profession in its attempt to teach intercultural communication is Scollon and Scollon (2001), whose "basic interest is in face-to-face conversation within speech events such as meetings, conversations, or interviews" (2001, p. 5) that take place in a professional context. They call their approach a *discourse approach* because instead of working with a broad entity called culture, they focus on what they call a *Discourse System* in which "the meaning intended is the broad range of everything which can be said or talked about or symbolized within a particular, recognizable domain" (p. 5). Examples of such recognizable discourse domains include *the discourse of law, the discourse of business, the discourse of entertainment*, etc.

Scollon and Scollon argued that within each Discourse System, what largely determines the relative success or failure of intercultural communication between individuals from different cultural backgrounds is the interpretive capacity they bring to bear on their

conversation. They illustrated this point with a typical, but hypothetical, example (p. 6):

> Mr Wong and Mr Richardson have a conversation. Mr Richardson
> has enjoyed this conversation and when they are ready to part he
> says to Mr Wong that they really should get together to have lunch
> sometime. Mr Wong says that he would enjoy that. After a few
> weeks Mr Wong begins to feel that Mr Richardson has been rather
> insincere because he has not followed up his invitation to lunch
> with a specific time and place.
>
> The difference in discourse patterns expected by many Asian
> speakers of English and by western speakers of English is the
> source of the problem between Mr Wong and Mr Richardson. The
> pattern which we have mentioned above of displacing important
> points until nearer the end of a conversation, which is often found
> in East Asian discourse, has led Mr Wong to think that this mention
> of lunch at the end of the conversation is of some importance to
> Mr Richardson. Whether it is important to Mr Wong or not, he be-
> lieves that Mr Richardson is seriously making an invitation to
> lunch. Mr Richardson, on the other hand, has made this mention of
> having lunch together sometime at the end of his conversation be-
> cause it is of little major significance. For him it does not signify
> any more than that he has enjoyed his conversation with Mr Wong.
> It is not a specific invitation, but just a conventional way of parting
> with good feelings toward the other.
>
> This difference in discourse patterns results in a confusion be-
> tween the two participants in this hypothetical conversation. The
> problem at root is that language is fundamentally ambiguous.
> While it is important for both speakers to distinguish between the
> main point and "small talk," there is nothing in the language used
> itself to say "This is the important point." That emphasis is supplied
> by the expectations each speaker has that the other speaker will use
> language in the same way that he or she does.

Therefore, Scollon and Scollon suggested that one solution to avoid
any possible misunderstanding "might be to teach both Mr Wong
and Mr Robertson what the other person's expectations are" (p. 22),
hoping that "they are both likely to pay closer attention to topics at
both the beginnings and the endings of their conversations" (p. 22).

In a further explication of this hypothetical conversation, Scollon
and Scollon reckoned that successful intercultural communication
relies on two factors: pragmatic effectiveness and cultural sensitivity. According to them, "pragmatic effectiveness in communication

means participating as fully as possible in the discourse systems of those with whom one is wishing to communicate, while never taking their requirements as simply self-evident. Cultural sensitivity means being conscious of the ways in which one's own communications may be perceived and also accepting the fact that one is never likely to be considered a full member of most of the discourse systems in which one will participate" (p. 134). Scollon and Scollon believed that "the most useful focus for research as well as for education and training are the actions people take in which differences produce sources of conflict in power or in understanding" (p. 267).

It is interesting to note that, in spite of their conceptual and methodological variations, Gumperz and Scollon and Scollon identified cultural assumptions and linguistic expectations as two central factors determining the effectiveness of intercultural communication. In other words, they both took a predominantly lingua-cultural orientation to their analysis and interpretation of interpersonal communication across cultures. (Kaplan did the same but his work is limited to written communication.) Any training based on such an orientation may promote a greater awareness of cultural assumptions one brings to an intercultural encounter, and it may also improve one's knowledge and use of appropriate linguistic and extralinguistic features. Together they carry the potential to reduce communication gap in the immediate interactive context. However, the lingua-cultural orientation cannot be considered to carry adequate explanatory power. For instance, even though Gumperz did not deny the pervasiveness of racial discrimination against Asians and other ethnic minorities in British society, and did consider it a factor in intercultural relationships, his theory of conversational inference did not address the issue at all.

What a predominantly lingua-cultural orientation does is to set aside social, political, and historical considerations governing intercultural communication. It is clearly inadequate to deal with the complexities of cultural globalization that are changing the cultural landscape by bringing into the encounter issues such as identity, agency, otherization, representation, etc. It is also limited in addressing changed patterns of communication brought about by globalization and "Internetization." There is, thus, a need to develop a framework for analyzing, interpreting, and teaching intercultural communication by taking into account the fast-changing global cultural environment.

One possible avenue is to take the cluster of five fundamental factors and five pedagogic priorities discussed in Chapter 9 as a point of departure. The fundamental factors of cultural connectivity, cultural complexity, cultural globality, cultural reality, and cultural identity collectively offer necessary conceptual underpinnings. The five pedagogic priorities that call for a shift of focus from target language community to targeted cultural community, from linguistic articulation to cultural affiliation, from cultural information to cultural transformation, from passive reception to critical reflection, and from interested text to informed context deal more specifically with policies and planning and with methods and materials. Together, they have the potential to provide the essentials of an intercultural communication framework that is sensitive to the development of global cultural consciousness. Clearly, serious and systematic exploration beckons the profession.

11.5. In Closing

In this chapter, I provided a detailed critique of traditional approaches to intercultural communication. I also touched upon poststructural/postcolonial perspectives that brought out the limitations of earlier approaches. I pointed out that if the traditional interculturalists emphasized the lingua-cultural orientation to the analysis and the teaching of intercultural communication, the poststructuralists and postcolonialists highlighted a broader sociopolitical orientation that sounds promising in the era of cultural globalization. I then argued that there are fast developing global imperatives that have to be taken into account for effective intercultural communication. Finally, I presented a brief account of the limited value of the current pedagogic insights and noted the need for developing a new framework that might open up possibilities for productive pedagogic intervention that is sensitive to the challenges of cultural globalization. Clearly, we need to rethink our theoretical principles and pedagogic practices by seeking out a meaningful articulation of the relationship between intercultural communication and cultural globalization.

CHAPTER 12

The Map of the Territory

I begin this final chapter with the same metaphor I presented to end the introductory chapter: travel. I promised to provide the reader with a general road map to culture, cultural concepts, cultural consciousness, cultural communication, and cultural globalization. The vast area I tried to map spans several disciplines including anthropology, applied linguistics, cultural studies, history, politics, and sociology. In order to provide a critical and comprehensive narrative, I had to cross disciplinary boundaries that are carefully gauged and jealously guarded. I found that there indeed are professional practitioners in these disciplines who themselves cross their disciplinary borders so as to map the cultural territory they survey.

We have, however, been wisely warned that *the map is not the territory*. This popular and productive concept started with the pioneering work done in general semantics by Alfred Korzybski (1933) and soon became a founding principle in Neuro-linguistic Programming before spreading to other academic areas as well. What does it mean to say that the map is not the territory? It means that our perception of reality is just our version of it, our map of it, and hence it is very different from the reality itself. It also means that a message does not consist of the object it denotes. The word *fire*, for instance, does not burn us. A popular artistic rendering of this concept is the famous painting by surrealist René Magritte (Figure 12.1). Titled *The Betrayal of Images* (1928–29), the painting bears a French text meaning "This is not a pipe."

Anthropologist Gregory Bateson elucidated the concept further: "we say the map is different from the territory. But what is the territory? Operationally, somebody went out with a retina or a measuring stick and made representations which were then put on paper.

Figure 12.1. René Magritte, *The Betrayal of Images* (1928–29)

What is on the paper map is a representation of what was in the retinal representation of the man who made the map; and as you push the question back, what you find is an infinite regress, an infinite series of maps" (1972, p. 454). Our mental representation is only a map of maps, ad infinitum. And hence, a map is far removed from the territory it purports to depict. And yet it is a very useful structure because it allows us to navigate the territory to begin to understand it. But, it cannot help us understand it fully because it is merely a representation.

The fact that a map is no more than a pale representation of the territory it portrays has resulted in contentious debates in the field where maps constitute the central focus: cartography. There have been several cartographic projections of the world, none satisfactory. Drawing an accurate map of the world is impossible for the simple reason that the earth is spherical and three-dimensional whereas its representation is flat and two-dimensional. It has not been feasible so far to accurately capture the properties of the earth in terms of equality of area, accuracy of shape, fidelity of north-south axis, etc. (Kaiser, 1987).

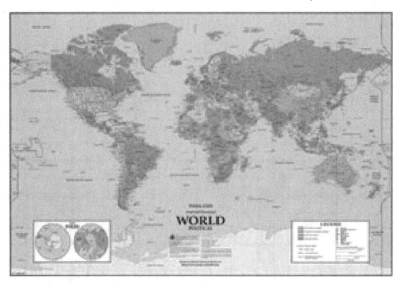

Figure 12.2. Mercator map (Gerhard Kremer, 1569)

The best-known world map is the Mercator map, created in 1569 by cartographer Gerhard Kremer (whose surname, meaning *merchant* in English, was translated as *Mercator* in Latin). He developed it mainly for use by professional navigators. Considered to be a cartographic achievement of the time, it has been criticized for seriously distorting size. Like all other maps, it puts the North Pole at the top and inflates the size of landmass according to its distance from the equator. It makes Europe, which has an area of 3.8 million square miles, look larger than South America with its area of 6.9 million square miles. Similarly, Africa, with its 11.6 million square miles, is shown as smaller than the former Soviet Union with its 8.7 million square miles. Because of such distortions, the map has even been branded as Eurocentric. But still it is used all over the world—in schools, colleges, and other institutions. It continues to be influential in shaping people's perception of the world.

An example of a map that effectively addresses the issue of distortion of size is the one developed by German historian Arno Peters; he proposed this map in 1974, and its English version was distributed in 1983. It was drawn mainly for the average person, not for navigators. Unlike the Mercator map, Peters's represents all areas

Figure 12.3. World map (Arno Peters, 1974)

according to relative size, that is, one square inch anywhere on the map represents a constant number of miles. A paramount criticism of this map is that it distorts shape. But it very effectively tackles the perceived Eurocentric bias, and so it has found favor with several socially and politically conscious groups.

I invoke cartographic projections not to join the contentious debate about which map better represents the world's countries, but to emphasize the point that if scientific cartography with all its instruments of measurement cannot accurately represent the geographical reality, then cultural cartography cannot be expected to capture the fullest extent of the cultural reality that exists in all its many dimensional splendor. Under these circumstances, what perhaps we should be conscious of are the limitations of fairly ethnocentric cultural representations that we have come to feel comfortable with. Mindful of the Batesonian elucidation of the relationship between the map and the territory, we should realize that the largely unchallenged cultural map that we have all along been using for our educational purposes was originally drawn by a few interculturalists with limited tools, and that the flawed map keeps getting replicated again and again, creating maps of maps, ad infinitum. Every time the map is uncritically replicated, it becomes more and more distant from the partial reality it originally represented. However, there is no gainsaying the fact that even this flawed cultural map, just like the flawed cartographic map, has its own structural use so long as we keep in mind its inherent inadequacies.

The language teaching profession has recently witnessed an impressive array of work on teaching culture and intercultural communication. However, as Michael Byram and Anwei Feng pointed out in an authoritative and comprehensive state-of-the-art essay, "the increase in the volume of work does not inevitably mean an improvement in quality, and there is a need to develop more systematically a programme of research rather than *ad hoc* efforts which may not have a lasting effect" (2004, p. 164). And they came to this conclusion without even considering the impact of the emerging forces of cultural globalization.

The inadequacies of the cultural maps that are currently in use are getting remarkably accentuated because of the emerging processes of cultural globalization. In the contemporary world, as Chief Rabbi Jonathan Sacks rightly observed in his award-winning book *The Dignity of Difference: How to Avoid the Clash of Civilizations*, "we live in the conscious presence of difference. In the street, at work and on the television screen we constantly encounter cultures whose ideas are unlike ours. That can be experienced as a profound threat to identity. One of the great transformations from the twentieth to the twenty-first centuries is that whereas the former was dominated by the politics of *ideology*, we are now entering an age of the politics of *identity*" (Sacks, 2003, p. 10, italics as in original). In order to cope with the tensions the great transformation has brought about, the Chief Rabbi advised us to "learn the art of conversation, from which truth emerges not, as in Socratic dialogues, by the refutation of falsehood but from the presence of others who think, act, and interpret reality in ways radically different from our own" (p. 23).

Recognizing the importance of fruitful conversations among all involved, the United Nations Organizations designated 2001 as the International Year of Dialogue Between Civilizations, and it continued its preoccupation with global culture by selecting "Cultural Liberty in Today's Diverse World" as its thematic focus for its *Human Development Report 2004*. The report defined cultural liberty as "the freedom to participate in society without having to slip off their chosen cultural moorings. It is a simple idea, but profoundly unsettling" (p. 1). This evocation is very much reflected in the overall approach to cultural identity formation pursued in this book: the twin path of rootedness and openness. Considered a vital part of human development, cultural liberty is "about expanding individual choices, not about preserving values and practices as an end in itself with blind allegiance to tradition" (p. 4). Warning that "cultural liberty will not just happen, any more than health, education and gender equity just happen" (p. 6), the U.N. called for concerted action by governmental and educational agencies.

I believe one way language educators can heed the clarion call is to try to create in their learners an educated mind rather than a schooled mind. In a newspaper column titled "Our Prejudices, Our Selves" that appeared a decade ago, I differentiated the schooled mind from the educated mind thus (Kumaravadivelu, 1997, pp. 1, 4):

> Schooling trains us for a particular profession. It equips us with knowledge and skills necessary to perform certain jobs with certain degree of success. Educating, on the other hand, deepens our understanding of who we are, what we wish to be and how we relate to others. It opens our minds and hearts to a multiplicity of perspectives and enables us to feel at home in a world of diversity. Schools do make us literate. But, a literate mind is not necessarily a liberated mind. . . .
>
> For the schooled mind, difference disturbs. But for the educated mind, difference delights. To the educated mind difference represents potential, and diversity represents possibility. . . .
>
> Since the educated mind is capable of discriminating truth from half-truths, it does not fall easy prey to sickening stereotypes. It acknowledges the good and the bad both in its own culture as well as in others. It is as willing to learn from others as it is to teach others. . . .
>
> We may never know the true measure of our strengths unless we also know the true measure of our weaknesses. And we can know this only if we have an open mind and are willing to learn about and from others.

Perhaps the last sentence points to the heart of the matter: a willingness to learn *from* other cultures, not just *about* them. Learning *about* other cultures may lead to cultural literacy; it is learning *from* other cultures that will lead to cultural liberty.

In order to navigate the difficult terrain of cultural liberty undulated by the centrifugal and centripetal forces of cultural globalization, we may need a cultural map that is different from the one

we have been using so far. In an earlier chapter I referred to a satiri-
cal narrative of what appeared to be the daily rituals of an alien
tribal culture, only to learn that the writer was, in fact, pulling our
leg by merely using the impressive vocabulary of anthropological
studies to describe our own normal activities such as tooth-brushing.
His spoof drives home the point that the familiar can easily be made
to look exotic. What the current phase of cultural globalization,
with its global flows of ideas, peoples, cultures, and conflicts, is beginning to do is to make the exotic look familiar. In doing so, it is
also beginning to render all the established cultural maps terribly
inadequate, if not totally ineffectual.

This book is based on the premise that it is time we charted a
new cultural map that helps us and our learners take a journey down
a whole new path, one that would take us all to a new destination.

Our destination is not just securing knowledge of the map, but
ensuring an understanding of the territory.

The road that might lead us to our destination is a less traveled
one. Let's dare ourselves to take the road less traveled.

References

Ahmed, A. (1992). *In Theory: Classes, Nations and Literatures.* London: Verso.

Alba, R., and V. Nee. (1999). "Rethinking Assimilation Theory for a New Era of Immigration." In C. Hirschman, P. Kasinitz, and J. DeWind (eds.). *The Handbook of International Migration: The American Experience.* New York: Russell Sage Foundation, 137–60.

Allwright, R. L., and K. M. Bailey. (1991). *Focus on the Language Classroom.* Cambridge: Cambridge University Press.

Alvares, C. (1979/1991). *Decolonizing History: Technology and Culture in India, China and the West 1492 to the Present Day.* New York: Apex Press, and Goa: The Other India Press.

Anderson, B. (1983/2005). *Imagined Communities: Reflections on the Origin and Spread of Nationalism.* 2d ed. London: Verso. (Originally published in 1983.) Citation is taken from Spencer and H. Wollman (eds.). (2005). *Nations and Nationalism: A Reader.* New Brunswick, NJ: Rutgers University Press, 48–59.

Appadurai, A. (1990). "Disjuncture and Difference in the Global Cultural Economy." In M. Featherstone (ed.). *Global Culture: Nationalism, Globalization and Modernity.* London: Sage, 295–310.

———. (1996). *Modernity at Large: Cultural Dimensions of Globalization.* Minneapolis, MN.: Minnesota University Press.

Appiah, K. A. (1991). "Is the Post- in Postmodernism the Post- in Postcolonial?" *Critical Inquiry* 17: 336–57.

———. (2005). *The Ethics of Identity.* Princeton and Oxford: Princeton University Press.

Ashcroft, B., G. Griffith, and H. Tiffin. (2001). *Postcolonial Studies: The Key Concepts.* London: Routledge.

Atkinson, D. (1997). "A Critical Approach to Critical Thinking in TESOL." *TESOL Quarterly* 31: 9–37.

———. (1999). "TESOL and Culture." *TESOL Quarterly* 33: 625–54.

Barber, B. (1996). *Jihad vs. McWorld: How Globalism and Tribalism Are Re-shaping the World.* New York: Ballantine Books.

Barro, A., S. Jordan, and C. Roberts. 1998. "Cultural Practice in Everyday Life: The Language Learner as Ethnographer." In M. Byram and M. Fleming (eds.). *Language Learning in Intercultural Perspective: Approaches Through Drama and Ethnography.* Cambridge: Cambridge University Press.

Bateson, G. (1972). *Steps to an Ecology of Mind.* New York: Ballantine Books.

Bateson, M. C. (2000). "Crossing Cultures: A Talk with Mary Catherine Bateson." *Edge* 76 (October 12, 2000). Retrieved on May 14, 2001, from www.edge.org/documents/archive/edge76.html.

Bauman, Z. (1995). *Life in Fragments: Essays in Postmodern Morality.* Oxford: Blackwell.

———. (1998). *Globalization: The Human Consequence.* New York: Columbia University Press.

Bennet, J. M., and M. J. Bennet. (2003). *Becoming a Skillful Intercultural Facilitator.* Portland, OR: Summer Institute for Intercultural Communication.

Bennett, J. M., M. J. Bennett, and W. Allen. (1998). "Developing Intercultural Competence in the Language Classroom." In D. L. Lange, C. A. Klee, R. M. Paige, and Y. A. Yershova (eds.). *Culture as the Core: Integrating Culture into the Language Curriculum.* Minneapolis, MN: The Regents of the University of Minnesota.

Bennett, M. J. (1998). *Basic Concepts of Intercultural Communication.* Yarmouth: Intercultural Press.

Bhabha, H. K. (1994). *The Location of Culture.* New York: Routledge.

Billig, M. (1995/2005). *Banal Nationalism.* London: Sage. (Originally published in 1995.) Citation is taken from P. Spencer and H. Wollman (eds.). (2005). *Nations and Nationalism: A Reader.* New Brunswick, NJ: Rutgers University Press, 184–97.

Block, D., and D. Cameron (eds.). (2002). *Globalization and Language Teaching.* New York: Routledge.

Blum-Kulka, S., J. House, and G. Kasper (eds.). (1989). *Cross-cultural Pragmatics: Requests and Apologies.* Norwood, NJ: Ablex.

Borofsky, R. (ed.). (1994). *Assessing Anthropology.* New York: McGraw-Hill.

Bourdieu, P. (1977). "The Economics of Linguistic Exchanges." *Social Sciences Information* 16: 645–68.

———. (1990). *In Other Words: Essays Towards a Reflexive Sociology.* Trans. M. Adamson. Stanford: Stanford University Press.

———. (1991). *Language and Symbolic Power.* Trans. G. Reymond and M. Adamson. Cambridge: Polity Press.

———. (2000). *Pascalian Meditations.* Stanford: Stanford University Press.

Boyer, E. L. (1987). *College: The Undergraduate Experience in America.* New York: Harper and Row.

Braddock, R. (1974). "The Frequency and Placement of Topic Sentences in Expository Prose." *Research in the Teaching of English* 8: 287–302.

Brah, A., and A. E. Coombs. (eds.). (2000). *Hybridity and Its Discontents: Politics, Science, Culture.* London: Routledge.

Brody, J. (2003). "A Linguistic Anthropological Perspective on Language and Culture in the Second Language Curriculum." In D. L. Lange and R. M. Paige (eds.). *Culture as the Core: Perspectives in Second Language Education.* Greenwich, CT: Information Age Publishing, 37–51.

Brooks, N. (1964/1960). *Language and Language Learning: Theory and Practice.* 2d ed. New York: Harcourt, Brace and World.

———. (1975). "The Analysis of Language and Familiar Cultures." In R. Lafayette (ed.). *The Cultural Revolution in Foreign Language Teaching. Reports of the Northeast Conference on the Teaching of Foreign Language.* Lincolnwood, IL: National Textbook.

Brown, D. (1994). *Teaching by Principles: An Interactive Approach to Language Pedagogy.* Englewood Cliffs, NJ: Prentice Hall.

Brown, S., and J. Eisterhold. (2004). *Topics in Language and Culture for Teachers.* Ann Arbor: The University of Michigan Press.

Buchanan, P. (1992). "Republican National Convention Speech." Dated August 17, 1992. Retrieved August 29, 2005, from www.buchanan.org/ pa-92–0817-rnc.html.

Bullivant, B. (1983). *The Pluralist Dilemma in Education: Six Case Studies.* Sydney: Allen and Unwin.

Byram, M. (1993). "Language and Culture Learning: The Need for Integration." In M. Byram (ed.). *Germany: Its Representation in Textbooks for Teaching German in Great Britain.* Frankfurt: Moritz Diesterweg, 13–18.

———. (1997). *Teaching and Assessing Intercultural Communicative Competence.* London: Multilingual Matters.

———. (1999). "Questions of Identity in Foreign Language Learning." In J. Lo Bianco, A. J. Liddicoat, and C. Crozet (eds.). *Striving for the Third Place: Intercultural Competence Through Language Education.* Melbourne: Language Australia, 91–101.

———. (ed.). (2000). *Routledge Encyclopedia of Language Teaching and Learning.* New York: Routledge.

Byram, M., and A. Feng. (2004). "Culture and Language Learning: Teaching, Research and Scholarship." *Language Teaching* 37: 149–68.

Byram, M., and M. Fleming (eds.). (1998). *Language Learning in Intercultural Perspective.* Cambridge: Cambridge University Press.

Byram, M., and C. Morgan. (1994). *Teaching and Learning Language and Culture.* Clevedon, U.K.: Multilingual Matters.

Cameron, D. (2002). "Globalization and the Teaching of 'Communication

Skills.'" In D. Block and D. Cameron (eds.). *Globalization and Language Teaching*. London: Routledge, 67–82.

Canagarajah, A. S. (1993). "Critical Ethnography of a Sri Lankan Classroom: Ambiguities in Student Opposition to Reproduction Through ESOL." *TESOL Quarterly* 27: 601–26.

———. (1997). "Safe Houses in the Contact Zone: Coping Strategies of African-American Students in the Academy." *College Composition and Communication* 48: 173–96.

———. (1999). *Resisting Linguistic Imperialism in English Teaching*. Oxford: Oxford University Press.

Canclini, N. G. (1990/1995). *Hybrid Cultures: Strategies for Entering and Leaving Modernity*. Minnesota: University of Minnesota Press.

Carr, J. (1999). "From 'Sympathetic' to 'Dialogic' Imagination: Cultural Study in the Foreign Language Classroom." In J. Lo Bianco, A. J. Liddicoat, and C. Crozet (eds.). *Striving for the Third Place: Intercultural Competence Through Language Education*. Melbourne: Language Australia, 103–12.

Carroll, J. B. (1956). Introduction. In J. B. Carroll (ed.). *Language, Thought, and Reality: Selected Writings by Benjamin Lee Whorf*. Cambridge, MA: MIT Press, 1–34.

Center for Critical Thinking. Sonoma State University. "Study of 38 Public Universities and 28 Private Universities to Determine Faculty Emphasis on Critical Thinking in Instruction." www.criticalthinking.org/school study.htm.

Cheah, P. (1998). "Given Culture: Rethinking Cosmopolitical Freedom in Transnationalism." In P. Cheah and B. Robbins (eds.). *Cosmopolitics*. Minneapolis, MN: Minnesota University Press, 246–64.

Cheng, X. (2000). "Asian Students' Reticence Revisited." *System* 28: 435–46.

———. (2002). "Chinese EFL Students' Cultures of Learning." In C. Lee and W. Littlewood (eds.). *Culture, Communication and Language Pedagogy*. Hong Kong: Hong Kong Baptist University, 103–16.

Chick, K. J. (1995). "The Interactional Accomplishment of Discrimination in South Africa." *Language in Society* 14: 229–326.

———. (1996). "Safe-Talk: Collusion in Apartheid Education." In H. Coleman (ed.). *Society and the Language Classroom*. Cambridge: Cambridge University Press, 21–39.

Chuang, R. (2003). "A Postmodern Critique of Cross-cultural and Intercultural Communication Research: Contesting Essentialism, Positivist Dualism, and Eurocentricity." In W. J. Starosta and G. Chen (eds.). *Ferment in the Intercultural Field: Axiology/Value/Praxis*. Thousand Oaks, CA: Sage, 24–53.

Clausen, C. (2000). *Faded Mosaic: The Emergence of Post-cultural America*. Chicago: Ivan R. Dee.

Clifford, J. (1986). "Introduction: Partial Truths." In J. Clifford and G. Marcus (eds.). *Writing Culture: The Poetics and Politics of Ethnography.* Berkeley, CA: University of California Press.

———. (1988). *The Predicament of Culture.* Cambridge: Harvard University Press.

———. (1993). *Routes: Travels and Translations in the Late Twentieth Century.* Cambridge: Harvard University Press.

Cohen, B. S. (1996). *Colonialism and Its Forms of Knowledge.* Princeton, NJ.: Princeton University Press.

Connor, U. (1996). *Contrastive Rhetoric: Cross-cultural Aspects of Second Language Writing.* New York: Cambridge University Press.

Connor, U., and P. McCagg. (1983). "Cross-cultural Differences and Perceived Quality in Writing Paraphrases of English Expository Prose." *Applied Linguistics* 4: 259–68.

Coombes, A. E., and A. Brah. (2000). "Introduction: The Conundrum of 'Mixing.'" In A. Brah and A. E. Coombes (eds.). *Hybridity and Its Discontents: Politics, Science, Culture.* London: Routledge, 1–16.

Corbett, J. (2003). *An Intercultural Approach to English Language Teaching.* Clevedon, U.K.: Multilingual Matters.

Cortazzi, M., and L. Jin. (1996). "Cultures of Learning: Language Classrooms in China." In H. Coleman (ed.). *Society and the Language Classroom.* Cambridge: Cambridge University Press, 169–206.

———. (1999). "Cultural Mirrors: Materials and Methods in the EFL Classroom." In E. Hinkel (ed.). *Culture in Second Language Teaching and Learning.* Cambridge: Cambridge University Press, 196–219.

Council of Europe. (2001). *Common European Framework of Reference for Languages: Learning, Teaching, Assessment.* Cambridge: Cambridge University Press, and Strasbourg: Council of Europe.

Crawford-Lange, L. M., and D. L. Lange. (1987). "Integrating Language and Culture: How to Do It." *Theory into Practice* 26: 258–66.

Crevecoeur, H. St. John de. (1782/1912). *Letters from an American Farmer.* As quoted by G. Gerstle (1999) in C. Hirschman, P. Kasinitz, and J. DeWind (eds.). *The Handbook of International Migration: The American Experience.* New York: Russell Sage Foundation, 274–93. (Originally published in 1782.)

Crozet, C., and A. J. Liddicoat. (1999). "The Challenge of Intercultural Language Teaching: Engaging with Culture in the Classroom." In J. Lo Bianco, A. J. Liddicoat, and C. Crozet (eds.). *Striving for the Third Place: Intercultural Competence Through Language Education.* Melbourne: Language Australia, 113–25.

Crozet, C., A. J. Liddicoat, and J. Lo Bianco. (1999). "Introduction: Intercultural Competence: From Language Policy to Language Education." In J. Lo Bianco, A. J. Liddicoat, and C. Crozet (eds.). *Striving for the Third Place: Intercultural Competence Through Language Education.* Melbourne: Language Australia, 1–20.

Cummins, J. (2000). "Negotiating Intercultural Identities in the Multilingual Classroom." *The Catesol Journal* 12: 164–66.

Davies, I. (1998). "Negotiating African Culture: Toward a Decolonization of the Fetish." In F. Jameson and M. Miyoshi (eds.). *The Cultures of Globalization*. Durham, NC: Duke University Press, 125–45.

de Certeau, M. (1984). *The Practice of Everyday Life*. Berkeley: University of California Press.

Delk, D. L. (1997). *Discovering American Culture*. Ann Arbor: The University of Michigan Press.

Dharampal. (1983). *The Beautiful Tree: Indigenous Indian Education in the Eighteenth Century*. New Delhi: Bibla Impex Private.

Dirlik, A. "'Empire?'" *Interventions* 5: 207–17.

Dissanayake, W. (ed.). (1988). *Communication Theory: The Asian Perspective*. Singapore: Asian Mass Communication Research and Information Center.

Du Bois, W. E. B. (1940). *Dusk of Dawn: An Essay Toward an Autobiography of a Race Concept*. New York: Library of America.

Dunn, R. (1998). *Identity Crises: A Social Critique of Postmodernity*. Minneapolis, MN.: University of Minnesota Press.

Eckert, P., and S. McConnell-Ginet. (1992). "Think Practically and Look Locally: Language and Gender as Community-based Practice." *Annual Review of Anthropology* 21: 461–90.

Edwards, D., and J. McCaffery. (1981). *Cross-Cultural Training for Peace Corps Volunteers*. Washington, DC: Peace Corps, Information Collection and Exchange.

Ellis, C., and A. Bochner. (2000). "Autoethnography, Personal Narrative, Reflexivity: Researcher as Subject." In N. Denzin and Y. Lincoln (eds.). *The Handbook of Qualitative Research*. 2d ed. Thousand Oaks, CA: Sage, 733–68.

Ellison, R. (1964). *Shadow and Act*. New York: Random House.

Emeneau, M. B. (1955). "India and Linguistics." *Journal of the American Oriental Society* 75: 143–53.

Fanon. F. (1952/1967). *Black Skin White Masks*. New York: Grove Press.

———. (1961/1963). *The Wretched of the Earth*. New York: Grove Press.

Fantini, A. F. (1997). "Developing Intercultural Competence: A Process Approach." In A. F. Fantini (ed.). *New Ways in Teaching Culture*. Washington DC: Teaching English to Speakers of Other Languages, 40–44.

———. (ed.). (1997). *New Ways in Teaching Culture*. Washington DC: Teaching English to Speakers of Other Languages.

Fink, J. N. (1999). "Conclusion. Pushing Through the Surface: Notes on Hybridity and Writing." In M. Joseph and J. N. Fink (eds.). *Performing Hybridity*. Minneapolis: University of Minnesota Press, 247–52.

Fish, S. (1999). *The Trouble with Principle*. Cambridge, MA.: Harvard University Press.

Fishman, J. (1980). "The Whorfian Hypothesis—Varieties of Valuation, Confirmation and Disconfirmation." *International Journal of the Sociology of Language* 26: 25–40.

Flowerdew, J., and L. Miller. (1995). "On the Notion of Culture in L2 Lectures." *TESOL Quarterly* 29: 345–73.

Foucault, M. (1970). *The Order of Things: An Archeology of Human Sciences.* Trans. A. M. Sheridan-Smith. New York: Pantheon Books.

———. (1972). *The Archeology of Knowledge.* Trans. A. M. Sheridan Smith, New York: Pantheon.

———. (1980). *Power/Knowledge: Selected Interviews and Other Writings. 1972–1977.* New York: Pantheon.

———. (1984). *The History of Sexuality: The Use of Pleasure.* Vol. 2. Penguin: Harmondsworth.

Fox, H. (1994). *Listening to the World.* Urbana, IL: National Council of Teachers of English.

Friedman, J. (1997). "Global Crises, the Struggle for Cultural Identity and Intellectual Porkbarrelling: Cosmopolitans Versus Locals, Ethnics and Nationals in an Era of De-hegemonisation." In P. Werbner and T. Modood (eds.). *Debating Cultural Hybridity.* London: Zed, 70–89.

Friedman, T. L. (2005). *The World Is Flat: A Brief History of the Twenty-first Century.* New York: Farrar, Straus and Giroux.

Fukuyama, F. (1999). *The Great Disruption: Human Nature and the Reconstruction of Social Order.* New York: The Free Press.

Gaertner, J. F., and J. F. Dovidio. (1986). "Changes in the Expression and Assessment of Racial Prejudice." In H. J. Knopke, R. J. Norrell, and R. W. Rogers (eds.). *Opening Doors: Perspectives on Race Relations in Contemporary America.* Tuscaloosa: The University of Alabama Press, 119–48.

Gandhi, M. K. (1921). "English Learning." (Entry dated September 1, 1921.) *Young India.* 170.

———. (1927/1997). *An Autobiography, Or the Story of My Experiments with Truth.* Ahmedabad: Navjivan Publishing House. (Originally published in 1927.)

Gans, H. J. (1999). "Toward a Reconciliation of "Assimilation" and "Pluralism": The Interplay of Acculturation and Ethnic Retention." In C. Hirschman, P. Kasinitz, and J. DeWind (eds.). *The Handbook of International Migration: The American Experience.* New York: Russell Sage Foundation, 161–71.

Gee, J. (1993). *An Introduction to Human Languages: Fundamental Concepts in Linguistics.* Upper Saddle River, NJ: Prentice Hall.

Geertz, C. (1973/2000). *The Interpretation of Cultures.* New York: Basic Books.

Giddens, A. (1991). *Modernity and Self-identity.* Stanford, CA: Stanford University Press.

———. (2000). *Runaway World*. New York: Routledge.

Gilroy, P. (1987). *There Ain't No Black in the Union Jack: The Cultural Politics of Race and Nation*. Chicago: University of Chicago Press.

———. (1992). "It's a Family Affair." In G. Dent (ed.). *Black Popular Culture*. Seattle: Bay Press, 303–16.

Gimenez, M. E. (1989). "Silence in the Classroom: Some Thoughts About Teaching in the 1980's." *Teaching Sociology* 17: 184–91.

Glazer, N. (1993). "Is Assimilation Dead?" *Annals of the American Academy of Political and Social Sciences* 530: 122–36.

———. (1997). *We Are All Multiculturalists Now*. Cambridge, MA: Harvard University Press.

Glazer, N., and D. Moynihan. (1963). *Beyond the Melting Pot: The Negroes, Puerto Ricans, Jews, Italians, and Irish of New York City*. Cambridge, MA: MIT Press.

Goldberg, D. T. (1994). "Introduction: Multicultural Conditions." In D. T. Goldberg (ed.). *Multiculturalism: A Critical Reader*. Oxford: Blackwell, 1–41.

Goldschmidt, W. (1977). "Anthropology and the Coming Crisis: An Autoethnographic Appraisal." *American Anthropologist* 79: 293–308.

Grillo, R. D. (1998). *Pluralism and the Politics of Difference*. Oxford: Clarendon Press.

Guest, M. (2002). "A critical 'checkbook' for Culture Teaching and Learning." *ELT Journal* 56: 158–61.

Gumperz, J. (1982). *Discourse Strategies*. Cambridge: Cambridge University Press.

Gutmann, A. (1994). Introduction. In A. Gutmann (ed.). *Multiculturalism and the Politics of Recognition*. Princeton, NJ: Princeton University Press, 1–14.

Hall, E. T. (1959). *The Silent Language*. New York: Doubleday.

Hall, E. T., and G. L. Trager. (1953). *The Analysis of Culture*. Washington, DC: Foreign Service Institute/American Council of Learned Societies.

Hall, J. K. (2002). *Teaching and Researching Language and Culture*. London: Longman.

Hall, S. (1991). "The Local and the Global: Globalization and Ethnicity." In A. King (ed.). *Culture, Globalization and the World-System*. London: Macmillan, 19–39.

———. (1996). "Who Needs 'Identity'?" In S. Hall and P. Du Gay (eds.). *Questions of Cultural Identity*. London: Sage, 1–17.

———. (1997). "The Spectacle of the 'Other.'" In S. Hall (ed.). *Representation: Cultural Representations and Signifying Practices*. London: Sage/Open University, 22–29.

Halpern, D. F. (1997). *Critical Thinking Across the Curriculum: A Brief Edition of Thought and Knowledge*. Mahwah, NJ: Lawrence Erlbaum.

Handlin, O. (1957). *Race and Nationality in American Life.* Boston: Little, Brown.

Harris, R., and B. Rampton. (2003). *The Language, Ethnicity and Race Reader.* London: Routledge.

Heath, S. B. (1983). *Ways with Words: Language and Work in Communities and Classrooms.* Cambridge: Cambridge University Press.

Heath, S. B., and M. B. Mongiola. (1991). *Children of Promise: Literate Activity in Linguistically and Culturally Diverse Classroom.* Washington, DC: National Education Association Publications.

Held, D. (1999). "The Transformation of Political Community: Rethinking Democracy in the Context of Globalization." In I. Shapiro and C. Hacker-Cordon (eds.). *Democracy's Edges.* Cambridge: Cambridge University Press, 84–111.

Heller, M. (2002). "Globalization and the Commodification of Bilingualism in Canada." In D. Block and D. Cameron (eds.). *Globalization and Language Teaching.* London: Routledge, 47–63.

Hibler, K. (1998). "Inter/cultural Communication and the Challenge of Postcolonial Theory." *The E-Journal of Intercultural Relations* 1 (Spring 1998): 2.

Higham, J. (1965). *Strangers in the Land: Patterns of American Nativism, 1860–1925.* New York: Atheneum.

———. (1999). "Instead of a Sequel, Or How I Lost My Subject." In C. Hirschman, P. Kasinitz, and J. DeWind (eds.). *The Handbook of International Migration: The American Experience.* New York: Russell Sage Foundation, 383–89.

Hinkel, E. (ed.). (1999). *Culture in Second Language Teaching and Learning.* Cambridge: Cambridge University Press.

Hirschman, C., P. Kasinitz, and J. DeWind (eds.). (1999). *The Handbook of International Migration: The American Experience.* New York: Russell Sage Foundation.

Hitler, A. (1925/1969). *Mein Kampf.* Trans. R. Manheim. London: Hutchingson. (Originally published in 1925.)

Hobsbawm, E. (1966). "Language, Culture, and National Identity." *Social Research* 63: 1065–80.

———. (1990). *Nations and Nationalism Since 1780.* Cambridge: Cambridge University Press.

Hoddad, Y., and J. Smith. (1996). "Islamic Values and American Muslims." In B. C. Aswad and B. Bilge (eds.). *Family and Gender Among American Muslims.* Philadelphia: Temple University Press, 16–27.

Hofstede, G. (1980). *Culture's Consequences: International Differences in Work-related Values.* Beverly Hills: Sage.

———. (1986). "Cultural Differences in Teaching and Learning." *International Journal of Intercultural Relations* 10: 301–20.

Holliday, A., M. Hyde, and J. Kullman. (2004). *Intercultural Communica-
  tion: An Advanced Resource Book.* New York: Routledge.
Hollinger, D. A. (1995). *Postethnic America: Beyond Multiculturalism.* New
  York: Basic Books.
Human Development Report 1999. (1999). "Globalization with a Human
  Face." New York: United Nations Development Programme and Oxford
  University Press.
Human Development Report 2004. (2004). "Cultural Liberty in Today's
  World." New York: United Nations Development Programme.
Huntington, S. (1993). "The Clash of Civilizations?" *Foreign Affairs* 72: 23–49.
———. (1998). *The Clash of Civilizations: The Remaking of the World Order.*
  New York: Simon and Schuster.
———. (2004). *Who Are We? The Challenges to America's National Identity.*
  New York: Simon and Schuster.
Jakubowicz, A. (1984). "State and Ethnicity: Multiculturalism as an Ideol-
  ogy." *Australia and New Zealand Journal of Sociology* 17: 3.
Jameson, F. (1991). *Postmodernism, Or, the Cultural Logic of Late Capital-
  ism.* Durham, NC: Duke University Press.
———. (1998). "Notes on Globalization and Philosophical Issues." In
  F. Jameson and M. Miyoshi (eds.). *The Cultures of Globalization.*
  Durham, NC: Duke University Press, 54–77.
Jones, G. L. (1998). "Mexico Is Right at Home in Win." *Los Angeles Times,*
  February 16, 1998, C1; "This Is Much Worse Than Trash Talking," C7.
Joseph, J. E. (1996). "The Immediate Sources of the 'Sapir-Whorf Hypothesis.'" *Historiographia Linguistica* 23: 365–404.
———. (1997). "The Misery and the Splendour of Multiculturalism: A Response to Michael Clyne." *Current Issues in Language and Society* 4, no.
  2: 129–34.
———. (2004). *Language and Identity: National, Ethnic, Religious.* London:
  Palgrave Macmillan.
Joseph, L. (1957). *Israel Zangwill.* New York: Thomas Yoseloff, 255. Cited
  in N. Glazer and D. Moynihan. (1963). *Beyond the Melting Pot: The Negroes, Puerto Ricans, Jews, Italians, and Irish of New York City.* Cambridge, MA: MIT Press, 290.
Joseph, M. (1999). "Introduction: New Hybrid Identities and Performance." In M. Joseph and J. N. Fink (eds.). *Performing Hybridity.* Minneapolis: University of Minnesota Press, 1–24.
Joseph, M., and J. N. Fink. (eds.). (1999). *Performing Hybridity.* Minneapolis: University of Minnesota Press.
Journal of Cross-Cultural Psychology 31, no. 1 (2000). January 2000. Millennium special issue.
Kaiser, W. L. (1987). *A New View of the World.* Amherst, MA: Freedom Press.
Kalantzis, M., and B. Cope. (1999). "Multicultural Education: Transform-

ing the Mainstream." In S. May (ed.). *Critical Multiculturalism: Rethinking Multicultural and Antiracist Education.* London/Philadelphia: Falmer Press, 245–76.

Kallen, H. (1924). *Culture and Democracy in the United States.* New York: Boni and Liveright.

Kang, L. (1998). "Is There an Alternative to (Capitalist) Globalization? The Debate About Modernity in China." In F. Jameson and M. Miyoshi (eds.). *The Cultures of Globalization.* Durham, NC: Duke University Press, 164–88.

Kaplan, R. B. (1966). "Cultural Thought Patterns in Intercultural Education." *Language Learning* 16: 1–20.

———. (1987). "Cultural Thought Patterns Revisited." In U. Connor and R. B. Kaplan (eds.). *Writing Across Languages: Analysis of L2 Text.* Reading, MA: Addison-Wesley, 9–21.

———. (1988). "Contrastive Rhetoric and Second Language Learning: Notes Toward a Theory of Contrastive Rhetoric." In A. C. Purves (ed.). *Writing Across Languages and Cultures: Issues in Contrastive Rhetoric.* Newbury Park, CA: Sage, 275–304.

Kasper, G., and S. Blum-Kulka (eds.). (1993). *Interlanguage Pragmatics.* Oxford: Oxford University Press.

Kelly, L. G. (1969). *25 Centuries of Language Teaching.* Rowley, MA.: Newbury House.

Kelly, W. (1999). "Postcolonial Perspective on Intercultural Relations: A Japan-U.S. Example." *The Edge, The E-Journal of Intercultural Relations* 2, no. 1 (Winter).

Ki, A., and C. Yeh. (2002). "Stereotypes of Asian American Students." ERIC document no. 172, February 2002.

Kim, M. S. (2002). *Non-western Perspectives on Human Communication: Implications for Theory and Practice.* Thousand Oaks: Sage.

Kim, U., Y. Park, and D. Park. (2000). "The Challenge of Cross-cultural Psychology." *Journal of Cross-cultural Psychology* 31: 63–75.

Kim, Y. Y. (2001). *Becoming Intercultural: An Integrative Theory of Communication and Cross-cultural Adaptation.* Thousand Oaks, CA: Sage.

Kivisto, P. (2002). *Multiculturalism in a Global Society.* Oxford: Blackwell Publishers.

Kluver, R. (2000). "Globalization, Informatization, and Intercultural Communication." *American Communication Journal* 13, no. 3. Retrieved May 21, 2001, from http://www.acjournal/holdings/vo13/Iss3/spec/kluver.htm.

Korzybski, A. (1933). *Science and Sanity: An Introduction to Non-Aristotelian Systems and General Semantics.* New York: Institute of General Semantics.

Kowal, K. (1998). *Rhetorical Implications of Linguistic Relativity.* New York: Peter Lang.

Kramsch, C. (1993). *Context and Culture in Language Teaching.* Oxford: Oxford University Press.

———. (1998). *Language and Culture.* Oxford: Oxford University Press.

———. (1999). "Thirdness: The Intercultural Stance." In T. Vestergaard (ed.). *Language, Culture and Identity.* Aalborg, Denmark: Aalborg University Press, 41–58.

———. (2002). "Intercultural Communications." In R. Carter and D. Nunan (eds.). *The Cambridge Guide to Teaching English to Speakers of Other Languages.* Cambridge: Cambridge University Press, 201–6.

———. (2003). "Teaching Language Along the Cultural Faultline." In D. L. Lange and R. M. Paige (eds.). *Culture as the Core: Perspectives in Second Language Education.* Greenwich, CT: Information Age Publishing, 19–35.

Kramsch, C., and S. L. Thorne. (2002). "Foreign Language Learning as Global Communicative Practice." In D. Block and D. Cameron (eds.). *Globalization and Language Teaching.* London: Routledge, 83–100.

Krishnaswamy, R. (1998). *Effeminism: The Economy of Colonial Desire.* Ann Arbor: University of Michigan Press.

Kristol, W. (2006). "Y is for Yahoo." (Editorial.) *The Weekly Standard* 11, no. 28: 7.

Ksmberelis, G. (2001). "Producing Heteroglossic Classroom (Micro)cultures Through Hybrid Discourse Practice. *Linguistics and Education* 21: 85–125.

Kubota, R. (1999). "Japanese Culture Constructed by Discourses: Implications for Applied Linguistics Research and ELT." *TESOL Quarterly* 33: 9–35.

———. (2001). "Discursive Construction of the Images of U.S. Classrooms." *TESOL Quarterly* 35: 9–38.

———. (2002). "The Impact of Globalization on Language Teaching in Japan." In D. Block and D. Cameroon (eds.). *Globalization and Language Teaching.* New York: Routledge, 13–28.

———. (2004). "Critical Multiculturalism and Second Language Education." In B. Norton and K. Toohey (eds.). *Critical Pedagogies and Language Learning.* Cambridge: Cambridge University Press, 30–52.

Kumaravadivelu, B. (1990). "Ethnic Variation and Classroom Interaction: Myth or Reality." *RELC Journal* 21: 45–54.

———. (1997). "Our Prejudices, Our Selves." *San Jose Mercury News,* 1P and 4P. May 18, 1997.

———. (1999). "Critical Classroom Discourse Analysis." *TESOL Quarterly* 33: 453–84.

———. (2000). "The Gift of One Another's Presence: Culture and Language Teaching." Keynote address delivered at The 13th Educational Conference, October 12–14, 2000, Fremantle, Australia.

———. (2002). "Paying Attention to *Inter-* in Intercultural Communication." *TESOL Journal* 11: 3–4.

———. (2003a). "Problematizing Cultural Stereotypes in TESOL." *TESOL Quarterly* 37: 709–18.

———. (2003b). *Beyond Methods: Macrostrategies for Language Teaching.* New Haven: Yale University Press.

———. (May 2003c). "Cultural Globalization and Individual Identity." Plenary address delivered at the 19th Communication Skills Conference, May 16–18, 2003, Helsinki, Finland.

———. (July 2006). "(Ex)tensions: The Cultural Logic of the Global and the Local." Plenary address delivered at the Applied Linguistics Association of Australia International Conference, July 5–8, 2006, Brisbane, Australia.

Lado, R. (1957). *Linguistics Across Cultures.* Ann Arbor: University of Michigan Press.

Landis, D., J. M. Bennett, and M. J. Bennett (eds.). (2004). *Handbook of Intercultural Training.* 3d ed. Thousand Oaks: Sage.

Lange, D. L. (2003). "Implications of Theory and Research for the Development of Principles for Teaching and Learning Culture in Second Language Classrooms." In D. L. Lange and R. M. Paige (eds.). *Culture as the Core: Perspectives in Second Language Education.* Greenwich, CT: Information Age Publishing, 271–336.

Lange, D. L., and R. M. Paige. (2003). "Interdisciplinary Perspectives on Culture Learning in the Second Language Curriculum: Introduction." In D. L. Lange and R. M. Paige (Eds.), *Culture as the Core: Perspectives in Second Language Education.* Greenwich, CT: Information Age Publishing, ix–xvii.

———. (eds.). (2003). *Culture as the Core: Perspectives in Second Language Education.* Greenwich, CT: Information Age Publishing.

Larsen-Freeman, D., and M. H. Long. (1991). *An Introduction to Second Language Acquisition Research.* London: Longman.

Lee, S. J. (1996). *Unraveling the "Model Minority" Stereotype: Listening to Asian American Youth.* New York: Teachers College Press.

Leki, I. (1991). "Twenty-five Years of Contrastive Rhetoric: Text Analysis and Writing Pedagogies." *TESOL Quarterly* 25: 123–43.

Lessow-Hurley, J. (1991). *A Commonsense Guide to Bilingual Education.* Alexandria, VA: Association for Supervision and Curriculum Development.

Lin, A. M. Y., and W. Martin (eds.). (2005). *Decolonisation, Globalisation: Language-in-Education Policy and Practice.* Clevedon: Multilingual Matters.

Lippmann, W. (1922). *Public Opinion.* New York: The Free Press.

Littlewood, W. (2000). "Do Asian Students Really Want to Listen and Obey?" *ELT Journal* 54: 31–36.

————. (2001). "Students' Attitudes to Classroom English Learning: A Cross-cultural Study. *Language Teaching Research* 5: 3–28.

Liu, J. (2001). *Asian Students' Classroom Communication Patterns in U.S. Universities.* Westport, CT: Ablex.

Lo Bianco, J., A. J. Liddicoat, and C. Crozet (eds.). (1999). *Striving for the Third Place: Intercultural Competence Through Language Education.* Melbourne: Language Australia.

Lodge, A. (1998). "French Is a Logical Language." In L. Bauer and P. Trudgill (eds.). *Language Myths.* London: Penguin Books. 23–31.

Loughrin-Sacco, S. (1992). "More Than Meets the Eye: An Ethnography of an Elementary French Class." *Canadian Modern Language Review* 49: 80–101.

Luke, A. (1989). "Open and Closed Texts: The Ideological/Semantic Analysis of Textbook Narratives." *Journal of Pragmatics* 13: 53–80.

————. (1996). "Genres of Power? Literacy Education and the Production of Capital." In R. Hasan and G. Williams (eds.). *Literacy in Society.* London: Longman, 308–38.

————. (2003). "After the Marketplace: Evidence, Social Science and Educational Research." *Australian Educational Researcher* 30: 87–107.

————. (2004). "Two Takes on the Critical." In B. Norton and K. Toohey (eds.). *Critical Pedagogies and Language Learning.* Cambridge: Cambridge University Press, 21–29.

Maalouf, A. (2000.) *On Identity.* Trans. Barbara Bray. London: Havill Press.

Malcolm, I. G. (1987). "Continuities in Communicative Patterns in Cross-cultural Classrooms." In B. K. Das (ed.). *Communication and Learning in the Classroom Community.* Singapore: Singapore University Press, 37–63.

Marcus, G. (1998). *Ethnography Through Thick and Thin.* Princeton: Princeton University Press.

Martin, J. E. (1992). *Toward a Theory of Text for Contrastive Rhetoric.* New York: Peter Lang.

Martin, J. N., and T. K. Nakayama. (1997). *Intercultural Communication in Contexts.* Mountain View, CA: Mayfield Publishing Company.

————. (2000). *Intercultural Communication in Contexts.* 2d ed. Mountain View, CA: Mayfield Publishing Company.

Matilal, B. M., and A. Chakrabarti (eds.). (1994). Introduction. In B. M. Matilal and A. Chakrabarti (eds.). *Knowing from Words: Western and Indian Philosophical Analysis of Understanding and Testimony.* Boston: Kluwer Academic Publishers, 1–22.

Matsumoto, D. (1996). *Unmasking Japan: Myths and Realities About the Emotions of the Japanese.* Stanford, CA: Stanford University Press.

May, S. (1999). "Critical Multiculturalism and Cultural Difference: Avoiding Essentialism." In S. May (ed.). *Critical Multiculturalism: Rethink-*

ing Multicultural and Antiracist Education. London: Falmer Press, 11–41.

Mayntz, R. (1992). "Social Norms in the Institutional Culture of the German Federal Parliament." In R. Munch and N. Smelser (eds.). *Theory of Culture*. Berkeley, CA: University of California Press, 219–40.

McKay, S. L. (2000). "Teaching English as an International Language: Implications for Cultural Materials in the Classroom." *TESOL Journal* (Winter 2000): 7–11.

McLaren, P. (1994). "White Terror and Oppositional Agency: Towards a Critical Multiculturalism." In D. T. Goldberg (ed.). *Multiculturalism: A Critical Reader*. Oxford: Blackwell, 45–74.

———. (1995). "Collisions with Otherness: 'Traveling' Theory, Postcolonial Criticism, and the Politics of Ethnographic Practice—The Mission of the Wounded Ethnographer." In P. McLaren and J. Giarelli (eds.). *Critical Theory and Educational Research*. New York: State University of New York Press, 271–99.

McLaren, P., and R. Torres. (1999). "Racism and Multicultural Education: Rethinking 'Race' and 'Whiteness' in Late Capitalism." In S. May (ed.). *Critical Multiculturalism: Rethinking Multicultural and Antiracist Education*. London: Falmer Press, 42–76.

Memmi, A. (1957/1965). *The Colonizer and the Colonized*. Boston: Beacon Press.

Mignolo, W. (1998). "Globalization, Civilization Processes, and the Relocation of Languages and Cultures." In F. Jameson and M. Miyoshi (eds.). *The Cultures of Globalization*. Durham, NC: Duke University Press, 32–53.

———. (2000). *Local Histories/Global Designs: Coloniality, Subaltern Knowledges, and Border Thinking*. Princeton, NJ: Princeton University Press.

Miike, Y. (2003). "Beyond Eurocentrism in the Intercultural Field: Searching for an Asiacentric Paradigm." In W. J. Starosta and G. Chen (eds.). *Ferment in the Intercultural Field: Axiology/Value/Praxis*. Thousand Oaks, CA: Sage, 243–76.

Mills, S. (1997). *Discourse*. London: Routledge.

Miner, H. (1956). "Body Ritual Among the Nacirema." *American Anthropologist* 58: 503–7.

Minh-ha, T. T. (1989). *Woman, Native, Other: Writing Postcoloniality and Feminism*. Bloomington: Indiana University Press.

Miyahara, A. (2000). "Toward Theorizing Japanese Interpersonal Communication Competence from a Non-Western Perspective." *American Communication Journal* 13, no. 3. Retrieved May 21, 2001, from http://www.acjournal/holdings/vo13/Iss3/spec/kluver.htm.

Mohan, B. A., and W. A.-Y. Lo. (1985). "Academic Writing and Chinese

Students: Transfer and Developmental Factors." *TESOL Quarterly* 19: 515–34.

Montovani, G. (2000). *Exploring Borders: Understanding Culture and Psychology.* New York: Routledge.

Mootoo, S. (1999). "Hybridity and Other Poems." In M. Joseph and J. N. Fink (eds.). *Performing Hybridity.* Minneapolis: University of Minnesota Press, 106–11.

Morgan, B., and V. Ramanathan. (2005). "Critical Literacies and Language Education: Global and Local Perspectives." *Annual Review of Applied Linguistics* 25: 151–69.

Mukhopadhyay, C., R. Henze, and Y. Moses. (2007). *How Real Is Race?: A Sourcebook on Race, Culture, and Biology.* Lanham, MD: Rowman and Littlefield Education.

Nachbar, J., and K. Lause (eds.). (1992). *Popular Culture: An Introductory Text.* Bowling Green, OH: Bowling Green State University Popular Press.

National Standards for Foreign Language Learning Project. (1996). *Standards for Foreign Language Learning: Preparing for the 21st Century.* New York: National Standards for Foreign Language Learning Project.

Negroponte, N. (1995). *Being Digital.* London: Hodder and Stoughton.

Nehru, J. (1936/1980). *An Autobiography.* New Delhi: Oxford University Press. (Originally published in 1936.)

Nelson, G. (1998). "Intercultural Communication and Related Courses Taught in TESOL Masters' Degree Programs." *International Journal of Intercultural Relations* 22: 17–33.

New London Group. (1996). "A Pedagogy of Multiliteracies: Designing Social Futures." *Harvard Educational Review* 66: 60–92.

———. (2000). "A Pedagogy of Multiliteracies: Designing Social Futures." In B. Cope and M. Kalantzis (eds.). *Multiliteracies: Literacy Learning and the Design of Social Futures.* London: Routledge, 9–38.

Nicholls, J. (1995). "Cultural Pluralism and the Multicultural Curriculum: Ethical Issues and English Language Textbooks in Canada." In M. L. Tickoo (ed.). *Language and Culture in Multilingual Societies: Viewpoints and Visions.* Singapore: Sherson Publishing House, 112–21.

Norton, B. (2000). *Identity and Language Learning.* London: Longman.

Novak, M. (1971). *The Rise of the Unmeltable Ethnics.* New York: Macmillan.

Ong, A. (1998). "Flexible Citizenship Among Chinese Cosmopolitans." In P. Cheah and B. Robbins (eds.). *Cosmopolitics: Thinking and Feeling Beyond the Nation.* Minneapolis: University of Minnesota Press, 134–62.

Ortiz, F. (1947/1995). *Cuban Counterpoint: Tobacco and Sugar.* NY: Alfred Knopf. Republished in 1995 by Duke University Press.

Oxford English Dictionary. (1971). New York: Oxford University Press.

Oxford, R. L. (1995). *Patterns of Cultural Identity.* Boston: Heinle and Heinle.

Panetta, C. G. (ed.). (2001). *Contrastive Rhetoric Revisited and Redefined.* Mahwah, NJ.: Lawrence Erlbaum.

Park, R. E., and E. W. Burgess. (1969). *Introduction to the Science of Sociology.* Chicago: University of Chicago Press. (Originally published in 1921.)

Pavlenko, A. (1998). "Second Language Learning by Adults: Testimonies of Bilingual Writers." *Issues in Applied Linguistics* 9: 3–19.

———. (2002). "Poststructuralist Approaches to the Study of Social Factors in Second Language Learning and Use." In V. J. Cook (ed.). *Portraits of the L2 User.* Clevedon: Multilingual Matters, 275–302.

Pavlenko, A., and J. Lantolf. (2000). "Second Language Learning as Participation and the (Re)construction of Selves." In J. Lantolf (ed.). *Sociocultural Theory and Second Language Learning.* Oxford: Oxford University Press, 155–78.

Pennycook, A. (1994). *The Cultural Politics of English as an International Language.* London: Longman.

———. (1998). *English and the Discourses of Colonialism.* London: Routledge.

———. (2002). "Language Policy and Docile Bodies: Hong Kong and Governmentality." In J. W. Tollefson (ed.). *Language Policies in Education.* Mahwah, NJ.: Lawrence Erlbaum 91–110.

Phillips, J. K. (2003). "National Standards for Foreign Language Learning: Culture, the Driving Force." In D. L. Lange and R. M. Paige (eds.). *Culture as the Core: Perspectives in Second Language Education.* Greenwich, CT: Information Age Publishing, 61–171.

Pierson, H. D. (1996). "Learner Culture and Learner Autonomy in the Hong Kong Chinese Context." In R. Pemberton et al. (eds.). *Taking Control: Autonomy in Language Learning.* Hong Kong: Hong Kong University Press, 49–58.

Pieterse, J. N. (2001). "Hybridity, So What? The Anti-hybridity Backlash and the Riddles of Recognition." *Theory, Culture and Society* 18: 219–45.

Pinker, S. (1995). *The Language Instinct.* New York: HarperPerennial.

Pollock, S., H. K. Bhabha, C. A. Breckenridge, and D. Chakrabarty. (2002). "Cosmopolitanisms." In C. A. Breckenridge, S. Pollock, H. K. Bhabha, and D. Chakrabarty (eds.). *Cosmopolitanism.* Durham, NC: Duke University Press, 1–14.

Portes, A. (1999). "Immigration Theory for a New Century." In C. Hirschman, P. Kasinitz, and J. DeWind (eds.). *The Handbook of International Migration: The American Experience.* New York: Russell Sage Foundation, 21–33.

Portes, A., and M. Zhou. (1993). "The New Second Generation: Segmented Assimilation and Its Variants Among Post-1965 Immigrant Youth." *Annals of the American Academy of Political and Social Science* 530: 74–96.

Pratt, M. L. (1991). "Arts of the Contact Zone." *Profession* 91: 33–40.

———. (1992). *Imperial Eyes: Travel Writing and Transculturation*. London and New York: Routledge.

Prodromou, L. (1992). "What Culture? Which Culture? Cross-cultural Factors in Language Learning." *ELT Journal,* 46: 39–49.

Pusch, M. D. (2004). "Intercultural Training in Historical Perspective." In D. Landis, J. M. Bennett, and M. J. Bennett (eds.). *Handbook of Intercultural Training.* Thousand Oaks, CA: Sage, 13–36.

Radhakrishnan, R. (1993). "Postcoloniality and the Boundaries of Identity." *Callaloo* 16: 750–71.

———. (2003). *Theory in an Uneven World*. Oxford: Blackwell Publishing.

Rampton, B. (1995). *Crossing: Language and Ethnicity Among Adolescents.* London: Longman.

———. (2006). *Language in Late Modernity: Interaction in an Urban School.* Cambridge: Cambridge University Press.

Realo, A. (2003). "Comparison of Public and Academic Discourses: Estonian Individualism and Collectivism Revisited." *Culture and Psychology* 9: 47–77.

Reed-Danahay, D. E. (ed.). (1997). *Auto/Ethnography: Rewriting the Self and the Social*. Oxford and New York: Berg.

Remennick, L. (2005). "Cross-cultural Dating Patterns on an Israeli Campus: Why Are Russian Immigrant Women More Popular Than Men?" *Journal of Social of Personal Relations* 22: 435–54.

Risager, K. (1998). "Language Teaching and the Process of European Integration." In M. Byram and M. Fleming (eds.). *Language Learning in Intercultural Perspective.* Cambridge: Cambridge University Press, 242–54.

———. (1999). "Language and Culture: Disconnection and Reconnection." In T. Vestergaard (ed.). *Language, Culture and Identity*. Aalborg, Denmark: Aalborg University Press, 83–98.

Rischin, M. (1976). *Immigration and the American Tradition*. Indianapolis: Bobbs-Merrill.

Ritzer, G. (1993). *The McDonaldization of Society*. Thousand Oaks, CA: Pine Forge Press.

Robertson, Robbie. (2003). *Three Waves of Globalization: A History of a Developing Global Consciousness*. London: Zed Books.

Robertson, Roland. (1992). *Globalization, Social Theory and Global Culture*. London: Sage.

Robinson, G. (1991). "Second Culture Acquisition." In J. E. Alatis (ed.). *Georgetown University Round Table on Languages and Linguistics, 1991*. Washington, DC: Georgetown University Press, 114–22.

Rogers, E. M., W. B. Hart, and Y. Miike. (2002). "Edward T. Hall and the

History of Intercultural Communication: The United States and Japan." *Keio Communication Review* 24: 3–26.

Rose, K. R., and G. Kasper (eds.). (2001). *Pragmatics in Language Teaching.* Cambridge: Cambridge University Press.

Rumbaut, R. G. (1999). "Assimilation and Its Discontents: Ironies and Paradoxes." In C. Hirschman, P. Kasinitz, and J. DeWind (eds.). *The Handbook of International Migration: The American Experience.* New York: Russell Sage Foundation, 172–95.

Sacks, J. (2003). *The Dignity of Difference: How to Avoid the Clash of Civilizations.* New York: Plenum.

Said, E. (1978). *Orientalism.* New York: Pantheon.

Salins, P. (1999). *Assimilation, American Style.* New York: Basic Books.

Sampedro, R., and S. Hillyard. (2004). *Global Issues.* Oxford: Oxford University Press.

San Jose Mercury News, February 23, 2006. "Bush Insists Outsourcing to India Has Its Benefits," 1A, 5A.

Sanchez, G. J. (1999). "Face the Nation: Race, Immigration, and the Rise of Nativism in Later-twentieth Century America." In C. Hirschman, P. Kasinitz, and J. DeWind (eds.). *The Handbook of International Migration: The American Experience.* New York: Russell Sage Foundation, 371–82.

Sapir, E. (1949). *Selected Writings of Edward Sapir in Language, Culture, and Personality,* ed. D. G. Mendelbaum. Berkeley, CA: University of California Press.

Sato, C. (1981). "Ethnic Styles in Classroom Discourse." In M. Hines and W. Rutherford (eds.). *On TESOL '81.* Washington DC: TESOL, 11–24.

Scarcella, R. C., and R. L. Oxford. (1992). *The Tapestry of Language Learning.* Boston: Heinle and Heinle.

Schlesinger, A. M., Jr. (1998). *The Disuniting of America: Reflections on a Multicultural Society.* New York: W.W. Norton.

Schumann, J. (1976). "Second Language Acquisition: The Pidginization Hypothesis." *Language Learning* 26: 391–408.

———. (1978). "The Acculturation Model for Second Language Acquisition." In R. C. Gingras (ed.). *Second Language Acquisition and Foreign Language Teaching.* Washington, DC: Center for Applied Linguistics.

Scollon, R., and S. W. Scollon. (2001). *Intercultural Communication.* 2d ed. Malden: Blackwell Publishers.

Sercu, L. (2005). "The Future of Intercultural Competence in Foreign Language Education: Recommendations for Professional Development, Educational Policy and Research." In L. Sercu (ed.). *Foreign Language Teachers and Intercultural Competence.* Clevedon: Multilingual Matters, 160–81.

——— (ed.). (2005). *Foreign Language Teachers and Intercultural Competence*. Clevedon: Multilingual Matters.

Shohat, E., and R. Stam. (1994). *Unthinking Eurocentrism: Multiculturalism and the Media*. London: Routledge.

———. (2003). Introduction. In E. Shohat and R. Stam (eds.). *Multiculturalism, Postcoloniality, and Transnational Media*. New Brunswick, NJ: Rutgers University Press, 1–17.

Shulman, M. (1998). *Cultures in Contrast*. Ann Arbor: University of Michigan Press.

Skelton, T., and T. Allen. (1999). *Culture and Global Change*. London: Routledge.

Sokolik, M. E. (1999). *Rethinking America*. Boston: Heinle and Heinle.

Spivak, G. (1988). *In Other Words: Essays in Cultural Politics*. New York: Routledge.

Spivak, G. C. (1985). "Can the Subaltern Speak? Speculations on Widow Sacrifice." *Wedge* 7: 120–30.

———. (1986). "Imperialism and Sexual Difference." *Oxford Literary Review* 8: 1–2.

———. (1993). *Outside in the Teaching Machine*. New York: Routledge.

Starosta, W. J., and G. Chen (eds.). (2003). *Ferment in the Intercultural Field: Axiology/Value/Praxis*. Thousand Oaks, CA: Sage.

———. (2003a). "'Ferment,' an Ethic of Caring, and the Corrective Power of Dialogue." In W. J. Starosta and G. Chen (eds.). *Ferment in the Intercultural Field: Axiology/Value/Praxis*. Thousand Oaks, CA: Sage, 3–23.

———. (2003b). "On Theorizing Difference: Culture as Centrism." In W. J. Starosta and G. Chen (eds.). *Ferment in the Intercultural Field: Axiology/Value/Praxis*. Thousand Oaks, CA: Sage, 277–87.

Steger, M. (2003). *Globalization: A Very Short Introduction*. Oxford: Oxford University Press.

Stern, H. H. (1983). *Fundamental Concepts of Language Teaching*. Oxford: Oxford University Press.

———. (1992). *Issues and Options in Language Teaching*. Oxford: Oxford University Press.

Storti, C., and L. Bennhold-Samaan. (1997). *Culture Matters: The Peace Corps Cross-Cultural Workbook*. Washington, DC: Peace Corps, Information Collection and Exchange.

Street, B. V. (1993). "Culture Is a Verb: Anthropological Aspects of Language and Cultural Process." In D. Graddol, L. Thompson, and M. Bryman (eds.). *Language and Culture*. London: Multilingual Matters, 23–43.

Sugimoto, Y. (1997). *An Introduction to Japanese Society*. Cambridge: Cambridge University Press.

Taylor, C. (1989). *Sources of the Self: The Making of the Modern Identity*. Cambridge, MA: Harvard University Press.

Threadgold, T. (1997). *Feminist Poetics*. London: Routledge.

Tickoo, M. L. (1995). "Authenticity as a Cultural Concern: A View from the Asian English-language Classroom." In M. L. Tickoo (ed.). *Language and Culture in Multilingual Societies: Viewpoints and Visions*. Singapore: Sherson Publishing House, 95–112.

Tomlinson, J. (1999a). *Globalization and Culture*. Cambridge: Blackwell Publishers.

———. (1999b). "Globalised Culture: The Triumph of the West?" In T. Skelton and T. Allen (eds.). *Culture and Global Change*. London: Routledge, 22–29.

Tonnies, F. (1955). *Community and Association*. London: Routledge and Kegan Paul.

Torres, A. (2001). "Latino Cultural Identity and Political Participation: Scanning the Recent Literature," www.gaston.umb.edu/publications/gr/8xxnl/torres_cornell.html.

Triandis, H. C. (1995). *Individualism and Collectivism*. Boulder, CO.: Westview Press.

Tsui, A. B. M. (1996). "Reticence and Anxiety in Second Language Learning." In K. Bailey and D. Nunan (eds.). *Voices from the Language Classroom*. Cambridge: Cambridge University Press, 145–67.

Tyrrell, H. (1999). "Bollywood Versus Hollywood: Battle of the Dream Factories." In T. Skelton and T. Allen (eds.). *Culture and Global Change*. London: Routledge, 260–73.

Vestergaard, T. (ed.). (1999). *Language, Culture and Identity*. Aalborg, Denmark: Aalborg University Press.

Wallace, C. (2002). "Local Literacies and Global Literacy." In D. Block and D. Cameron (eds.). *Globalization and Language Teaching*. London: Routledge, 101–14.

Washington Post. "Karen Hughes to Work on the World's View of U.S." Dated March 12, 2005. Retrieved March 12, 2005, from http://www.washingtonpost.com/ac2/wp-dyn/A25347-2005Mar10.

Watkins, M. S., and S. N. Butler. (1999). "Understanding Classroom Realities: A Cultural Implications Role Play." *Multicultural Perspectives* 1: 27–30.

Watson-Gegeo, K. A., and D. W. Gegeo. (1995). "Understanding Language and Power in the Solomon Islands: Methodological Lessons for Educational Intervention." In J. W. Tollefson (ed.). *Power and Inequality in Language Education*. Cambridge: Cambridge University Press, 59–72.

Weedon, C. (1987). *Feminist Practice and Poststructuralist Theory*. London: Blackwell.

Wenger, E. (1999). *Communities of Practice: Learning, Meaning and Identity*. Cambridge: Cambridge University Press.

Werbner, P. (1997). "Introduction: The Dialectics of Cultural Hybridity." In

P. Werbner and T. Modood (eds.). *Debating Cultural Hybridity.* London: Zed, 1–26.

Whorf, B. (1956). *Language, Thought, and Reality: Selected Writings by Benjamin Lee Whorf,* ed. John B. Carroll. Cambridge, MA: MIT Press.

Wierzbicka, A. (1997). *Understanding Cultures Through Their Key Words.* Oxford: Oxford University Press.

Williams, R. (1976). *Keywords: A Vocabulary of Culture and Society.* Oxford: Oxford University Press.

Williams, R. (1977). *Marxism and Literature.* Oxford: Oxford University Press.

Wolf, A. (2004). "Native Son: Samuel Huntington Defends Homeland." *Foreign Affairs* (May/June 2004): 120–25.

Wolf, C., and S. Spencer. (1996). "Stereotypes and Prejudice: Their Overt and Subtle Influence in the Classroom." *American Behavioral Scientist* 40: 176–85.

Wright, A. R., and M. A. Hammons. (1970). *Guidelines for Peace Corps Cross-Cultural Training: Philosophy and Methodology.* Washington, DC: Office of Training Support, Peace Corps, and Estes Park, CO: Center for Research and Education.

Xiaoge, X. (2000). "Asian Perspectives in Communication: Assessing the Search." *American Communication Journal* 13: 3. Retrieved May 21, 2001, from http://www.acjournal/holdings/vo13/Iss3/spec/kluver.htm.

Young, D. (1990). "An Investigation of Students' Perspectives on Anxiety and Speaking." *Foreign Language Annals* 23: 539–53.

Young, R. (1995). *Colonial Desire: Hybridity in Theory, Culture and Race.* London: Routledge.

———. (2001). *Postcolonialism: An Historical Introduction.* Oxford: Blackwell.

Yuval-Davis, N. (1997). *Gender and Nation.* London: Sage.

Zamel, V. (1983). "The Composing Process of Advanced ESL Students: Six Case Studies." *TESOL Quarterly* 17: 165–87.

———. (1997). "Toward a Model of Transculturation." *TESOL Quarterly* 31: 341–52.

Zangwill, I. (1909/1923). *The Melting Pot.* As quoted in G. Gerstle (1999) in C. Hirschman, P. Kasinitz, and J. DeWind (eds.). *The Handbook of International Migration: The American Experience.* New York: Russell Sage Foundation, 274–93. (Originally published in 1909.)

Zarate, G. (1999). "French Linguistic and Cultural Politics Facing European Identity: Between Unity and Diversity." In J. Lo Bianco, A. J. Liddicoat, and C. Crozet (eds.). *Striving for the Third Place: Intercultural Competence Through Language Education.* Melbourne: Language Australia, 43–52.

Zhou, M. (1999). "Segmented Assimilation: Issues, Controversies, and Recent Research on the New School Generation." In C. Hirschman, P. Kasinitz, and J. DeWind (eds.). *The Handbook of International Migration: The American Experience.* New York: Russell Sage Foundation, 196–211.

Zolberg, A. R. (1999). "Matters of State: Theorizing Immigration Policy." In C. Hirschman, P. Kasinitz, and J. DeWind (eds.). *The Handbook of International Migration: The American Experience.* New York: Russell Sage Foundation, 71–93.

Index